GQ · Thomas Fink's compellingly brilliant guide…is a fascinating guide to being a man in the 21st century… It will make a wonderful present, or simply a great guide to the confusions of modern life.

Literary Review · Every now and then, a book comes along that makes you ask yourself: why didn't I think of that… [*The Man's Book*] is above all useful: it deserves to sell in truckloads, and it probably will.

New Statesman · Virile and proud of it.

Sunday Sport · What a man needs is an edge – and this book is it. Herein lies The Knowledge, a hoard of facts and info that'll make you look better than Brad Pitt, cooler than Johnny Depp and smarter than Stephen Hawking… A Godsend, fellas…

The Gerry Ryan Show · Every syllable is vital.

The Times · There are few more reassuring things in life than a dependable set of instructions. A new guide to the habits, protocols and pursuits of the modern man by Thomas Fink covers everything from marriage, to snuff, with firelighting and first dates in between.

The London Paper · An almanac of all things bloke-related…

Thomas Fink was a Junior Fellow at
Caius College, Cambridge. He is a theoretical
physicist at Institut Curie and lives in London.

Also by the author:
The 85 Ways to Tie a Tie

THE
MAN'S BOOK

Thomas Fink

PHOENIX

LONDON

First published in Great Britain in
2006 by Weidenfeld & Nicolson

This edition published in 2007
by Phoenix, an imprint of
Orion Books Ltd

Orion House
5 Upper Saint Martin's Lane
London, WC2H 9EA

3 5 7 9 10 8 6 4 2

A CIP catalogue record for this book is
available from the British Library.

ISBN 978 0 7538 2216 6

Printed in Great Britain
by Mackays of Chatham plc,
Chatham, Kent

www.orionbooks.co.uk

'It'll be a man's world.
That's the fashion.'

CONTENTS

PREFACE

The Man's Book is the authoritative handbook for men's customs, habits and pursuits – a vade-mecum for modern-day manliness. It comprehensively examines the essential elements of a man's life and provides a guide to the year ahead. It is systematic in spirit, system being a masculine strength: it records unspoken customs, separates the essential from the incidental and simplifies what from the outset can seem complex. It is also up to date: it notes the latest trends and considers upcoming events.

This is the second edition of *The Man's Book*. It has been completely revised and expanded, and includes some 30 new sections and four new chapters (Sports, Smoking, Cooking and Idling). Updated throughout, *The Man's Book* remains the essential road map for the modern man. It also has a new look, having been completely re-typeset by the author.

At a time when the sexes are muddled and masculinity is marginalized, *The Man's Book* unabashedly celebrates being male. Chaps, cads, blokes and bounders, rejoice: *The Man's Book* will bring you back to where you belong.

Thomas Fink
London, July 2007

THE
MAN'S BOOK

HEALTH

♂ · The symbol for man is an arrow emanating from a circle in a northeast direction, believed to represent a shield and spear. It is also the symbol for the planet Mars, named after the Roman war god of the same name, and is associated with the male connector, iron and Volvo cars.

Ian Fleming · You only live twice: / Once when you are born / And once when you look death in the face. (*You Only Live Twice*, 1964)

Arnold Schwarzenegger · If you want to be a champion you cannot have any kind of an outside negative force coming in and affect you. Let's say before a contest, if I get emotionally involved with a girl – that can have a negative effect on my mind and therefore destroy my workout. So I have to cut my emotions off and be kind of cold, in a way… That's what you do with the rest of the things. If somebody steals my car outside of my door right now I don't care… I trained myself for that. To be totally cold and not have things go into my mind. (*Pumping Iron*, 1977)

♀ · Loo man is best known as the male public loo symbol. Unlike the Mars symbol for man, it is a pictogram – its meaning can be deduced from its shape. The male loo symbol differs from the female one in having broader shoulders and straight legs as opposed to a flared dress (See Public Loos, p 10.)

Samuel Johnson · It is so *very* difficult (said he, always) for a sick man not to be a scoundrel. (Mrs Piozzi, *Anecdotes*)

Benjamin Franklin · He's a fool that makes his doctor his heir. ❧ Keep your mouth wet, feet dry. ❧ Beware of the young doctor and the old barber. ❧ A good wife and health is a man's best wealth. ❧ There's more old drunkards than old doctors. (*Poor Richard's Almanack*, 1732–1757)

❦IDEAL MAN

VITRUVIAN MAN

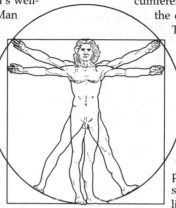

Leonardo da Vinci's well-known Vitruvian Man is based on the ancient ideal proportions of man written down by the Roman architect Vitruvius. Man's outstretched span is equal to his height, marking out a square, and his spreadeagled body marks the circumference of a circle with the origin at his navel. These are not the only mathematical symmetries present in da Vinci's study of the ideal man. According to the architect and the text accompanying the drawing, the proportions of man also satisfy the following linear relations.

PROPORTIONS OF MAN

1 height	= 4 nipples up	= 8 upper arms	= 30 ears
= 1 arms out	= 5 forearms	= 10 hands	= 30 foreheads
= 2 halves	= 7 feet	= 10 faces	= 30 mouths
= 4 widths	= 8 heads	= 24 palms	= 96 fingers

where half = beginning of genitals to top of head ❧ width = width at shoulders ❧ nipples up = centre of nipples to top of head ❧ forearm = elbow to tip of hand ❧ head = bottom of chin to top of head ❧ upper arm = elbow to armpit ❧ hand = length of hand ❧ face = bottom of chin to hairline ❧ palm = width of palm ❧ ear = length of ear ❧ forehead = eyebrows to hairline ❧ mouth = bottom of chin to bottom of nose ❧ finger = width of finger

MODULOR

The Swiss architect and designer Le Corbusier (Charles-Edouard Jeanneret) developed the Modulor, 'a measure based on mathematics and the human scale: it is constituted of a double series of numbers, the red series and the blue'. The blue series is twice the red, and any two consecutive lengths in the same series differ by a factor of the Golden ratio (see Colophon, p 212), making the series infinitely extendable.

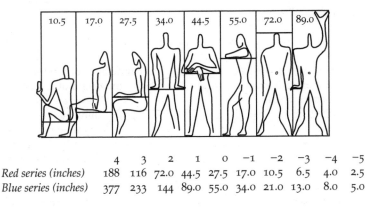

	4	3	2	1	0	−1	−2	−3	−4	−5
Red series (inches)	188	116	72.0	44.5	27.5	17.0	10.5	6.5	4.0	2.5
Blue series (inches)	377	233	144	89.0	55.0	34.0	21.0	13.0	8.0	5.0

BODY MASS INDEX

The ideal relationship between height and weight can be quantified by the body mass index (BMI). The BMI is the number obtained by taking your weight in kilograms divided by your height in metres squared. For example, a 5 ft 10 in (1.78 m) man weighing 160 lb (73 kg) has a BMI of 23. For men, 23 to 25 is ideal (highlighted below), although there is some room for fluctuation. An endomorphic (broadset) build might be just above this range; an ectomorphic (slim) build, just below. James Bond (p 180), who is known to have a lanky frame, has a BMI of 22.4. Below is a table of values for different heights and weights. There may be slight discrepancies due to rounding.

Height								Weight (lb)										Height
(ft in)	130	135	140	145	150	155	160	165	170	175	180	185	190	195	200	205	210	(cm)
5'5"	22	22	**23**	**24**	**25**	26	27	27	28	29	30	31	32	32	33	34	35	165
5'6"	21	22	**23**	**23**	**24**	**25**	26	27	27	28	29	30	31	31	32	33	34	168
5'7"	20	21	22	**23**	**23**	**24**	**25**	26	27	27	28	29	30	31	31	32	33	170
5'8"	20	21	21	22	**23**	**24**	**24**	**25**	26	27	27	28	29	30	30	31	32	173
5'9"	19	20	21	21	22	**23**	**24**	**24**	**25**	26	27	27	28	29	30	30	31	175
5'10"	19	19	20	21	22	22	**23**	**24**	**24**	**25**	26	27	27	28	29	29	30	178
5'11"	18	19	20	20	21	22	22	**23**	**24**	**24**	**25**	26	26	27	28	29	29	180
6'0"	18	18	19	20	20	21	22	22	**23**	**24**	**24**	**25**	26	26	27	28	28	183
6'1"	17	18	18	19	20	20	21	22	22	**23**	**24**	**24**	**25**	26	26	27	28	185
6'2"	17	17	18	19	19	20	21	21	22	22	**23**	**24**	**24**	**25**	26	26	27	188
6'3"	16	17	17	18	19	19	20	21	21	22	22	**23**	**24**	**24**	**25**	26	26	190
6'4"	16	16	17	18	18	19	19	20	21	21	22	**23**	**23**	**24**	**24**	**25**	26	193
	59	61	64	66	68	70	73	75	77	79	82	84	86	88	91	93	95	

Weight (kg)

❦BEARDS

Though not widely seen today, one of the most striking visual differences between the sexes is man's natural display of facial hair. The beard 'is the badge of a man', wrote St Clement of Alexandria. 'Whatever smoothness or softness there was in him God took from him when he fashioned the delicate Eve from his side…'

BEARD LENGTH

On average, facial hair grows as long as it is wide every three hours. It grows about 0.4 inches a month, or 0.013 inches a day. A more natural unit for beard length can be borrowed from typography: the point, where 72.3 points = 1 inch. Beards grow 1 point per day. Different lengths of facial hair have different names, as follows:

Name	Days	Length (in points)	Notes
Shadow	<1	<1	change of shade; whiskers not noticeable
Umbra	1–2	1–2	worn with impunity: 'I've been very busy'
Stubble	3–4	3–4	ambiguous: 'Did he forget to shave?'
Designer stubble	5–8	5–8	stubble with intent; no longer negligence
Bristle	9–16	9–16	most awkward stage of growing a beard
Beard	17+	17+	will continue to grow at 5 inches a year

BEARD TRIMMING

Trimming a beard not only reduces its length but also makes it thicker: the surface of an untrimmed beard is sparse, because not all hairs grow at the same rate. Most men shave the hair below the neckline, even in the case of full beards. The only facial hair allowed in the British armed forces is the moustache, except in the Royal Navy, which permits a 'full set', that is, a moustache and beard combined. At one point, the Catholic Church allowed priests to have facial hair only on the condition that they did not trim it – this being a sign of vanity. The fashion for facial topiary during the 1990s now seems rather studied, and today the most accepted form of facial hair is a full set not longer than ¾ inch = 54 points = 54 days.

There are two myths about beards which should be dispelled. The first is that shorter hair grows faster. This is not possible, since the hair follicle cannot tell how long the hair has been cut: there is no communication along the hair shaft, which is dead. But the follicle does know how old the hair is, and after a fixed period the hair is expelled and a new hair emerges, which is why hair does not grow beyond a fixed length. The second myth is that shaved hair grows back thicker. This is only partly true, in that the first growth from a follicle is fine and tapers to a point, with further growth of normal thickness. Cutting off the tip makes the new end thicker, but cutting it again has no effect.

BEARD TYPES

Here is a classification of facial hair, redrawn from a print from the Yale University November Beard Club.

Hollywoodian

Mutton Chops

A la Souvarov

French Fork

Handlebar
and Chin Puff

Van Dyke

Friendly
Mutton Chops

Balbo

Short Boxed Beard

Goatee

Chin Curtain

Hulihee

Petit Goatee

Franz-Josef

Anchor

Napoleon III
Imperial

❦SHAVING

A typical man will shave his beard approximately 12,000 times in his life-time, which is the equivalent of being a full-time barber for six months. For most men, shaving is their most practised skill outside of their profession, so it is worth considering how this masculine ritual is best executed.

RAZOR

Wet shaving Shaving razors fall into two categories: traditional straight and safety razors, which must be regularly sharpened on a leather strop or stone; and razors that are never sharpened but instead thrown out when dull. Disposable razors have advanced considerably since Gillette introduced the disposable blade in 1903. Despite the superior aesthetic of using a straight razor, today disposable razors are invariably the superior choice.

Dry (electric) shaving Shaving with an electric razor is analogous to wearing wrinkle-free polyester shirts – an inferior product driven by a philosophy of comfort and pragmatism. Because the lubricant in a wet shave causes the whiskers to swell, it is unlikely that dry shaving will ever compete with the closeness of a razor. Use an electric razor if you must – for example, if you have particularly sensitive skin. But don't tell anyone about it.

LUBRICANT

Shaving with a razor is sometimes called wet shaving, because it requires the use of a lubricant to reduce the friction between the razor and the skin. There are two kinds of common lubricant: foams and gels, which can be applied to the skin directly from the source; and creams and soaps, which must first be whisked into a foam with hot water and a shaving brush.

Foams and gels A comparatively recent innovation, these are the most popular and convenient. A small shot from the can is spread over the face with the hand. There is not much difference between a foam and a gel: both produce a thick white lather on application.

Creams and soaps Cream comes in a tub, and a wet brush is dipped into it and whisked into a foam in the palm of the other hand or directly on to the face. Shaving soap has the consistency of hand soap when dry, but lathers into a dense foam with a brush and a shaving pot (a small bowl in which it is mixed). For those who have sensitive skin, it is wise to use a cream mixed with an equal part of skin lotion, which is then lathered as usual.

SHAVING BRUSHES

These are used to whisk creams and soaps. They can be made from several kinds of bristle, but the best bristle comes from badgers. Badger hair is flexible, stores heat and retains water. But not all badger bristles are equal; the softest, finest-tipped hairs are found around the badger's neck, and only in winter. A brush of these materials makes anything lather.

Name	Source	Texture and colour	Animal rights activist response
Boar	various	coarse, white or dark	tepid
Dark badger	underbelly	coarse, nearly black	threatening stares
Pure badger	tail	medium, grey	hate mail
Best badger	back	fine, light-dark-light	prick car tyres
Super badger	neck	very fine, silver-tipped	tar & feather owner

INSTRUCTIONS FOR WET SHAVING

Wet shaving comprises three steps: preparing the whiskers with lather, shaving them with a razor, and rinsing and assessing the skin.

Lather up The most important ingredient for shaving with a razor is water. Not only should the face be wet, but the skin and whiskers should also have absorbed water. If you can't shave right after a shower, rinse your face generously with hot water a couple of minutes before shaving. Then, using your hand or a brush, apply foam or gel, or whisked cream or soap, on to your face for 15 seconds.

Shave Using a sharp razor, apply short strokes along the direction of growth. Don't press down – a light contact will do if the blade is sharp. 'The rhythm of a morning shave is a slow blues – a quiet, solitary, contemplative experience', explain B. Sloan and S. Guarnaccia in *A Stiff Drink and a Close Shave*. There is a natural order of which parts to shave when. Begin with the least dense areas and finish with the densest: first the sides, then cheeks, neck, upper lip, lower lip and chin. While shaving against the grain may cause irritation, the best barbers finish by shaving across the grain.

Rinse and assess Rinse your face with cold water to remove cream and close the pores. Press small cuts with wet paper, then dry paper, or apply an alum stick. A skin cream at this stage would not go amiss (though no eyebrow plucking). If using a shaving brush, rinse it in water, shake out any excess and stand it up or, preferably, hang it upside down on a holder to dry.

❦PUBLIC LOOS

There is an unstated code of behaviour in men's public loos which, while more instinctive than prescriptive, is surprisingly universal.

RULES OF CONDUCT

No pairing Unlike women, men visit the lavatory entirely for practical reasons, and it is suspect to immediately follow a friend to the loo.

No talking Terse conversation in the loo can take place before and after, but not during, use of the urinals.

No looking Eyes should be aimed straight ahead or down in concentration; glances towards your neighbour are very suggestive.

No touching Hands should be in front of you. A bump of the elbows can be deflated by a sober apology, but without turning the head.

OPTIMAL STRATEGY

When faced with an array of urinals to choose from, which one should you take? The basic idea is that the distance between users should be maximized, at the same minimizing a newcomer's chance of getting too close. The latter makes the endmost urinals highly desirable. Never go between two men if it can be avoided. Below are sample situations and the best strategy for each, where ○ means vacant and ♱ occupied. (Assume that any man following you chooses a vacant urinal at random.)

1	2	3	4	5	6	
○	○	○	○	○	○	Urinals 1 and 6 are correct, and every man knows this.
♱	○	○	○	○	○	6 is correct, but 5 is sometimes picked to avoid showing paranoia.
♱	○	○	○	○	♱	3 and 4 maximize the distance from others.
♱	○	○	♱	○	♱	Urinal 2 offers a slight advantage over 3.
○	♱	♱	○	○	♱	Urinal 1 is the surprise correct answer.
♱	○	♱	○	♱	♱	An unpleasant scenario, but 2 is the lesser of two evils.

URINAL TEST

Below is a test of where to stand along a line-up of seven urinals. It includes all possible configurations with two or more vacancies, excluding mirror images. What is the optimal choice for each? The answers are on p 13.

	1	2	3	4	5	6	7
1	o	o	o	o	o	o	o
2	♦	o	o	o	o	o	o
3	o	o	o	o	♦	o	o
4	o	♦	o	o	o	o	o
5	o	o	o	♦	o	o	o
6	o	o	o	o	o	♦	♦
7	o	♦	o	♦	o	o	o
8	o	♦	o	o	o	o	♦
9	o	o	o	♦	♦	o	o
10	o	o	♦	o	o	o	♦
11	♦	o	o	♦	o	o	o
12	o	o	♦	o	o	♦	o
13	♦	o	o	o	o	o	♦
14	♦	o	♦	o	o	o	o
15	o	o	o	o	♦	♦	o
16	o	♦	o	o	o	♦	o
17	o	o	♦	o	♦	o	o
18	♦	♦	♦	o	o	o	o
19	♦	o	o	o	o	♦	♦
20	♦	o	o	o	♦	o	♦
21	o	o	♦	♦	♦	o	o
22	o	o	o	♦	♦	♦	o
23	♦	♦	o	o	o	♦	o

	1	2	3	4	5	6	7
24	o	o	♦	♦	o	♦	o
25	o	♦	o	♦	o	o	♦
26	o	♦	o	♦	o	♦	o
27	♦	♦	o	♦	o	o	o
28	o	o	♦	o	♦	♦	o
29	o	♦	o	o	♦	o	♦
30	o	♦	♦	o	o	o	♦
31	♦	o	o	♦	o	o	♦
32	♦	o	♦	♦	o	o	o
33	o	o	♦	o	o	♦	♦
34	o	o	♦	o	♦	o	♦
35	o	♦	o	o	♦	♦	o
36	o	o	♦	♦	o	o	♦
37	o	o	o	♦	♦	♦	♦
38	o	o	♦	♦	♦	♦	o
39	♦	o	♦	o	o	♦	♦
40	♦	♦	o	o	o	♦	♦
41	o	♦	♦	♦	o	o	♦
42	♦	o	♦	♦	o	o	♦
43	♦	♦	♦	o	o	♦	o
44	♦	♦	♦	o	o	o	♦
45	o	♦	o	♦	♦	o	♦
46	♦	o	o	♦	o	♦	♦

	1	2	3	4	5	6	7
47	o	♦	♦	o	♦	♦	o
48	o	♦	♦	o	o	♦	♦
49	o	♦	♦	o	♦	o	♦
50	♦	♦	♦	o	♦	o	o
51	o	o	♦	♦	o	♦	♦
52	♦	o	♦	♦	♦	o	o
53	♦	o	♦	o	♦	o	♦
54	♦	♦	o	o	♦	♦	o
55	o	♦	o	♦	♦	♦	o
56	♦	♦	♦	♦	♦	o	o
57	o	♦	♦	♦	o	♦	♦
58	♦	o	o	♦	♦	♦	♦
59	♦	♦	o	♦	o	♦	♦
60	o	♦	o	♦	♦	♦	♦
61	♦	o	♦	o	♦	♦	♦
62	o	♦	♦	♦	♦	♦	o
63	o	♦	♦	♦	♦	o	♦
64	♦	♦	♦	o	o	♦	♦
65	♦	o	♦	♦	o	♦	♦
66	♦	♦	♦	o	♦	♦	o
67	♦	o	♦	♦	♦	o	♦

AN EQUATION FOR THE BEST URINAL

Let N be the total number of urinals, labelled from left to right by $k = 1, 2, ..., N$, of which $q + 1$ are vacant. Assume on average one new man approaches a random vacant urinal (without applying any strategy) during the typical period of occupation. As he may come in at any point after you, the average intersection of his and your occupation time is $\frac{1}{2}$. Further assume the interaction between men is repulsive with an inverse square law. Then the optimal unoccupied urinal k_{opt} is the one which minimizes $E(k)$ below:

$$E(k) = 1/(2q) \sum_{i \neq k} 1/(k - i)^2 + (2q - 1)/(2q) \sum_{i \ occupied} 1/(k - i)^2.$$

❦ FAMILY JEWELS

HIGH BALL

Zoe: How's the nuts? / Bloom: Off side. Curiously they are on the right. Heavier I suppose. One in a million my tailor, Mesias, says. (James Joyce, *Ulysses*)

The Ancient Greeks were well aware that a man's testicles were not symmetrical, but that one – usually the left – descended lower than the other. This anatomical subtlety is borne out in their sculpture. Of 187 statues considered by the psychologist I. C. McManus, 51% show the left testicle to be lower and 22% the right, the remainder being of equal descent ('Right-left and the scrotum in Greek sculpture', *Laterality*, **9**, 189 (2004)). This correlates with modern-day observations. Chang et al. (*Journal of Anatomy*, **94**, 543 (1960)) found the left testicle to be lower in 62% of subjects and the right in 27%, the rest being indistinguishable. The reason for this bias is not known, but Bloom's explanation above can be dismissed. It is widely accepted that, surprisingly, the right testicle tends to be heavier and larger. (For the cylindrical drinking vessel highball, see Glasses, p 124.)

DRESSING

Dressing is the persistent self-positioning of a man's jewels to the same side of his trousers. A man is said to 'dress to the left' or 'dress to the right' if he predominantly falls to the left or right trouser leg. The best time to tell which side you're on is while sitting down. When making a suit (p 53), some tailors assemble the crotch of the trousers asymmetrically to account for this bias. There are a number of theories to account for dressing, none of which has been substantiated: the direction of dress corresponds with left-/right-handedness; it is the side of the lower testicle (see High ball, above); it is a by-product of wearing trousers twisted round the waist.

VARICOCELE

Generally harmless, a varicocele is the enlargement of the blood vessels that drain blood from one of the testicles. As with varicose veins common in women, a varicocele is caused by the malfunction of the one-way valves in the vessels. When the valves can no longer counteract the force of gravity, blood pools in the lower veins. The condition affects around 15% of men, the bulk of cases involving the left testicle, and feels like a soft testicular lump. There are usually no symptoms, although the varicocele may seem to disappear while lying down when the blood drains away from it.

CIRCUMCISION

The ancient Egyptians practised circumcision, and the Book of Jeremiah (9:26) adds the Jews, Edomites, Ammonites and Moabites. On the other hand, the ancient Greeks thought circumcision unbecoming, and associated it with satyrs, the promiscuous man-goat race that wandered the forest. The early Christian Church frowned on the practice, and by medieval times it was prohibited: '[The Holy Roman Church] strictly orders all who glory in the name of Christian not to practise circumcision either before or after baptism, since…it cannot possibly be observed without loss of eternal salvation', declared Pope Eugenius IV in his 1442 papal bull. The curious popularity of circumcision in the English-speaking world largely originated in the late 19th century in the United States, where the removal of the foreskin was associated with all sorts of remedial and preventive medicine. Although circumcision is now believed to confer no significant medical benefits, the majority of males are circumcised for non-religious reasons in the United States, the Philippines and South Korea.

BLUE BALLS

Although sometimes dismissed as an old wives' – or rather husbands' – tale, blue balls is well recognized, if not fully understood or documented. It is a painful ache in the scrotum, caused by prolonged arousal, and affects many adolescent and mature men, though infrequently. While the pathophysiology is not understood, J. M. Chalett and L. T. Nerenberg conjecture that, in tandem with persistent pelvic venous dilation, 'testicular venous drainage is slowed, pressure builds and causes pain' ('Blue Balls', *Pediatrics*, **106**, 843 (2000)). The discomfort ceases on release or subsides on its own after one or two hours. Circumstantial evidence suggests that the name may derive from a blue tint in the scrotum caused by reduced circulation – de-oxygenated blood being darker than oxygenated.

ANSWERS TO THE URINAL TEST (ON P 11)

1. 1,7	9. 1	17. 1,7	25. 1	33. 1	41. 1	49. 1	57. 1	65. 2
2. 7	10. 1	18. 7	26. 1,7	34. 1	42. 6	50. 7	58. 2	66. 7
3. 1	11. 7	19. 3	27. 7	35. 1	43. 7	51. 1	59. 3,5	67. 2,6
4. 7	12. 1	20. 3	28. 1	36. 1	44. 5	52. 7	60. 1	
5. 1,7	13. 4	21. 1,7	29. 1	37. 1	45. 1	53. 2,6	61. 2	
6. 1	14. 7	22. 1	30. 5	38. 1	46. 2	54. 7	62. 1,7	
7. 7	15. 1	23. 4	31. 2,6	39. 4	47. 1,7	55. 1	63. 1	
8. 5	16. 4	24. 1	32. 7	40. 4	48. 1	56. 7	64. 5	

❦ HAIR LOSS

Given that two-thirds of men will suffer from hair loss at some point in their lives, it is puzzling to find the subject so full of misinformation, pseudo-science and charlatanism. In part this is explained by a limited understanding of what causes – and prevents – the spontaneous thinning of hair. The rest is due to opportunistic marketing of alternative and quack medicines to gullible and often desperate men. Differentiating fact from fiction and finding reliable, transparent information on the subject remains difficult.

HEALTHY HAIR GROWTH

Healthy hair on the scalp has a two-stage life cycle: a growth period of two to six years, during which hair grows about 0.3 mm per day, followed by a dormant period of two to four months. After this the hair falls out, and a new hair emerges from the same hair follicle. (Hair on other parts of the body has a shorter life cycle and therefore does not grow as long.) Different hairs are in different phases in this cycle, so that on any given day only about 50–150 hairs fall out, which is less than 0.1% of the total number of hairs on the scalp.

MALE PATTERN BALDNESS

The dominant form of hair loss in men is called androgenetic alopecia, more commonly known as male pattern baldness. It generally follows a fixed pattern of progression: the corners of the hairline recede first, giving rise to an 'M'-shaped hairline. This is followed by a thinning of the hairline generally and also the crown (the top of the head). Eventually the exposed areas of the hairline and crown join, leaving hair at the back and sides only, which itself may continue to thin. This is the course to total baldness; in most men hair loss will tail off at some intermediate point. The type and degree of hair loss can be classified using the Hamilton-Norwood scale (opposite), first devised by James Hamilton and later revised by O'Tar Norwood in 1975. The scale ranges from HN 1 (a full head of hair; not shown) to HN 7; higher numbers correspond to more severe cases.

In male pattern baldness, hair loss is not caused by the sudden loss of hair but rather increasingly diminished growth of individual hairs over time. In the early stages, the number of hairs remains constant, and what appears as hair loss is in fact a reduction in the thickness and rate of growth of new hairs. Each generation of new hair grows back finer, shorter, often lighter-coloured than before. As the condition progresses, hair appears wispy, then like peach fuzz and eventually cannot be seen at all.

HAMILTON-NORWOOD SCALE

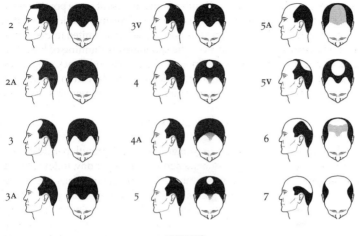

MYTHS

There are several commonly held myths about hair loss. One is that the incidence of hair loss in a man is solely determined by the maternal grandfather. Although it is heritable, there is at present no way to accurately predict who will lose his hair or when he will lose it. A recent study has found that men whose fathers exhibit hair loss are 2–2.5 times as likely to suffer from hair loss as those whose fathers have a full head of hair. Another myth is that wearing hats, caps or bandannas promotes hair loss, for which there is no support. It is often claimed that stress or significant mental exercise can initiate or hasten hair loss, but the evidence for this too is scant.

TREATMENTS

All hair-loss drugs are more successful at preventing the decay of healthy hair follicles than reviving dormant follicles which produce fine, wispy hair. So the earlier hair loss is treated, the greater is the amount of hair that is likely to be maintained. For the time being, baldness is more preventable than reversible.

The primary contributing factor in male pattern baldness is believed to be the androgenic hormone dihydrotestosterone (DHT). Increased levels of DHT are known to inhibit hair growth, although how this occurs remains poorly understood. Higher testosterone levels are not in themselves correlated with increased likelihood of hair loss.

In what might appear to be a stroke of fortune for drug companies, hair-loss treatments do not cure hair loss once and for all; rather the medicine has to be taken indefinitely. If the treatment is terminated, the rate of hair loss will return to its pre-treatment levels. Bear in mind, however, that the way baldness is treated is changing rapidly, and today's maintenance will likely prove to be a stop-gap until the arrival of superior, possibly permanent treatments.

PROPECIA

Finasteride, marketed as Propecia, is, along with Minoxidil (see below), the only US Food and Drug Administration-approved hair-loss drug. This does not imply that other treatments are not effective; gaining FDA approval is expensive and requires additionally that a drug's side-effects are understood and minimal. Propecia is currently accepted as the most effective treatment for hair loss, with 30–75% of users reporting constant or increased hair levels. It works by inhibiting the production of DHT, and is administered in the form of a pill taken daily.

MINOXIDIL

Minoxidil, marketed as Regaine in most countries except the US (where it is known as Rogaine), has been shown to slow or stop hair loss in 25–40% of patients. It was originally developed as a high-blood-pressure treatment, with increased hair growth an unintended side-effect. Despite its commercial success, how it fights hair loss is not well understood. It is applied as a solution or cream directly to the afflicted area once or twice a day. Despite Homer Simpson's immediate results with Dimoxinil (Simpson and Delilah, episode 7F02, 1990), both Propecia and Regaine require three to six months' use before clear results appear.

BOLD

Despite the relative advances in dealing with baldness, I admire the man who resolutely refuses to resort to medicine to halt hair loss. And even a strict regimen of treatments cannot reverse stubborn genetics. As with most aspects of men's appearance, an air of indifference is essential to wearing thin hair well. At some point, manipulating sparse hair to hide the head must come to an end. Yul Brynner shaved his head completely and made baldness chic. Zinedine Zidane knew when to make the cut, as did Andre Agassi, both of whom keep their hair close-cropped. John Malkovich and Sean Connery kept their hair mid-length but never wore a comb-over.

SPORTS

Samuel Johnson · I take the true definition of exercise to be labour without weariness. (Boswell, *Life of Johnson*, 1791)

Olympic oath · In the name of all the competitors I promise that we shall take part in these Olympic Games, respecting and abiding by the rules which govern them, committing ourselves to a sport without doping and without drugs, in the true spirit of sportsmanship, for the glory of sport and the honour of our teams. (Last modified at Sydney, 2000)

Izaak Walton · As inward love breeds outward talk, /The hound some praise, and some the hawk; / Some, better pleased with private sport, / Use tennis; some a mistress court; / But these delights I neither wish / Nor envy, while I freely fish. (The Angler's Song, *The Compleat Angler*, 1653)

Vince Lombardi · Show me a good loser, and I'll show you a loser.

Ernest Hemingway · There are only three sports: bullfighting, motor racing and mountaineering; all the rest are merely games. (Attributed to Hemingway but likely derived from *Blood Sport* by Ken Purdy, 1957)

The first Lord Brabazon of Tara · The Cresta is like a woman with this cynical difference – to love her once is to love her always.

Arnold Schwarzenegger · Pain divides a champion from someone who is not a champion. That's what most people lack, having the guts to go on and just say they'll go through the pain no matter what happens. I have no fear of fainting. I do squats until I fall over and pass out. So what? It's not going to kill me. I wake up five minutes later and I'm OK. A lot of other athletes are afraid of this. So they don't pass out. They don't go on.

Ron Atkinson · Well, either side could win it, or it could be a draw.

❦EXERCISES AT HOME

James Bond (p 180), often away from home for days at a time, occasionally exercises in his room in the mornings to rouse himself from self-pity or (more often) a hangover. A typical routine, described in Ian Fleming's *From Russia with Love*, is as follows:

> Bond went down on his hands and did twenty slow press-ups, lingering over each one so that his muscles had no rest. When his arms could stand the pain no longer, he rolled over on his back and, with his hands at his sides, did the straight leg-lift until his stomach muscles screamed. He got to his feet and, after touching his toes twenty times, went over to arm and chest exercises combined with deep breathing until he was dizzy.

Despite the modern obsession with exercising in a gym, it is possible to do a serious workout at home with no equipment apart from two sturdy chairs and a bar or broomstick.

PRESS-UPS

This is the most versatile weights-free exercise of all. With the hands directly under the shoulders, the triceps are emphasized; a wider placement works the pectoral muscles. The difficulty can be increased by raising the feet off the ground: for example, on the front of a chair or, higher still, the back of a chair. As the body approaches vertical (a handstand), this exercise approaches a military press with the body's own weight – not easy. In *The Education of a Bodybuilder* (Books, p 172), Arnold Schwarzenegger advises 'Do not let your ego get in the way of your progress. Perhaps somebody told you you should do 20 or 50 push-ups. Put it out of your mind… The important thing is to do the exercise correctly; that counts for everything.'

PULL-UPS

This is one of the most effective of all exercises, and the most difficult of those without weights. 'This is probably the only exercise you can do without gym equipment to build impressive biceps,' writes Schwarzenegger. To do it, you need a raised, fixed bar to grab hold up. One option is to place bar inside a door jamb. Alternatively, a horizontal tree branch can work. There are two kinds of pull-ups: hands facing in (also known as chin-ups) with a closer grip, and hands facing out, with a wider grip. Hands-in mainly works the biceps, then lats, and also expands the chest. Hands-out works the lats then biceps. If you can do three sets of 12 in five minutes, rejoice.

CHAIR DIPS

Chair dips are excellent for working the triceps and also the deltoid (the main muscle of the shoulder). Find two chairs with sturdy, straight backs, and place them back-to-back, just further apart than the width of your shoulders. Standing between them, put your hands on the top of the chair backs and, keeping your legs bent, rest your entire weight on the chairs. Lower yourself as much as possible by bending your arms, then extend your arms to lift your weight. Keep your head and back straight. This exercise will be difficult at first but you will improve quickly. Aim for sets of 20.

REVERSE BENCH (ROWS)

This exercise is good for the back, similar in its effect to seated rows. Put two chairs back-to-back, four feet apart, and place a bar or broomstick across the backs of both. Lie on your back with your chest under the bar and hold it overhand with a wide grip, pulling yourself slowly to the top; your legs should be straight with your feet acting as a pivot point. The resistance can be increased by putting your feet on a chair, thereby starting from a decline position. The back should not touch the floor between repetitions.

TRICEPS EXTENSIONS

This is another focus on the triceps, but also works the back and lats. Put two chairs front-to-front, three or four feet apart. Place your heels on the seat of one, and your hands, behind your back, on the corners of the seat of the other. The idea is to use your arms to lower and raise your body with the feet stationary and acting as the pivot point. Lower yourself as far as you can and then fully extend your arms, all the while keeping your legs as straight as possible. Work towards sets of 30; if these become easy, put a couple of heavy books on your lap for added resistance.

BENT-KNEE SIT-UPS

Sit-ups are one of the best exercises for the upper abdominals. Keep your knees bent and fix your feet under, say, a sofa. Put your hands at your sides, or against the sides of your neck for added resistance. 'It is not necessary to lie back fully – only about three-quarters of the way – but the movement should be very smooth and rhythmical. With abdominals all you need is contraction. It's actually one of the few sets of muscles we don't give a full movement,' explains Schwarzenegger. If you can do 50 in one go, hold a couple of books against your chest.

❦EXERCISES IN A GYM

The most effective method of lifting weights – and by this is meant high-resistance anaerobic exercise for size and strength – is to use free weights instead of machines where possible. Of course, some exercises are difficult or impossible to perform without machines – leg curls, for instance. But free weights or the body's own weight should be used for most exercises. Part of the reason is that machines invariably lock the motion into a fixed path, negating the subconscious effort put into symmetry and balance. This means that the auxiliary muscles that keep the motion from wandering off course are neglected. The result is a body without tie-ins between muscle groups and left–right symmetry. As a practical advantage, free weights are universal in the sense that they can be done identically in any gym.

ROUTINE

Weight training is usually organized by a fixed routine, repeated each week:

Session	Visit to the gym	2–6 times per week
Exercise	Focus on specific muscles (see pp 21–2)	6–12 per session
Set	Period of continuous exertion	3–5 per exercise
Rep	Repetition of the same movement	7–12 per set

Sessions may incorporate a fixed set of exercises, or cycle through different major muscle groups: legs and abdominals one session, arms and shoulders the next, for example. The number and intensity of repetitions is determined by the weight-training goal: higher numbers of repetitions to increase strength; lower numbers, done to failure, to increase bulk.

SINGLE-REPETITION MAXIMUM

The single-repetition maximum is the highest weight you can push, pull or lift. It can be calculated for any exercise from your performance at a lower weight as follows. Let r be the maximum number of repetitions that can be done at some weight w. Then $C(r) \times w$ is your single-repetition maximum, where $C(r)$ is given in the table below:

Reps r	2	3	4	5	6	7	8	9	10
$C(r)$	1.062	1.109	1.152	1.191	1.227	1.259	1.287	1.311	1.332

For example, if you can bench-press 135 lb just 8 times, then your maximum for a single repetition is 1.287 × 135 lb = 173.7 lb.

LOADING WEIGHTS

Standard Olympic bars have a solid 1-inch-diameter central segment and 2-inch-diameter ends for loading appropriately fitted metal plates. The bar itself weighs 20 kg. Despite being 44.1 lb, 20-kg plates are usually taken to be 45 lb for the purposes of reckoning. (As a rule of thumb, a fit man should be able to bench-press his own weight.) Plates are available in the various weights below:

Plate sizes	(kg)	20	10	5	2½	1¼
	(lb)	44.1	22.0	11.0	5.51	2.75

This binary system has the advantage that all resistance levels, from 20 kg to 97.5 kg in 2.5-kg intervals, can be symmetrically loaded with only two plates of each size. For any given total weight, including the 20 kg bar, the optimal loading of plates per side is shown below:

Plates per side

Total	20	10	5	2½	1¼
20					
22.5					1
25			1		
27.5			1		1
30		1			
32.5		1			1
35		1	1		
37.5		1	1		1
40	1				
42.5	1				1

Total	20	10	5	2½	1¼
45		1		1	
47.5		1		1	1
50		1	1		
52.5		1	1		1
55		1	1	1	
57.5		1	1	1	1
60	1				
62.5	1				1
65	1			1	
67.5	1			1	1
70	1		1		

Total	20	10	5	2½	1¼
72.5	1		1		1
75	1		1	1	
77.5	1		1	1	1
80	1	1			
82.5	1	1			1
85	1	1		1	
87.5	1	1		1	1
90	1	1	1		
92.5	1	1	1		1
95	1	1	1	1	
97.5	1	1	1	1	1

EXERCISES BY PRINCIPAL MUSCLE WORKED

Below are 30 classic lifting exercises. A moderate routine might be 3–4 sets per exercise, 8 exercises per session and 3 sessions per week; for intensive training, 10 exercises per session and 6 sessions per week. The 10 most essential exercises are marked ★.

Biceps

★ Standing barbell curls — A bent barbell works best. Keep elbows fixed.
Seated dumbbell curls — Rest elbow in hand, one arm at a time.
Dumbbell curl on incline bench — Keep upper arms vertical with floor.
Pull-ups — With palms facing in and a close grip (see p 18).

Triceps

★ Tricep extensions   Use bent grip from overhead cable. Elbows fixed.
  French press   Lock elbows straight above, lower barbell to back of neck.
  Parallel bar dips   Isolates triceps with body's own weight (see p 19).

Forearms

★ Wrist curls   With forearms flat on bench lift barbell with palms-up grip.
  Reverse wrist curls   Like wrist curls but with palms-down grip.

Chest

★ Bench press   Wider grip for pectorals, closer grip for triceps.
  Incline press   Works upper pecs for armour-plated look.
  Bent-arm flyes   Lying on bench, lift dumbbells from sides to over chest.
  Machine flyes   Start with arms 180 degrees apart. Good for definition.

Shoulders

★ Military press (a.k.a. Shoulder press)   In front of or behind neck.
  Dumbbell lateral raises   While standing, raise dumbbells to horizontal.
  Upright rows   While standing, lift barbell with close grip to chest.
  Bent-over cable laterals   With arms crossed, use two floor-level pulleys.

Calves

  Standing calf raises   Keep knees locked. Beware of back strains.
★ Seated calf raises   Use heavy loads. Do not rock back and forth.
  Calf-extensions on leg press   Balls of feet on lower edge of foot plate.

Thighs

  Leg press   Contract until legs are 70 or 80 degrees at the knee.
★ Squats   Foundation exercise for working the quadriceps.
★ Leg curls   Isolates the back of the thighs.
  Leg extensions   Focuses on the front of the thigh and above the knee.

Abdominals

★ Sit-ups   When performed on a decline adds considerable resistance.
  Crunches   Either lying on your back or with a vertical bench.
  Bent-knee leg raises   Lying on back, lift and contract legs.

Back (including lats)

★ Wide-grip chins   With palms facing out. Also try behind neck.
  Bent-over rows   With back parallel to floor lift barbell to waist.
  Seated rows   Done with cable and T-bar with close grip.

❦ SPORTS CALENDAR

Below are sports highlights for 2008. Events that were not scheduled by July 2007 are not included. Bear in mind that the dates are subject to change, especially those set far in advance.

Because 2008 is an Olympic year, some international competitions have merged with the corresponding Olympic event. For details of the 2008 Olympics, see p 28.

KEY   tba = to be announced   tbc = to be confirmed

American football	*in 2008*
American Football Conference Championship Game, *tba, US*	20 Jan
National Football Conference Championship Game, *tba, US*	20 Jan
Super Bowl XLII (AFC vs NFC champions), *Glendale, Arizona, US*	3 Feb
Pro Bowl (AFC vs NFC All-Stars), *Honolulu, Hawaii, US*	10 Feb

Archery	
Archery World Cup Stage 1, *Dominican Republic*	1–8 Apr
World Cup Stage 2, *Porec, Croatia*	15–19 Apr
World Cup Stage 3, *Antalya, Turkey*	27–31 May
World Cup Stage 4, *Boe, France*	23–29 Jun
World Field Archery Championships, *Llwynypia, Wales*	1–6 Sep

Athletics	
World Indoor Athletics Championships, *Valencia, Spain*	7–9 Mar
World Cross Country Championships, *Edinburgh, Scotland*	30 Mar
African Athletics Championships, *Addis Ababa, Ethiopia*	1–5 May
World Race Walking Cup, *Cheboksary, Russia*	15–16 May
European Athletics Cup, *Annecy, France*	21–22 Jun
World Athletics Final, *Stuttgart, Germany*	20–21 Sep
World Road Running Championships, *Rio de Janeiro, Brazil*	tba, Oct

Badminton	
European Badminton Championships, *Herning, Denmark*	tbc, 16–20 Apr
Thomas and Uber Cup Finals, *Jakarta, Indonesia*	11–18 May

Basketball	
NBA All-Star Game, *New Orleans, Louisiana, US*	17 Feb
NCAA Basketball Final Four, *San Antonio, Texas, US*	5, 7 Apr
Olympic Test Event, *Beijing, China*	19–25 Apr
Euroleague Final Four, *Madrid, Spain*	2–4 May

Bodybuilding

Arnold Classic, *Columbus, Ohio, US*	29 Feb–2 Mar
Mr Olympia, *Las Vegas, Nevada, US, tbc*	tba, Sep

Cricket

Triangular One Day International Series (Australia, India and Sri Lanka), *various*	tbc, begins 3 Feb
Triangular One Day International Series (Bangladesh, India and South Africa), *various*	tba, begins Mar
ICC Champions Trophy, *Pakistan, tbc*	tba, Sep

Cycling

Cyclo-Cross World Championships, *Treviso, Italy*	26–27 Jan
Track World Championships, *Manchester, England*	26–30 Mar
Giro d'Italia, *Italy*	10 May–1 Jun
BMX World Championships, *Taiyuan, China*	30 May–1 Jun
Mountain Bike World Championships, *Val di Sole, Italy*	16–22 Jun
Tour de France, *France*	5–27 Jul
Mountain Bike Marathon World Championships, *Villabassa, Italy*	6 Jul
Road World Championships, *Varese, Italy*	24–28 Sep
Indoor Cycling World Championships, *Ballerup, Denmark*	22–24 Nov

Darts

World Darts Championship, *London, England*	17 Dec 2007–1 Jan
World Prof. Darts Championship, *Frimley Green, England*	5–13 Jan

Flat racing

2000 Guineas, *Newmarket, Suffolk, England*	tba, May
1000 Guineas, *Newmarket, Suffolk, England*	tba, May
The Oaks, *Epsom Downs, Surrey, England*	6 Jun
The Derby, *Epsom Downs, Surrey, England*	7 Jun
Gold Cup, *Ascot, Berkshire, England*	tba, Jun
Eclipse, *Sandown Park, Surrey, England*	tba, Jul
King George VI & Queen Elizabeth, *Ascot, Berkshire, England*	tba, Jul
St Leger, *Doncaster, Yorkshire, England*	tba, Sep
Champion, *Newmarket, Suffolk, England*	tba, Oct

Football

African Cup of Nations, *Ghana*	20 Jan–10 Feb
UEFA Cup Final, *Manchester, England*	14 May
FA Cup Final, *London, England*	17 May
UEFA Champions League Final, *Moscow, Russia*	21 May

Games

Olympic Games, *Beijing, China*	8–24 Aug
Paralympic Games, *Beijing, China*	6–17 Sep
Commonwealth Youth Games, *Pune, India*	12–18 Oct
Pan Pacific Masters Games, *Gold Coast, Australia*	1–9 Nov

Golf

US Masters, *Augusta, Georgia, US*	10–13 Apr
US Open, *La Jolla, California, US*	12–15 Jun
British Open, *Southport, England*	17–20 Jul
US PGA Championship, *Bloomfield Township, Michigan, US*	4–10 Aug
Ryder Cup, *Louisville, Kentucky, US*	16–21 Sep

Ice hockey

NHL All-Star Game, *Atlanta, Georgia, US*	16 Jan
World Championship, *Quebec City and Halifax, Canada*	1–18 May

Marathons

London Marathon, *London, England*	13 Apr
Boston Marathon, *Boston, Massachusetts, US*	21 Apr
Berlin Marathon, *Berlin, Germany*	28 Sep
Chicago Marathon, *Chicago, Illinois, US*	12 Oct
New York City Marathon, *New York City, New York, US*	tba, Nov

Motor racing

Daytona 500, *Daytona Beach, Florida, US*	17 Feb
Indianapolis 500, *Speedway, Indiana, US*	25 May
24 Hours of Le Mans, *Le Mans, France*	14–15 Jun
Goodwood Festival of Speed, *Goodwood House, West Sussex, England*	tba, late Jun/early Jul
Le Mans Classic, *Le Mans, France*	11–13 Jul
British Grand Prix, *Silverstone, England*	11–13 Jul
London to Brighton Veteran Car Run, *London, England*	2 Nov

Rowing

The Boat Race (Oxford vs Cambridge), *River Thames, London, England*	29 Apr
Rowing World Cup, *Munich, Germany*	9–11 May
Rowing World Cup, *Poznan, Poland*	30 May–1 Jun
Rowing World Cup, *Lucerne, Switzerland*	20–22 Jun
Henley Royal Regatta, *Henley-on-Thames, Oxfordshire, England*	2–6 Jul
World Rowing Championships, *Ottensheim, Austria*	22–27 Jul
European Rowing Championships, *Marathon, Greece*	tba, Sep

Rugby

The Varsity Match (Oxford vs Cambridge), *Twickenham, England* 6 Dec 2007
Six Nations Championship   2 Feb–15 Mar
   (England, France, Ireland, Italy, Scotland, Wales)

Ireland	vs	Italy	2 Feb	France	vs	England	23 Feb
England	vs	Wales	2 Feb	Ireland	vs	Wales	8 Mar
Scotland	vs	France	3 Feb	Scotland	vs	England	8 Mar
Wales	vs	Scotland	9 Feb	France	vs	Italy	9 Mar
France	vs	Ireland	9 Feb	Italy	vs	Scotland	15 Mar
Italy	vs	England	10 Feb	England	vs	Ireland	15 Mar
Wales	vs	Italy	23 Feb	Wales	vs	France	15 Mar
Ireland	vs	Scotland	23 Feb				

Heineken Cup Final, *Cardiff, Wales*   tba, 24 or 25 May
Guinness Premiership Final, *Twickenham, England*   31 May
Rugby League World Cup, *Australia*   25 Oct–22 Nov

Sailing

Barcelona World Race, *Barcelona, Spain*   11 Nov 2007–Feb 2008
Tornado World Championship, *Auckland, New Zealand*   22 Feb–1 Mar
Star World Championship, *Miami, Florida, US*   7–18 Apr
Cowes Week, *Cowes, Isle of Wight, England*   2–9 Aug
Volvo Ocean Race, *Alicante, Spain*   4 Oct–20 Jun 2009

Snooker

The Masters, *London, England*   13–20 Jan
World Snooker Championships, *Sheffield, England*   19 Apr–5 May

Squash

British Open, *Liverpool, England*   tba, May
World Open Championships, *Manchester, England*   12–19 Oct
World Masters Championships, *Christchurch, New Zealand*   20–25 Oct

Swimming

European Championships, *Eindhoven, The Netherlands*   13–24 Mar
  (Swimming, Diving, Synchronized Swimming)
FINA World Short Course Swimming Championships,   9–13 Apr
  Manchester, England

Tennis

Australian Open, *Melbourne, Australia*   14–27 Jan
French Open, *Paris, France*   25 May–8 Jun
Wimbledon Championships, *London, England*   23 Jun–6 Jul

US Open, *New York City, New York, US*	25 Aug–7 Sep
Davis Cup Final, *tba*	week beginning 24 Nov or 1 Dec

Triathlon

Winter Triathlon World Championships, *Freudenstadt, Germany*	22 Feb
Triathlon World Championships, *Vancouver, Canada*	7 Jun
Long Dist. Triathlon World Championships, *Almere, Netherlands*	30 Aug

Weightlifting

Pan-American Championships, *Callao, Peru*	18–22 Mar
Oceania Championships, *Auckland, New Zealand*	26–29 Mar
European Championships, *Rome, Italy*	11–20 Apr
Asian Championships, *Ishikawa, Japan*	27 Apr–1 May
African Championships, *Johannesburg, South Africa*	7–11 May

Winter sports

Alpine Skiing World Cup, *various*	27 Oct 2007–16 Mar
Cresta Run University Week, *St Moritz, Switzerland*	7–9 Jan
Iditarod Trail Sled Dog Race, *Alaska, US*	1–16 Mar
World Figure Skating Championships, *Gothenburg, Sweden*	17–23 Mar
World Men's Curling Championship, *Grand Forks, N. Dakota, US*	5–13 Apr

OTHER SPORTS

World Table Tennis Championships, *Guangzhou, China*	24 Feb–2 Mar
Men's Water Polo Olympic Qualifying Event, *Oradea, Romania*	2–9 Mar
WWE WrestleMania 24, *Orlando, Florida, US*	30 Mar
Fencing Olympic Test Event, *Beijing, China*	18–20 Apr
Real Tennis World Championships, *Fontainebleau, France*	20, 22, 24 May
Men's Champions Trophy, *Rotterdam, The Netherlands*	21–29 Jun
National Rifle Association Imperial Meeting, *Bisley, England*	12–26 Jul
Major League Baseball All-Star Game, *The Bronx, New York, US*	15 Jul
World Ten Pin Bowling Men's Championship, *Bangkok, Thailand*	20–31 Aug

UK sports customs

Olney Pancake Race, *Olney, Buckinghamshire*	5 Feb
Scoring the Hales (Shrovetide Football), *Alnwick, Northumberland*	5 Feb
Cheese Rolling, *Cooper's Hill, Gloucestershire*	26 May
Woolsack Race, *Gumstool Hill, Tetbury, Gloucestershire*	26 May
World Conker Championships, *Ashton, Northamptonshire*	12 Oct
Tar Barrel Rolling, *Ottery St Mary, Devon*	5 Nov
Peter Pan Cup Swimming Race, *Serpentine, Hyde Park, London*	25 Dec

❦ 2008 OLYMPICS

The 2008 Summer Olympics, also known as the Games of the XXIX Olympiad, will be held in Beijing, China, from 8 to 24 August. There will be 302 events in 31 sports: 165 events for men, 127 for women and 10 open. Compared to the 2004 Olympics, eight events have been discontinued, and nine added: men's and women's BMX cycling, 10 km swimming and team table tennis; and women's 3,000 m steeplechase, team foil and team sabre.

SUMMARY OF SPORTS SCHEDULE

Sport	Aug 9	10	11	12	13	14	15	16	17	18	19	20	21	22	23	24	Tot.
Archery	•	1	1	•	•	1	1										4
Athletics							2	4	6	6	5	3	6	7	7	1	47
Badminton	•	•	•	•	•	•	•	1	2	2							5
Baseball				•	•	•	•	•		•	•	•		•	1		1
Basketball	•	•	•	•	•	•	•	•	•	•	•	•	•	•	1	1	2
Boxing	•	•	•	•	•	•	•	•	•	•	•	•		•	5	6	11
Canoe/Kayak			•	2	•	2				•	•	•		•	6	6	16
Cycling	1	1		2			1	3	1	2	3	•	2	1	1		18
Diving		1	1	1	1		•	•	1	•	1	•	1	•	1		8
Equestrian	•	•	•	2	•	1	•	•	•	1	1		1				6
Fencing	1	1	1	1	2	1	1	1	1								10
Field hockey		•	•	•	•	•	•	•	•	•	•	•	•	•	1	1	2
Football	•	•		•	•				•	•	•		1	•	1		2
Gymnastics	•	•		1	1	1	1	•	4	4	4		•	•	1	1	18
Handball	•	•	•	•	•	•	•	•	•	•	•	•	•	•	1	1	2
Judo	2	2	2	2	2	2	2										14
Mod. pentathlon													1	1			2
Rowing	•	•	•	•	•	•	7	7									14
Sailing	•	•	•	•	•	•	•	2	1	2	2	2	2				11
Shooting	2	2	2	2	1	2	1	2	1								15
Softball				•	•	•	•	•	•	•		•	1				1
Swimming	•	4	4	4	4	4	4	4	4			1	1				34
Synch. swimming										•	•	1		•	1		2
Table tennis				•	•	•	•	•	1	1	•	•	•	1	1		4
Taekwondo												2	2	2	2		8
Tennis		•	•	•	•	•	•	•	2	2							4
Triathlon										1	1						2
Volleyball	•	•	•	•	•	•	•	•	•	•	•	•	1	1	1	1	4
Water polo		•	•	•	•	•	•	•	•	•	•	•	1	•		1	2
Weightlifting	1	2	2	2	2		2	1	1	1	1						15
Wrestling			2	2	3		2	2		2	2	3					18

KEY   • = *matches*   *number = number of finals*

THE 302 OLYMPIC EVENTS

ARCHERY (4)

	Individual	♂ ♀
	Team	♂ ♀

ATHLETICS (47)

Track events	100 m	♂ ♀
	200 m	♂ ♀
	400 m	♂ ♀
	800 m	♂ ♀
	1,500 m	♂ ♀
	5,000 m	♂ ♀
	10,000 m	♂ ♀
	100 m hurdles	♀
	110 m hurdles	♂
	400 m hurdles	♂ ♀
	3,000 m steeplechase	♂ ♀
	4 × 100 m relay	♂ ♀
	4 × 400 m relay	♂ ♀
Field events	High jump	♂ ♀
	Pole vault	♂ ♀
	Long jump	♂ ♀
	Triple jump	♂ ♀
	Shot put	♂ ♀
	Discus throw	♂ ♀
	Hammer throw	♂ ♀
	Javelin throw	♂ ♀
Combined	Decathlon	♂
events	Heptathlon	♀
Road events	20 km race walk	♂ ♀
	50 km race walk	♂
	Marathon	♂ ♀

BADMINTON (5)

	Singles	♂ ♀
	Doubles	♂ ♀
	Mixed doubles	open

BASEBALL (1)

	8-team tournament	♂

BASKETBALL (2)

	12-team tournament	♂ ♀

BOXING (11)

	Light fly	< 48 kg ♂
	Fly	< 51 kg ♂
	Bantam	< 54 kg ♂
	Feather	< 57 kg ♂
	Light	< 60 kg ♂
	Light welter	< 64 kg ♂
	Welter	< 69 kg ♂
	Middle	< 75 kg ♂
	Light heavy	< 81 kg ♂
	Heavy	< 91 kg ♂
	Super heavy	> 91 kg ♂

CANOE/KAYAK (16)

Flatwater	K single 500 m	♂ ♀
	K single 1,000 m	♂
	K double 500 m	♂ ♀
	K double 1,000 m	♂
	K four 500 m	♀
	K four 1,000 m	♂
	C single 500 m	♂
	C single 1,000 m	♂
	C double 500 m	♂
	C double 1,000 m	♂
Slalom	K single	♂ ♀
	C single	♂
	C double	♂

CYCLING (18)

Track	Sprint	♂ ♀
	Individual pursuit	♂ ♀
	Points race	♂ ♀
	Keirin	♂
	Team sprint	♂
	Team pursuit	♂
	Madison	♂
Road	Mass start	♂ ♀
	Time trial	♂ ♀
Mount. bike	Cross-country	♂ ♀
BMX	Individual	♂ ♀

DIVING (8)

Indiv. springboard	♂ ♀
Indiv. platform	♂ ♀
Synch. springboard	♂ ♀
Synch. platform	♂ ♀

EQUESTRIAN (6)

Jumping	Team	open
	Individual	open
Dressage	Team	open
	Individual	open
Eventing	Team	open
	Individual	open

FENCING (10)

Foil, individual	♂ ♀
Epée, individual	♂ ♀
Sabre, individual	♂ ♀
Epée, teams	♂
Sabre, teams	♂ ♀
Foil, teams	♀

FIELD HOCKEY (2)

12-team tournament	♂ ♀

FOOTBALL (2)

16-team tournament	♂
12-team tournament	♀

GYMNASTICS (18)

Artistic	Team	♂ ♀
	Individual	♂ ♀
	Floor	♂ ♀
	Pommel horse	♂
	Rings	♂
	Vault	♂ ♀
	Parallel bars	♂
	Horizontal bar	♂
	Uneven bars	♀
	Balance beam	♀
Rhythmic	Individual	♀
	Group	♀
Trampoline	Individual	♂ ♀

HANDBALL (2)

12-team tournament	♂ ♀

JUDO (14)

Men	Women	
< 60 kg	< 48 kg	♂ ♀
< 66 kg	< 52 kg	♂ ♀
< 73 kg	< 57 kg	♂ ♀
< 81 kg	< 63 kg	♂ ♀
< 90 kg	< 70 kg	♂ ♀
< 100 kg	< 78 kg	♂ ♀
> 100 kg	> 78 kg	♂ ♀

MODERN PENTATHLON (2)

Individual	♂ ♀

ROWING (14)

	Single sculls	♂ ♀
	Pair	♂ ♀
	Double sculls	♂ ♀
	Four	♂
	Quadruple sculls	♂ ♀
	Eight	♂ ♀
Lightweight events	Double sculls	♂ ♀
	Four	♂

SAILING (11)

One person dinghy	♂ ♀
Two person dinghy	♂ ♀
Heavywgt dinghy	open
Windsurfer	♂ ♀
Keelboat	♂ ♀
Multihull	open
Skiff	open

SHOOTING (15)

Rifle	50 m rifle prone	♂
	50 m rifle 3 positions	♂ ♀
	10 m air rifle	♂ ♀
Pistol	50 m pistol	♂
	25 m rapid fire pistol	♂
	25 m pistol	♀
	10 m air pistol	♂ ♀

Shotgun   Trap   ♂ ♀
Double trap   ♂
Skeet   ♂ ♀

SOFTBALL (1)
8-team tournament   ♀

SWIMMING (34)
50 m freestyle   ♂ ♀
100 m freestyle   ♂ ♀
200 m freestyle   ♂ ♀
400 m freestyle   ♂ ♀
800 m freestyle   ♀
1,500 m freestyle   ♂
100 m backstroke   ♂ ♀
200 m backstroke   ♂ ♀
100 m breaststroke   ♂ ♀
200 m breaststroke   ♂ ♀
100 m butterfly   ♂ ♀
200 m butterfly   ♂ ♀
200 m indiv. medley   ♂ ♀
400 m indiv. medley   ♂ ♀
4 × 100 m freestyle   ♂ ♀
4 × 200 m freestyle   ♂ ♀
4 × 100 m medley   ♂ ♀
Marathon 10 km   ♂ ♀

SYNCHRONIZED SWIMMING (2)
Duet   ♀
Team   ♀

TABLE TENNIS (4)
Singles   ♂ ♀
Team   ♂ ♀

TAEKWONDO (8)

Men	Women	
< 58 kg	< 49 kg	♂ ♀
< 68 kg	< 57 kg	♂ ♀
< 80 kg	< 67 kg	♂ ♀
> 80 kg	> 67 kg	♂ ♀

TENNIS (4)
Singles   ♂ ♀
Doubles   ♂ ♀

TRIATHLON (2)
Olympic distance   ♂ ♀

VOLLEYBALL (4)
Indoor   12-team tournament   ♂ ♀
Beach   24 pairs   ♂ ♀

WATER POLO (2)
12-team tournament   ♂
8-team tournament   ♀

WEIGHTLIFTING (15)

Men	Women	
< 56 kg	< 48 kg	♂ ♀
< 62 kg	< 53 kg	♂ ♀
< 69 kg	< 58 kg	♂ ♀
< 77 kg	< 63 kg	♂ ♀
< 85 kg	< 69 kg	♂ ♀
< 94 kg	< 75 kg	♂ ♀
< 105 kg	> 75 kg	♂ ♀
> 105 kg		♂

WRESTLING (18)

	Men	Women	
Freestyle	< 55 kg	< 48 kg	♂ ♀
	< 60 kg	< 55 kg	♂ ♀
	< 66 kg	< 63 kg	♂ ♀
	< 74 kg	< 72 kg	♂ ♀
	< 84 kg		♂
	< 96 kg		♂
	< 120 kg		♂
Greco-Roman	< 55 kg		♂
	< 60 kg		♂
	< 66 kg		♂
	< 74 kg		♂
	< 84 kg		♂
	< 96 kg		♂
	< 120 kg		♂

❦ SPORTS RECORDS

Below are the principal men's sports world records. For races, the average speed decreases as distance increases, apart from the track 100 m to 200 m, where speed improves due to the relative decrease in time lost accelerating.

Event	Record	Speed (mi/hr)	Name	Country	Year
Track					
100 m	9.77 s	22.9	Asafa Powell	Jamaica	2006
200 m	19.32 s	23.2	Michael Johnson	USA	1996
400 m	43.18 s	20.7	Michael Johnson	USA	1999
800 m	1:41.11	17.7	Wilson Kipketer	Denmark	1997
1,500 m	3:26.00	16.3	Hicham El Guerrouj	Morocco	1998
1 mile	3:43.13	16.1	Hicham El Guerrouj	Morocco	1999
Half marathon	58:35	13.4	Samuel Wanjiru	Kenya	2007
Marathon	2:04:55	12.6	Paul Tergat	Kenya	2003
110 m hurdles	12.88 s	19.1	Liu Xiang	China	2006
400 m hurdles	46.78 s	19.1	Kevin Young	USA	1992
Field					
High jump	2.45 m		Javier Sotomayor	Cuba	1993
Pole vault	6.14 m		Sergei Bubka	Ukraine	1994
Long jump	8.95 m		Mike Powell	USA	1991
Triple jump	18.29 m		Jonathan Edwards	UK	1995
Discus	74.08 m		Jürgen Schult	E. Germany	1986
Shot put	23.12 m		Randy Barnes	USA	1990
Hammer	86.74 m		Yuriy Sedykh	USSR	1986
Javelin	98.48 m		Jan Zelezný	Czech Rep.	1996
Swimming					
50 m	21.64 s	5.2	Alexander Popov	Russia	2000
100 m	47.84 s	4.7	P. v. d. Hoogenband	Netherlands	2000
200 m	1:43.86	4.3	Michael Phelps	USA	2007
400 m	3:40.08	4.1	Ian Thorpe	Australia	2002
800 m	7:38.65	3.9	Grant Hackett	Australia	2005
1,500 m	14:34.56	3.8	Grant Hackett	Australia	2001
Cycling					
hr best effort	56.38 km	35.0	Chris Boardman	UK	1996
hour record	49.70 km	30.9	Ondřej Sosenka	Czech Rep.	2005
Weightlifting					
Snatch	213 kg		Hossein Reza Zadeh	Iran	2003
Clean and jerk	263 kg		Hossein Reza Zadeh	Iran	2004
Bench press	458 kg		Gene Rychlak	USA	2006

WOMEN

Homer Simpson · Son, a woman is a lot like a refrigerator. They're about six feet tall, 300 pounds. They make ice. (*The Simpsons*, New Kid on the Block, episode 9F06, 1992)

Samuel Johnson · Marriage, Sir, is much more necessary to a man than to a woman; for he is much less able to supply himself with domestick comforts... I had often wondered why young women should marry, as they have so much more freedom, and so much more attention paid to them while unmarried. (Boswell, *Life of Johnson*, 1791)

Naff dear Johns · I've been thinking about us... ❧ We're not going anywhere... ❧ You'll always be very special to me. ❧ I hope we can always be friends. ❧ I'm leaving you, Simon. I want to discover who I really am. ❧ (*The Complete Naff Guide*, 1983)

Lord Chesterfield · There are but two objects in marriage, love or money.

If you marry for love, you will certainly have some very happy days, and probably many uneasy ones; if you marry for money, you will have no happy days and probably no uneasy ones. (*Lord Chesterfield's Letters*, 1776)

Hardy Amies · I never see any elegant dressed young women. They don't try hard enough.

Benjamin Franklin · Happy's the wooing that's not long a doing. ❧ Love well, whip well. ❧ Keep your eyes open wide before marriage, half shut afterwards. ❧ Pretty & witty will wound if they hit ye. ❧ Good wives and good plantations are made by good husbands. ❧ He that takes a wife, takes care. ❧ An undutiful daughter, will prove an unmanageable wife. ❧ If Jack's in love, he's no judge of Jill's beauty. ❧ Let thy maid-servant be faithful, strong and homely. ❧ There are no ugly loves, nor handsome prisons. (*Poor Richard's Almanack*, 1732–1757)

❦ B E A U T Y

A woman's beauty is notoriously difficult to define, dependent as it is on non-physical attributes such as style and demeanour. Jacqueline Kennedy and Princess Diana, not classically beautiful, were two of the most photographed women of the 20th century. Even a strict physical interpretation of beauty must concede that it waxes and wanes with a woman's effort.

QUANTIFYING BEAUTY

Without attempting to define beauty, we can nevertheless quantify it. Our starting point is Helen of Troy, the offspring of the Greek god Zeus and Leda, wife of the king of Sparta. Helen, whose abduction sparked the Trojan War, was the most beautiful woman in the world around the 12th century BC. In Christopher Marlowe's *The Tragical History of Doctor Faustus*, Mephistopheles calls up a vision of Helen, and Faustus reponds:

> Was this the face that launched a thousand ships
> And burned the topless towers of Ilium?

From this we can deduce two things: the extent of Helen's beauty, and its effect. The population of the earth in the 12th century BC is estimated to be at most 100 million, making her the most beautiful of 50 million women. If Helen's beauty launched a thousand ships, we may infer that the most beautiful of 50,000 women would launch a single ship. The military vessels of the time were simple galleys powered by 25 oarsmen on each side. Accordingly, the pick of a thousand women would bring a single oarsman to risk his life in war. Let such a beauty be the colloquial 'perfect 10' on a scale of 0 to 10. We call a single point on this scale a Helena (Ha).

The beauty of a thousand women is not, of course, uniformly distributed; there are invariably more 8s than 9s, more 7s than 8s, and so on. Like the Richter scale for measuring earthquakes, beauty is logarithmic, but with a base of 2 rather than 32. This means that, for beauty to increase by one Helena, the woman must be the most beautiful of twice as many women. Thus if a woman is the most striking of 2 women, her beauty is 1 Helena; of 4 women, 2 Helenas; of 8 women, 3 Helenas; and, in general, of 2^N women, N Helenas. While 10 Helenas would cause a man to risk his life, a woman's beauty does occasionally exceed 10. The beauty of Helen herself is $\log_2 (50,000,000) = 25.6$ (50 million is $2 \times 2 \times \ldots \times 2$, between 25 and 26 times). Thus we define one Helen (H) to be 25.6 Helenas (Ha).

Of any large population of women, $\frac{1}{2}$ of the women have beauty 0 Ha, $\frac{1}{4}$ have 1 Ha, $\frac{1}{8}$ have 2 Ha, and so on. This contrasts with the more common but less systematic beauty scale in which 0 is plain, 5 average and 10 stunning. Alas, Helenas can only measure beauty, not homeliness.

Woman	Number	Ha	H
Best of a dozen	12	3.6	0.14
Most beautiful of a martyr's 72 virgins	72	6.2	0.24
Would cause a man to risk his life	1,000	10.0	0.39
Best beauty seen in a lifetime	10^5	16.6	0.65
Helen of Troy	5×10^7	25.6	1.00
Miss World	3.2×10^9	31.6	1.23
Most beautiful woman who ever lived	2×10^{10}	34.2	1.34

FLATTERY

It is one thing to believe a woman to be beautiful, another to proclaim it. Flattery is best offered to the intermediate, not the extreme.

> Women who are either indisputably beautiful, or indisputably ugly, are best flattered, upon the score of their understandings; but those who are in a state of mediocrity, are best flattered upon their beauty, or at least their graces; for every woman who is not absolutely ugly thinks herself handsome; but not hearing often that she is so, is the more grateful and the more obliged to the few who tell her so; whereas a decided and conscious beauty looks upon every tribute paid to her beauty only as her due; but wants to shine, and to be considered on the side of her understanding; and a woman who is ugly enough to know that she is so, knows that she has nothing left for it but her understanding, which is consequently and probably…her weak side.
>
> *Letters to His Son*, Philip Stanhope, 4th Earl of Chesterfield

Paradoxically, beauty seems to safeguard modesty. The more a woman is admired and surrounded by men, the less likely she is to indulge in casual passion; whereas a woman whose beauty is contested, finding herself unable to compete with the beautiful head-on, will compensate by offering easy access. Beauty has its price, of course. As a kept animal, used to daily provision without toil, loses its instinct to find food in the wild, a beautiful woman, accustomed to men's attention, can forget how to earn it through kindness. Perhaps this explains Shakespeare's inversion of Marlowe in the *History of Troilus and Cressida*:

> Is she worth keeping? Why, she is a pearl
> Whose price hath launch'd above a thousand ships.

❦ CHIVALRY

The word chivalry – meaning disinterested courage, honour and courteousness, according to the *Oxford English Dictionary* – is rather out of fashion, ripe as it is with conflict between modern feminism and accepted custom. It is fundamentally predicated on an asymmetry between the sexes.

PRECEDENCE

All else being equal, women take precedence over men, and this is the basis of a number of customs. Men are introduced to women, as in 'Daisy Buchanan, may I introduce Jay Gatsby', or, more simply, 'Marge, this is Homer.' It is the woman rather than the man who initiates, and thereby determines, the form of recognition – a kiss, a handshake or a glance – on greeting and departing. Women are in general served food before men, and their glasses are filled first (unless the table is large, in which case wine is served around the table clockwise). It is correct for men to rise when a woman arrives or departs, although the coming and going of a man does not justify this. A man lights a woman's cigarette (see p 129), carries her heavy bags and offers his seat if she is forced to stand, though the last can be dispensed with in busy settings, such as the underground.

Walking with a woman can be easily formulated. In general, a man walks to the right of a woman, unless the couple is walking beside a road, in which case the man puts himself between the woman and the road. If the couple passes another man, the man keeps to the side of the woman and allows the man to walk into the street, but if they pass a woman the man walks into the street himself.

The etiquette of opening doors is motivated first by considerations of labour, then of precedent. Thus if the door opens in, the man opens it and allows the woman to walk through first. But if the door opens out, the man walks through and the women follows. If others are coming from the opposite side, in the first case the man holds the door open and the others take precedence, but in the second the woman then the man precede. In the case of revolving doors, both on account of labour and of them opening out, the man is the first to enter.

PROVISION

One of the most innate chivalric tendencies is the provision – though not necessarily the preparation – of food. This can be seen in the actual procurement of fish and fowl, of course, but is also symbolized by the carving of meat at the dinner table (see p 142 for instructions).

Today provision often takes the form of paying for dinner and drinks. Whatever the arguments might be for going Dutch, a woman who insists on splitting the bill is either romantically uninterested or tedious. In early courtship it is correct to pay even when a woman offers once or twice, though if three times a man must concede. The foxiest females seem most willing to let men cover the costs. French women never offer to pay for dinner – nor lunch, for that matter – and are certainly no less desirable than *les Anglaises*. In the case that a woman thinks it her due, a casual suggestion to split the bill is often more likely to secure a second date (*cf.* flattery, p 35).

A constant outlay on women can cause near-bankruptcy, and for men who find themselves pinching pennies it is advisable to *only pay for women you fancy*. A thoughtful woman will recognize any financial disparity and contribute accordingly after the first few outings.

Wine remains a male preserve, despite the increasing number of female oenologists. At a restaurant the man chooses the wine; though he may ask the woman for input, he is under no obligation to do so. He fills the woman's glass when low and each time he fills his own, even if only symbolically. A sensitive woman will nurse a half-full glass rather than refuse when she has had her fill.

PROTECTION

The custom of returning a woman home after an evening out remains correct in principle, but varies in practice according to the circumstances. It is correct to walk or drive a woman to her door if she does not live far away, but if she does it is impractical to make a long detour, as well as alarming from the woman's point of view. Better to send her home in a taxi. The man is not required to pay, unless he insists on her taking a taxi as opposed to, say, a bus. When entertaining a group, a man's first priority is to his guests, and it is his guests who should look after the safe return of any women.

When is a man welcome inside a woman's house after returning her? 'If a woman does not want a man to come in, then gentle but clear suggestions…should be put into the conversation', explains John Morgan in *Debrett's New Guide to Etiquette and Modern Manners*. 'If a man is asked in, he must not assume that he has the green light for sex, although a woman who does this shouldn't be surprised if he does.'

An insult to a man's girlfriend or wife in his presence is always a gross offence. The Code Duello, the most widely accepted set of prescriptions on duelling and honour, states: 'Any insult to a lady under a gentleman's care or protection [is] to be considered as, by one degree, a greater offence than if given to the gentleman personally, and to be regulated accordingly.' Offences are, in increasing order of severity, an insult, a lie and a blow.

❦FIRST DATE

The first thing to keep in mind in early courtship is that men chase and women are chased. A man finds this both pleasurable and instinctive; he is:

> Like the hunter who chases the hare
> Through heat and cold, o'er hill and dale,
> Yet, once he has bagged it, he thinks nothing of it;
> Only while it flees away does he pound after it.
>
> Ariosto, *Orlando Furioso*, X, vii, translated by M. A. Screech

Men chase what they desire. Intelligent women recognize this, and invert it: a man who does not chase does not desire. The best-selling book *The Rules* by Ellen Fein and Sherrie Schneider lists 'time-tested secrets for capturing the heart of Mr Right', shown below. The central message is that playing hard to get provides a litmus test for a man's interest. The chase-chased courtship asymmetry is not male chauvinism – it is an essential ritual in forming stable matches.

The second thing is that men fall in love more quickly than women. Where a woman takes her time and considers what is real, a man runs with first impressions and invents the rest according to his fantasy. This invention is both intoxicating and intimidating; ultimately it makes men fear women. In Lermontov's *A Hero of Our Time*, the practised seducer Pechorin tells us: 'Women ought to wish that all men knew them as well as I because I have loved them a hundred times better since I have ceased to be afraid of them and have comprehended their little weaknesses.' Hence the importance in early conquest of approaching women with insouciance, as one might a potential male friend. This requires acting, but the game is short-lived – it need only last until love (or its absence) has replaced infatuation.

THE RULES FOR WOMEN

Don't talk to a man first (and don't ask him to dance). ❧ Don't stare at men or talk too much. ❧ Don't meet him halfway or go Dutch on a date. ❧ Don't call him and rarely return his phone calls. ❧ Always end phone calls first. ❧ Don't accept a Saturday night date after Wednesday. ❧ Always end the date first. ❧ Stop dating him if he doesn't buy you a romantic gift for your birthday or Valentine's Day. ❧ Don't see him more than once or twice a week. ❧ No more than casual kissing on the first date. ❧ Don't tell him what to do. ❧ Let him take the lead. ❧ Don't expect a man to change or try to change him. ❧ Don't open up too fast. ❧ Don't live with a man (or leave your things in his apartment). ❧ Don't date a married man. ❧ Be easy to live with.

LOGISTICS

Except perhaps on Sadie Hawkins Day (p 201), on a first date a man invites a woman by suggesting a fixed plan, without negotiation as to where to meet or what to do. It is not a time to be original in your choice of venue. A first date should merely be a setting for easy and unimpeded conversation, hence the custom of having it in a public place. Dinner is ideal: it is conducive to talking; it affords the chance to drink alcohol; and there is no set time to finish by. If you do not have plans for afterwards, such as music or the theatre or the cinema, it is wise to begin with separate drinks beforehand, which brings a sense of motion to the evening.

While it remains correct to collect a girl by car, it is more common – and often more practical in a big city – to meet her at a pre-arranged location. In this case it is essential to arrive ten minutes early. By the time the girl arrives, you should be seated and have in hand a drink and a slim novel (Pushkin or Turgenev is ideal). In any event do not talk to others or use your mobile phone; you may appear interested in things, not other people.

You should have a reservation at a restaurant and know how to get there, which may require reconnaissance beforehand. (If you find yourself stuck with nowhere in mind, choose one on the spot using the algorithm below.) A schoolboy error is the over-ambitious choice of restaurant. Apart from being expensive, it is intimidating for the woman, who tends to think that allowing you to pay a large bill obligates her affection, and usually has the reverse effect. On whether and when to pay the bill, see p 37.

The end is as important as the beginning. The essential thing – and remember we are talking about the *first* date – is to show no interest in her physically. Your restraint should grow in proportion to her beauty. A pretty girl considers a man's affection her due (p 35). Her desirableness rebuffed, a man becomes more, not less, fascinating to her. Which makes a second date straightforward by comparison.

CHOOSING THE BEST RESTAURANT

Consider the familiar experience of walking down a street looking for somewhere to eat. One would like, on the one hand, to sample many restaurants before making a choice, and on the other, to avoid passing a good candidate in the hope of something better. What strategy maximizes the probability of choosing the best restaurant? If there are numerous restaurants on the street, the optimal policy is to walk past the first $37\% = 1/e$, then pick the next one better than all of those. (Here e is the base of the natural logarithm, 2.718.) This is a universal strategy, and can be equally applied to accepting an offer or buying a house or, in the case of women, accepting a marriage proposal.

❦ MARRIAGE

WEDDING ANNIVERSARIES

The first widely accepted list of wedding anniversary gifts was published by Emily Post in her best-selling book *Etiquette* in 1922. It listed eight anniversaries: 1, 5, 10, 15, 20, 25, 50 and 75. '[The gifts] need not, however, be of value; in fact the paper, wooden and tin wedding presents are seldom anything but jokes. Crystal is the earliest that is likely to be taken seriously by the gift-bearers. Silver is always serious, and the golden wedding a quite sacred event.' In later editions Post increased the list to the years 1–15, and multiples of 5 up to 60. Today these are the only years for which broad conventions exist. Some freedom in choosing what to give can be had by giving two or three alternative objects whose sum is the requisite anniversary. Thus cotton and bronze might be given for a 10th anniversary instead of tin.

1	paper	7	wool	13	lace	35	coral
2	cotton	8	bronze	14	ivory	40	ruby
3	leather	9	pottery	15	crystal	45	sapphire
4	linen	10	tin	20	china	50	gold
5	wood	11	steel	25	silver	55	emerald
6	iron	12	silk	30	pearl	60	diamond

ENGAGEMENT RINGS

An engagement ring is normally given to a woman on or soon after proposing. While there is much talk today about letting the woman choose the design, I admire the man who without warning proposes with ring in hand. There are various rules of thumb as to how much an engagement ring should cost, ranging from two weeks' to two months' salary. In the UK, two-thirds of a month is more typical.

Often an engagement ring is flanked by one of the five cardinal gemstones: amethyst, diamond, emerald, ruby and sapphire (amethyst is no longer considered valuable following the discovery of large deposits in Brazil and elsewhere). During the 19th century a popular form of engagement ring made use of different gemstones to form an acrostic, a sequence of words whose initial letters form a message. The most popular spelled REGARDS, making use of the five cardinal stones and garnet: ruby, emerald, garnet, amethyst, ruby, diamond, sapphire. Another spells LOVE: lapis lazuli, opal, vermarine, emerald, though the colour coordination and inclusion of vermarine makes such a combination suspect. Much better is EROS: emerald, ruby, opal, sapphire. See p 168 for a list of birthstones.

WHOM TO MARRY

Consanguinity has always constrained who can marry whom. According to *The Book of Common Prayer*, by tradition a man may not marry his:

mother	wife's mother	mother's father's wife
daughter	wife's daughter	wife's father's mother
sister	father's wife	wife's mother's
father's mother	son's wife	mother
mother's mother	father's sister	wife's son's daughter
son's daughter	mother's sister	wife's daughter's
daughter's daughter	brother's daughter	daughter
father's daughter	sister's daughter	son's son's wife
mother's daughter	father's father's wife	daughter's son's wife

In the UK laws prohibiting some of the more arcane combinations above have been relaxed. Despite popular belief, a man may marry his cousin, and first-cousin marriage is legal in most countries. Laws prohibiting first-cousin marriage usually predate modern genetic theory, although one-half of American states has yet to repeal them.

WHEN TO MARRY

The most common rule of thumb for the ideal age of your bride at marriage is ½ your age + 7. For women readers, it's (your age − 7) × 2. Thus for a man of 30, a bride of 22 is most suitable; for a man of 40, a bride of 27. The formula adjusts for women's comparatively advanced emotional strength and matches the fertile period of a woman (14–47) to that of a man (14–80). Proponents suggest it also reduces the risk of later infidelity on the side of men: 'I like my whiskey old and my women young,' in the words of Errol Flynn. (For a list of single malts, see p 114.)

Man's age at marriage (a):	16	24	32	40	48	56	64	72
Woman's age at marriage (½ a + 7):	15	19	23	27	31	35	39	43

An alternative guide to marriage ages, and one which gives less disparate numbers, matches the Fibonacci numbers (1 + 2 = 3, 2 + 3 = 5, 3 + 5 = 8...) and the Lucas numbers (1 + 3 = 4, 3 + 4 = 7, 4 + 7 = 11...). These sequences mark the notable stages of a man's and woman's life, respectively.

Man's age at marriage (F_n):	21	34	55	89
Woman's age at marriage (L_{n-1}):	18	29	47	76

❦SAYING GOODBYE

In English there is a broad range of customary closings, particularly for men, who do not end the bulk of their correspondence with *Love* or a string of xs. Some are more appropriate on paper; others are best suited to digital communication. Which variations mean what, and which parts are made explicit, is a subject of some subtlety, conveying as much about the sender as about his relationship with the recipient. Here is a guide.

XXX

The emoticon x is mostly used by women at the end of text messages and emails. An x, of course, denotes a kiss, but what do these kisses convey? Affection grows with the number of xs, but only up to a point; after, say, four, the intended intimacy *decreases*. One x is often considered a minimum civilized closing, but there is no set convention, and it is only the relative increase of xs that is significant.

x = friendship   xxx = eros?   xxxxx = friendship

POSTAL ACRONYMS

Although the recent surge of interest in abbreviations and acronyms was motivated by text messaging, it is not unprecedented. During the Second World War, servicemen adopted a number of sentimental acronyms in their censored letters home to spouses. Unlike FUBAR and SNAFU, these were usually in the form of place names. One theory holds that they were originally written out in full as a means of communicating where the men were stationed, which they were not allowed to disclose. Only later was their usage reversed, with the acronyms written to indicate the full expressions.

BOLTOP	Better on lips than on paper
BURMA	Be undressed ready my angel
CHINA	Come home I need affection
HOLLAND	Hope our love lasts and never dies
ITALY	I trust and love you
MALAYA	My ardent lips await your arrival
MEXICO CITY	May every x I can offer carry itself to you
NORWICH	[K]nickers off ready when I come home
SIAM	Sexual intercourse at midnight
SWALK	Sealed with a loving kiss
WALES	With a love eternal sweetheart

DICTIONARY OF CLOSINGS

In essence, the closing of letters, email and text messages indicates how *I* relate to *you*, with the basic formulae being *I* [verb] *your* [noun phrase]; or *I* [verb] *yours* [modifier]. The verb is usually *am* or *remain*; the noun phrase might be *humble subject* or *friend* or *affectionate brother*; the modifier can be an adverb, like *sincerely*, or an adverbial clause, usually *with…*, as in *with best wishes*. Today these formulae are usually not written out in full but implied, and we are left with such familiar artefacts as *Yours sincerely* or *With best wishes*. (Note that only the first word is capitalized.)

Closings range from chav to non-chav as follows (chav means roughly the equivalent of trailer trash in the US or bogan in Australia):

Chav	C	→	c	→	~	→	N	→	N	Non-Chav

Adieu	N	Literally, to God (see you in Heaven). Used when the next meeting is distant or uncertain.
All good wishes	N	Curiously warmer than *Best wishes*, perhaps because it is less common.
All my love	N	For romantic or familial contexts. Simple but effectual.
All the best	C	Naff, although *All best* is not. The latter is frequently used by those in the literary business.
Best	C	Short for *With best wishes* or *With best regards*. OK for short emails; clumsy when written.
Best regards	~	One of the most common closings. More familiar than *Best wishes*, but unoriginal.
Best wishes	~	*With best wishes* is more intimate.
Cheerio	~	'A parting exclamation of encouragement', according to the *Oxford English Dictionary*. Now it is outdated *Famous Five* speech.
Cheers	C	In writing, mostly used by the French and Americans, thinking it is colloquial among the British. In Britain it is mainly spoken as a mild expression of thanks. Sometimes extended to *Cheers, mate* (C), also used in speech.
Ciao	~	From the Italian *schiavo* (servant), it now means hello or goodbye. In English it first appeared in Hemingway's *A Farewell to Arms*.
Farewell	N	In correspondence it suggests finality.
Fond regards	N	*Fond* once suggested doting, but now means affectionate, loving. It can imply mild romantic interest.
I have the…	N	*…honour to remain, Madam, Your Majesty's most humble and obedient servant*. When addressing the Queen.

I remain, Sir…	N	…*your obedient servant*. Once widely used, now rare.
Kind regards	N	Often cool. But *Kindest regards* (N) is meant to be warm.
Lots of love	C	From women. Less intimate than *Love*, it is an example of a phrop – a phrase which means the opposite of what it says. Sometimes abbreviated by LOL.
Love	N	Apart from romantic contexts, indiscriminate use can have camp associations.
Luv	C	Tries to deflate the meaning by a parody of spelling.
Regards	~	Literally affection and good wishes. Cool if unqualified.
See you later	C	This and its derivatives (*See you soon*) are part of the letter proper, not closings. *See you later, alligator* (~), on the other hand, is a closing, and invites the response *In a while, crocodile*.
Take care	C	From women or metrosexuals; less grating when spoken rather than written.
TTYL, TTFN	C, N	Initialisms for *Talk to you later* (text-message speak) and *Ta ta for now* (twee). TTFN was popularized in the 1940s and was later adopted by the animated Tigger.
Warm regards	N	Hearty. Used both with friends and acquaintances.
Yours	C	*I am* or *I remain* is implied. Informal, if somewhat cool.
Yours affectionately	N	Sometimes used between family members or friends. Attributed to the writer John Gay (1685–1732).
Yours aye	N	*Aye* means always, ever. Used in the military and by Scots between close acquaintances.
Yours cordially	C	Meant to be between *Yours sincerely* and *Yours affectionately*, but self-conscious and pretentious.
Yours ever	N	Between friends. The variation *As ever*, short for *Yours as ever*, suggests frequent correspondence.
Yours faithfully	N	The correct closing when a letter begins *Dear Sir*.
Yours in Christ	N	Apart from by clerics, indiscriminate use can be awkward. *Yours in Jesus* (C) suggests a Protestant sender.
Yours in haste	N	A handy construction for short notes. Note the change of adverbial clause from the usual *with…* to *in…*
Yours respectfully	N	To Catholic clergy. In letters to the pope, brother bishops close with *Yours devotedly in Christ*.
Yours sincerely	~	*Sincerely* means honestly, without pretence. The correct closing when a letter begins *Dear Mr Simpson*. Americans frequently use *Sincerely yours*.
Yours truly	C	Earnest or American.
–	~	No closing. Many people sign emails with only their name, and text messages with only their initial.

DRESS

Lord Chesterfield • Take great care always to be dressed like the reasonable people of your own age, in the place where you are, whose dress is never spoken of one way or another, as either too negligent or too much studied. (*Lord Chesterfield's Letters*, 1776)

P. G. Wodehouse • [Jeeves lugged my purple socks] out of the drawer as if he were a vegetarian fishing a caterpillar out of the salad. (*Death At The Excelsior*, 1914)

Hardy Amies • A man should look as if he had bought his clothes with intelligence, put them on with care and then forgotten all about them. (*ABC of Men's Fashion*, 1964)

Umberto Angeloni • The most challenging part to dressing well is knowing how to be elegant while being casual.

George Meredith • Cynicism is intellectual dandyism.

F. Scott Fitzgerald • Can't repeat the past? Why, of course you can! (*The Great Gatsby*, 1925)

Kotzebue • Everything a man of fashion puts on his body must be broken in, nothing should appear new. (1804)

George Bryan 'Beau' Brummell • If John Bull turns round to look after you, you are not well dressed, but either too stiff, too tight or too fashionable.

Alfred, Lord Tennyson • What profits now to understand / The merits of a spotless shirt – / A dapper boot – a little hand – / If half the little soul is dirt? (*Punch*, 1846)

August Luchet • Last briefly and change often, appear rather than be – that is what suffices. (*L'Art Industriel à l'Exposition Universelle de 1867*)

Paris Hilton • The only rule is don't be boring and dress cute wherever you go.

❦ SHOES

There is a well-known saying that the best way to tell whether a man is well dressed is to look down. Hardy Amies, recent dressmaker to Queen Elizabeth II, concurs: 'It is totally impossible to be well dressed in cheap shoes. To buy the best you can afford, to go for what you really can't afford, is not extravagance. But to fail to look after shoes is profligacy.' Looking after shoes requires a modest amount of effort: regular polishing (p 78) and the use of shoe trees are key. The shoes' life will be much extended if you can avoid wearing the same pair two days in a row.

A short word on which shoes should be worn with what. The rule is simple: black shoes with black, blue and grey trousers; brown shoes with anything but black trousers. All other coloured shoes are of questionable taste, apart from trainers and white canvas. Disregard the dictum that brown shoes should not be worn with a blue suit. Many of the best dressed men, especially Italians, have always worn brown brogues or suede toe-caps with their navy suits. Of more concern is the wearing of black shoes with casual clothes, such as jeans, chinos and cords. Apart from black penny loafers, this is in bad taste.

SHOE SIZE

Shoe size is one of the least standardized of all measurements, largely because, for a given size, the length of the foot and the length of the last are not the same. (The last is the shape that a shoe is made around.) The most common units of shoe size are the barleycorn (⅓ inch) and the Paris point (⅔ cm). In the UK, shoe size is equal to the length of the last in barleycorns minus the constant 25.25. The same applies to the US, except that the constant is 24.75. In Europe, shoe size is the length of the last in Paris points. Thus the equivalence between UK and US sizes and EU sizes is only approximate.

last (in.)	UK size	US size	EU size	last (cm)	last (in.)	UK size	US size	EU size	last (cm)
10.25	5½	6	39	26.0	11.58	9½	10	44	29.3
10.42	6	6½	40	26.7	11.75	10	10½	45	30.0
10.58	6½	7	40	26.7	11.92	10½	11	45	30.0
10.75	7	7½	41	27.3	12.08	11	11½	46	30.7
10.92	7½	8	42	28.0	12.25	11½	12	47	31.3
11.08	8	8½	42	28.0	12.42	12	12½	47	31.3
11.25	8½	9	43	28.7	12.58	12½	13	48	32.0
11.42	9	9½	44	29.3	12.75	13	13½	49	32.7

SHOELACES

There are many different ways of lacing a shoe, and the number of ways grows quickly with the number of eyelets. According to a mathematical study by B. Polster ('What is the best way to lace your shoes?', *Nature* **420**, 476 (2002)), for two pairs of eyelets, there are three ways; for four pairs, 1,080 ways; for the six pairs shown below, 43,200 ways.

Below are some of the more interesting shoe-lacing methods. According to Polster, the criss cross and shoe shop lacings are the strongest possible, and the bow tie is the shortest – useful when the laces are too short. The bow tie and straight European lacings show only crosses and horizontal lines, respectively, whereas the Roman lacing shows an alternating series of lines and crosses (Is and Xs). All three are particularly suitable for dress shoes. The lattice, double back and double cross lacings exhibit a woven pattern and, apart from being decorative, are useful for taking up long laces. More lacing possibilities can be found at www.fieggen.com/shoelace.

As for the actual tying of shoes, the reef bow (see Knots, p 92) is the standard method, although many men mistakenly use the granny bow.

EIGHT WAYS TO TIE YOUR SHOES

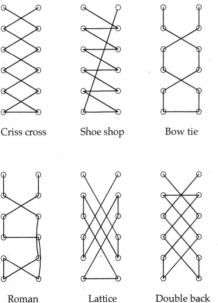

Criss cross   Shoe shop   Bow tie   Straight European

Roman   Lattice   Double back   Double cross

❦ SHIRTS

The original function of the shirt was to protect the expensive and difficult-to-clean suit from the body. Hence the popularity of cotton – easily laundered and pleasant against the skin. Silk remains an indulgence, wool a mortification. Today a shirt (and here we limit ourselves to shirts with buttons) serves two purposes: as an undergarment with a suit or jacket, and as an outer garment without one.

WITH A JACKET

Worn with a suit, a shirt should contrast with its dark cloth and therefore be light-coloured – white and light blue and pink, for example. Checks and stripes on a light background are popular, especially in Britain. There should be no breast pocket, and embroidered initials, if present, should never be seen. Short-sleeved shirts are worn at barbecues and the beach; with a suit it is an act of sartorial terrorism, even if Ian Fleming always wore them thus (he found cuffs uncomfortable and inconvenient). Rolling up your sleeves, on the other hand, is to be encouraged, with both button and double-cuffed shirts alike. Chaps roll to below the elbow, blokes to above.

Of particular importance are the collar and cuffs which, when wearing a jacket, are the shirt's most prominent parts. Collars come in a wide range of varieties. Cutaway collars look handsome with tie knots of all sizes; less widely spread collars require smaller knots (see Tie knots, p 64). Cuffs should always 'show', which means they should extend a half inch beyond the jacket sleeve. Double cuffs, also known as French cuffs, though the French infrequently wear them, are worn with cuff links (see Jewellery, p 71). They are more formal than button cuffs but are sometimes worn casually with a pair of jeans.

WITHOUT A JACKET

Without a jacket, the shirt becomes the outer garment, and for this reason undershirts are sometimes seen, especially among Americans and Italians in Britain they are considered incorrect. A breast pocket is handy, if not particularly smart – it takes the place of the pockets on the jacket. The tie is usually discarded and the collar, no longer framing a knot, may be buttoned down. The top placket buttons are invariably undone, exposing the top of the chest. One open button is safe; two suggests insouciance; three is warm on the chav scale. More casual cloths, stronger colours and the bold checks favoured by Americans are all on display alongside the more civilized colours of 'dress' shirts.

NUMBER OF SHIRTS

Here is a rule of thumb for what to pack when travelling. The minimum number of shirts and trousers to pack (in addition to clothes worn) on a trip lasting 'Days' days is:

$$\text{Shirts} = \sqrt{\text{Days}} \quad \text{and} \quad \text{Trousers} = \sqrt[3]{\text{Days}}$$

Thus, for 1, 2, 3, 4,…, 365 days, you should pack 1, 1, 2, 2,…, 19 shirts and 1, 1, 1, 2,…, 7 pairs of trousers. Thus the relationship between the number of shirts and trousers in your possession is:

$$\text{Shirts}^2 = \text{Trousers}^3$$

For example, a man with 3 pairs of trousers should have 5 shirts; with 6 pairs of trousers, 15 shirts; with 9 pairs of trousers, 27 shirts.

ESSENTIAL SHIRTS

According to the first rule above, a man needs a minimum of 19 shirts over 365 days. In an ideal wardrobe, this is what they should be:

Ordinary	W	broadcloth	a plain white shirt is the most essential
	W	twill	a heavier, ribbed diagonal weave
	B	broadcloth	the most formal of blue shirts
	B	end-on-end	woven from blue and white threads
	B *or* P	twill	best if weft & warp are blue or pink & white
	BW	stripe	pin, pencil or butcher stripes
	BW	fine check	one of the most versatile of shirts
	BW	coarse check	gingham or windowpane checks
	PW	fine check	gone are the days when pink meant wink
Formal	W	marcella	with turn-down collar, for dinner jacket
	W	marcella	with detachable wing collar, for tail coat
	BW	fine check	with white turn-down collar, for morning suit
	W	silk	plain off-white, like Bond's
Informal	W	oxford	a long-lasting, heavy, informal weave
	B *or* P	oxford	best worn with jeans or khakis
	B	chambray	a coarse, uneven weave for the country
	W	linen	an essential shirt for summer and the tropics
	B	linen	worn with cotton trousers or a linen suit
	any	check	muted checks on white ground, for tweeds

KEY   W = white   B = light blue   P = pink   BW = B and W   PW = P and W

❦ JEANS

Although the origin of denim work clothes is disputed, it was during the second half of the 19th century that they became widespread. The invention of jeans arguably came with the introduction of copper reinforcing rivets by Jacob Davis and Levi Strauss in 1873. It was not until the 1950s, however, that jeans were in any sense fashionable and worn outside their manual labour context. Wearing jeans was a minor act of rebellion, a supposed association with the proletariat.

Jeans today are so ingrained in popular culture that it is difficult to view their symbolism objectively. The old motivation – association with Everyman – remains partially true. Today part of their attraction is that jeans attenuate the formality of the overall costume, thereby allowing you to dress smartly with impunity. Andy Warhol was not the first man to combine jeans with a suit jacket and tie, but he made the juxtaposition popular. Today a blazer with a worn pair of jeans does not draw attention. It suggests spontaneity – not for the first time we see the desire for studied indifference.

DEFINITION

Along with the other quintessentially male garment, the suit, jeans are the most common element of Western men's dress. Everyone knows about jeans, but few understand them. A fair definition is close-fitting, blue denim trousers, which we consider in detail.

Close-fitting Despite the short-lived popularity of bagginess in the 1990s jeans are fundamentally close-fitting. A slim fit is inherent in their design; jeans do not have pleats; they grip the hips rather than suspend from the natural waist; the generous vertical pockets found on suit trousers are replaced with horizontal ones; jeans conform rather than drape, and for this reason need not be ironed. The narrow cut emphasizes a man's breadth of chest and muscularity. 'The tightness of fit, the showing of a good leg, fitted in with the Edwardian look of the modern dandy and the humble Teddy Boy. The shape of course affected that of all trousers which were belted low over the hips', writes Hardy Amies.

Blue The vast majority of jeans are blue jeans. Black and white jeans resurface once a decade or so, but in such small numbers as to be negligible. It is perhaps not coincidental that blue is the dominant colour of the suit. In jeans the blue is made from indigo, a natural dye derived from plants in the genus *Indigofera*, or a synthetic equivalent. The exposed thread (weft) is dyed blue and the perpendicular, covered thread (warp) is left white, tell-tale sign of which is the diagonal stripe pattern on the reverse. It is a common misconception that the fading of jeans results from the dark weft being worn through, exposing the white warp, which only happens with extreme wear. Fading is in fact the result of the poor adhesive properties of indigo dye. Tiny fragments of indigo are embedded in, rather than bonded to, the cotton fibres. Friction results in the loss of dye fragments, hence the particular fading properties of denim with washing and wearing.

Denim The cloth itself is a kind of heavy cotton twill with a pronounced diagonal rib. Denim is a contraction of *serge de Nîmes*: Nîmes is a southern French city; serge is a kind of weave with diagonal ribs, now used more to describe wool cloths (James Bond liked his suits made from blue serge, p 181). The cloth is known to shrink, usually about 3% over the first couple of years, which is about an inch for a 34-inch inseam. Denim shrinks further when dried at high temperature (although this is largely reversible through ordinary wear). For this reason jeans should be hung up to dry.

STYLE

Unlike with most clothes, with jeans the appearance of age through fading and wear is not only accepted but encouraged. This is not new: Jules Barbey d'Aurevilly, writing in 1844, describes Georgian swells who distressed the surface of their newly made clothes with glass-paper: 'They were at the end of their impertinence, they just couldn't go any further... They had their clothes distressed before they put them on, all over the cloth...' Today this worn look is more often ready-made, with jeans sold in various states of decline. Just how much wear is acceptable varies from year to year. The recent look of extreme distress, frayed edges and faded seat and legs has been replaced by more moderately worn cloth in uniform shades. The most flattering cut of jeans is straight-leg, with boot cut (though not flares) an acceptable and sometimes practical alternative. In either case, it is essential that jeans are worn slightly longer than your usual trousers.

BRANDS

The oldest jeans companies, Levi's, Lee and Wrangler, continue to be the most successful, though only Levi's are much seen in urban settings. Their straight-leg, undecorated jeans are perhaps the only branded article of clothing that is truly egalitarian. The most dramatic shift in how denim is worn has, of course, been the meteoric rise in popularity of high-end jeans like Diesel and True Religion. Designers are giving unprecedented attention to fit and details, while firmly maintaining the proletarian, utilitarian look. Importantly, the brand itself takes second place to cut and cloth, which discourages analogies with the designer-jeans fad 20 years earlier. The situation is more reminiscent of traditional men's tailoring, which relies on sober detailing and above all else fit; it too puts limited stock in labels. Will bespoke jeans be widely available soon?

❦ SUITS

The Western civilized world – and much of the Eastern – has adopted English national dress. In 1649 King Charles I was executed and with him went doublet and hose. The history of the suit – in its earliest form a knee-length coat, waistcoat and breeches – begins with the Restoration. Unlike in France, where the aristocracy was concentrated at court, the English nobility was scattered about the countryside. Sport played a decisive role in shaping fashion, and by the late 18th century the frock coat was cut away for riding. A hundred years later the tails were removed altogether and the suit in its modern form appeared.

DESCRIPTION

The suit is foremost a masculine garment, both in its simplicity of decoration and emphasis of the male form. Its matching fabric in muted colours forms the backdrop against which the colour and finery of women's clothes are displayed. The V shape rising from the tapered trousers to the jacket's padded shoulders sets man distinctly apart from woman.

The suit jacket comes in two varieties: single- and double-breasted. Single-breasted jackets have notched lapels and usually two or three or four buttons. Three buttons is classic, four showbiz and two making a comeback after being out of favour. Only the middle, middle two and top buttons are done up, respectively, these being level with the natural waist and the jacket's narrowest point. Double-breasted jackets have peaked lapels and the jacket fronts overlap, with only the top working buttons done up. The number of vents is largely a matter of taste, although single-breasted jackets tend to have none or one; double, none or two.

There is less scope for variation in trousers. Turn-ups (called cuffs in the US), while perfectly acceptable, are presently not *la mode*. If present, they are 1½ inches deep. Belts, appropriate with separate jacket and trousers, interrupt the matching fabric of the suit; in their place side fasteners or braces are preferable. Vertical front pockets, and one back pocket, are correct.

Waistcoats are made of the same fabric as the suit, except with morning coats (p 56). Like the jacket, a waistcoat should have (notched) lapels. By tradition the lowest waistcoat button is not fastened.

BUYING A SUIT

Like architecture and typography, a suit is built up out of minor variations on inherited wisdom. Small deviations speak loudly. 'Never in your dress altogether desert that taste which is general', advises Bulwer-Lytton (p 72). 'The world considers eccentricity in great things genius, in small things folly.' Your first couple of suits should be dark blue or dark grey. Black suits, apart from evening clothes, clothes for the clergy and at funerals (and even here navy is perfectly correct), look cheap. First learn to wear with ease a plain navy suit, white shirt and solid navy tie, which is not as easy as it sounds. Once you have developed an eye for the basics, you can turn to other cloths – chalk stripes, checks, Prince of Wales, tweeds, corduroy, even velvet.

Price does not guarantee that a suit will look good, and indeed the most expensive suits, selected without a practised eye, are often unattractive and ill-fitting. A number of details signify a well-made suit: pocket flaps; sewn rather than fused canvas lining; a button as opposed to zip fly; side adjusters instead of belt loops; working cuff buttons; matching lining inside the pocket flaps and jacket; a thread behind the lapel buttonhole to hold stems.

The single most important aspect of a good suit is fit. Always begin with the shoulders. Here the suit should be close-fitting, with little space for the cloth to indent against the arms. The collar must not gape at the back. The arm holes should be high and the sleeves narrow. The jacket should be just long enough to cover the seat entirely. A close-fitting garment around the legs has always been important in defining the masculine figure, first in the form of hose, then breeches, then trousers. Accordingly, trousers should be narrow through the seat and thigh and have one or no front pleats, not two.

HAVING A SUIT MADE

While most men's suits are ready-made, having a suit tailored brings with it the possibility of improved fit and the choice of cloth, lining, vents, pockets and button placement. There are two kinds of tailoring: made-to-measure and bespoke. A made-to-measure suit costs half again the price of a suit off-the-peg. The suit is made to a fixed pattern, but adapted to your basic measurements: chest, waist, arms, legs and back. These details are sent away and made into a suit. When the finished product is returned, only small further changes can be made, like waist size or trouser length. A bespoke suit, on the other hand, is stagewise assembled on site over the course of a number of fittings (and costs twice as much as made-to-measure). Attention to detail is paramount, and much effort will be made to ensure a perfect fit. But beware of the tailor's eye for human defects: few men are constructed in the image of Ideal Man (p 4), and the tailor will ruthlessly spot and adjust for any peculiarities.

Bear in mind that a tailor is only as demanding as his client, so it is important to be a stickler for details. When having clothes made you learn by mistakes, and your first suit will not be your favourite, so it is wise to begin with an inexpensive tailor. The principal signs that a suit has been tailored is the absence of a label and the choice of lining, which is customarily bolder than ready-made linings. Burgundy is the most traditional colour. Also smart are crimson, salmon pink and orange (blue suits) and bottle green, navy and ivory (grey suits). Light and royal blue linings tend to conflict with blue shirts.

IDEAL WARDROBE

How many suits does a man need? Hugh Holland, of the tailor Kilgour (8 Savile Row, London w1s, www.kilgour.eu), suggests the following comprehensive list. Keep in mind that they would normally be acquired over ten or so years.

Heavyweight suits

Purpose	Freezing days in London, New York and Moscow. Useful for cold-blooded businessmen.
Features	Excellent crease resistance, makes up beautifully, longevity.
Design	Pinstripe (blue and grey ground), charcoal-grey flannel, plain navy.
Style	Two double breasted (button two, show six) and two single breasted (button two).
Quantity	Ideally plan to have four suits at this weight.
Material	100% pure wool worsted, and flannels.
Weight	13 ounces to 16 ounces.

Mediumweight suits

Purpose	The perfect utility suit ideal for temperatures of 10–15° Celsius (50–60° Fahrenheit) and use in all environments from the office (standard materials) to the Opera (luxury fibres).
Features	Luxurious fabrics in a huge range of designs.
Quantity	We advise five suits in standard materials for business and five in finer materials for smart occasions. Extra trousers advisable.
Material	Pure wool worsted (cloth this weight drapes beautifully when cut in the English style).
Weight	10 ounces to 12 ounces.

Lightweight suits

Purpose	For warm spring and summer.
Features	Choose lighter coloured fabrics in keeping with the season

Beige and vanilla hues are particularly popular.

Quantity Again five suits in standard materials and five in finer materials such as silk, mohair and high twist fine wool.

Weight 7 ounces to 9 ounces.

Overcoats

Purpose For wearing outdoors in cold weather.

Features Camel, dark grey or navy.

Quantity Three should be plenty.

Material Wool worsted Crombie overcoating, pure cashmere and cashmere/wool mixes.

Weight 16 ounces to 26 ounces.

Sports jackets and blazers

Purpose Principally semi-informal, these garments can be worn on a huge variety of occasions. Dress-down Friday means sports jacket for many office workers. Blazers, which by no means have to be navy blue, are popular at club functions.

Quantity No limit!

Material Millionaire cashmere, silk and cashmere, pure silk, wools, tweeds and cheviots.

Trousers

Purpose Whenever shorts are inappropriate!

Features We favour plain colours with no limit to shade.

Quantity At least 20 pairs per season.

Material High twist woollens, cottons, flannels, cavalry twills and corduroys.

Dress wear

Dinner jacket and trousers Black barathea (one 10 ounces, one 12 ounces), midnight blue wool worsted.

Dinner jacket White wool worsted, worn with black trousers. The above can be styled single- or double-breasted, with peak, notch or Tautz lapel and a standard or shawl collar.

Black silk cummerbund To match silk facing on jacket.

Smoking jacket Navy, green or maroon silk velvet to be worn with trousers.

Morning-coat suit Black coat, beige waistcoat and grey-and-black striped trousers. Or matching grey coat, waistcoat and trousers.

Evening dress tails Matching black coat with silk facing and trousers, white marcella waistcoat.

❦ CLOTHES FOR WEDDINGS

Despite the American and to some extent European habit of wearing black tie to daytime weddings, the correct dress is a morning suit or, barring that, a suit. Black and white tie are worn in the evening only, usually taken to start at six o'clock. Even in America this is observed at traditional weddings: John Kennedy wore a morning suit, as did Arnold Schwarzenegger.

A morning suit is the most formal of daytime clothes, mostly worn at weddings but also at formal garden parties and the English horse-race meeting Ascot. The only alternative is an ordinary suit. We have discussed the suit on p 52, and here we focus on morning dress and its furnishings. But if you do wear a suit to a wedding, make sure it is of the plainest variety, which means dark blue or dark grey. Wear a shirt with double cuffs and a stiff turn-down collar.

JACKET AND TROUSERS

The morning coat has tails, of course, but it is not shaped like a tailcoat. It is closer to a frock coat with the corners cut away, with continuous curves from lapels to tail; hence a morning coat is sometimes called a cutaway. Morning coats come in two colours: grey, worn with matching grey trousers; or black, usually in a herringbone weave, worn with black-and-grey striped or black-and-white houndstooth trousers. A black coat is the smarter of the two, reminding us of the Regency coat and breeches from which it descends. These did not match either, the coat being dark and the trousers light. Unlike a tailcoat, the lapels do not have silk facings. The trousers should be worn with braces and have plain hems (no turn-ups).

SHIRT AND WAISTCOAT

A white shirt, dove-grey waistcoat and black-and-white tie are correct, if uninspired. Much more handsome is the incorporation of colour, which also helps dispel the hired look. Solid, checked and striped shirts are suitable in any light colour, although blue is a wise starting point. The collar, however, should be white, preferably stiff. A stiff turn-down collar is attached by studs, and weaving a necktie through it is not easy. A coloured shirt calls for a coloured waistcoat, in buff (a light brownish yellow) or cream or pale blue or pink even, preferably made of linen. The waistcoat should have lapels, but whether it is single- or double-breasted is purely a matter of taste; since the wedding of Charles, Prince of Wales and Camilla Parker Bowles, double has been somewhat more fashionable. Both the shirt and the waistcoat are closed with the usual buttons rather than studs.

TIE OR CRAVAT

A coloured shirt or waistcoat means that you can choose your tie more liberally, in navy or burgundy, for example, rather than in black and white. It should be in heavy silk and, if not plain, woven rather than printed, and fixed to the shirt with a tie tack (see p 71). It is acceptable to wear a cravat instead of a necktie, tied in an overhand knot and pinned in place with a stick pin. Nevertheless a tie is the less studied and smarter of the two. It forms a link between the morning coat and the modern suit, without which a morning suit risks looking like fancy dress. A man should feel as much at ease in formal clothes as in any others, but he needs reference points.

TOP HAT

Though not essential, a top hat is often worn or carried. In *The Englishman's Suit* (see Books, p 175), Hardy Amies advises how to wear it confidently:

> Wear the hat high on your head like a crown and not low down on your ears like a candle-snuffer. If you are hiring a 'topper', see that you tilt it well over your nose and never to the back of your head. It should look too small rather than too big… Squat crowns [make] you look, if you are not careful, like a doorman at a provincial hotel in Holland. The smartest top hat is indubitably that made of black silk. It is, of course, difficult to maintain with its surface unruffled. It is, I think, correct to wear it all the year round, whereas a grey topper looks silly in winter.

ET CETERA

Shoes should be well-polished black toecaps. As with white tie (p 60), a pocket watch can be worn. If ever there was a time to wear a buttonhole, this is it. But make sure it is a single flower, and not a miniature floral arrangement sometimes seen in American *boutonnières*.

Disregard the dictum that the principal male members of the wedding party should dress alike, probably inspired by the for-hire companies which rent to them. Indeed the opposite is true: exercising the limited freedoms in morning dress is one of the principal pleasures in wearing it. At the smartest weddings, there is a broad mix of pastel shirts and waistcoats, and no two ties are alike.

If buying a new morning suit is prohibitively expensive, fine old ones can be bought second-hand for little more than the cost of hiring. But if you do hire, go for the simplest design and try to get a buff waistcoat and wear your own coloured shirt and tie.

❦ BLACK TIE

Men's formal clothes invariably have their roots in sporting and military costume, first being accepted as day wear and eventually as clothes for the evening. The dinner jacket does not, as is often thought, derive from the evening tailcoat but from a Victorian lounge jacket popular in the late 1800s. The short jacket was later worn as informal evening wear and in the 1920s made a fashionable alternative to the tailcoat by the Prince of Wales.

Today black tie is worn in the evening when the occasion calls for clothes more formal than a suit. Black tie is also known as a dinner jacket, a tuxedo in America, and 'dress for dinner' – the last only found on invitations.

JACKET

Dinner jackets come in three varieties: single-breasted, with peaked lapels; single-breasted, with a round shawl collar; and double-breasted, which is always peaked. Unlike a black suit, a dinner jacket never has notched lapels, which is an immediate sign of a cheaply made garment. The silk facings of the lapels and collar are one of two types: satin – a smooth, glossy weave; or grosgrain – a matte silk weave with pronounced ribs. Both are permissible on all three jacket styles, with the exception of double-breasted, which today tends to show grosgrain. Dinner jackets are black, of course, but also sometimes midnight blue, which under artificial light appears blacker than black; true black by comparison can have a greenish tinge. A white dinner jacket should not be worn, not in the summer, not by the sea.

TROUSERS

Trousers are cut in the same material as the jacket with a silk braid running down the outside leg. They should be slim-fitting, straight-legged and have one or no pleats running from the waistband. Being formal, the trousers should not have turn-ups, and the hem should be slightly longer in the back than the front, reaching the heel of the shoe. Braces are normally worn; in their absence, there are often side fasteners. Belts are off limits, and indeed the trousers should not have belt loops.

WAISTCOAT OR CUMMERBUND

Formal clothes require that the place where the trousers and the shirt meet be covered. A double-breasted jacket looks after this itself. In the case of a single-breasted jacket, it is the job of a cummerbund or waistcoat. A cummerbund, originally an Indian sash wrapped around the waist (*kamar-band*), is worn with the folded pleats facing up. A waistcoat is equally correct, if slightly more formal, and ideally comes with a deep opening which displays a large expanse of shirt. The cummerbund or waistcoat should be plain and black; coloured or patterned varieties are questionable at a school leavers' ball, a solecism elsewhere.

SHIRTS

Dinner jackets are worn with a white marcella (piqué) shirt or, at a pinch, plain white broadcloth. Pleated shirts, while sometimes worn, have an aged look; ruffles suggest fancy dress. The unstarched shirt collar should turn down, although there remains an interest in stiff wing collars. Shirt studs and cufflinks are worn, usually in black and silver. The cufflinks should have faces on both sides.

BOW TIE

The bow tie comes today in three shapes (see p 66). Its weave should reflect the silk facings of the jacket: satin if the lapels are satin and barathea (a textured, basket weave) if the lapels are grosgrain. The bow should be tied by hand; for the clumsy there are ties that attach in the back which can be first tied around the leg in full view. As Hardy Amies notes in *The Englishman's Suit*, it must be undecorated and black:

> I now have to be severe with the young. You simply cannot wear a scarlet satin tie; it is overwhelmingly 'naff'. Nor may you wear any coloured or any patterned tie. European invitations say firmly 'black tie'. Colour blindness is not excused. And oldies must throw away that velvet butterfly tie. You can revive a passing fashion of 100 years; not one of ten.

ET CETERA

Shoes are of course black, with patent black lace-ups or black toecaps correct; black brogues, less so. Slip-ons (whether they bear a penny or a tassel or a snaffle) are in bad taste. Socks should be long enough to cover the calf, and may be black or coloured. Pocket handkerchiefs are essential and should be silk; a coloured one is ideal, but if you wear a white one, it should be off-white rather than bright white. Never wear a white silk scarf.

Few things are more ruined by poor fit than evening clothes. Secondhand dinner jackets seem to fit best, probably because they were hand-made by skilled tailors. But beware of the matching trousers, which are likely to have a hint of Oxford bagginess – a sartorial crime.

❦ WHITE TIE

Not often seen today, white tie is the most formal evening garment a man can wear. It is also known as a tailcoat or evening dress. The tailcoat descended from the double-breasted riding coat such that the two halves could never be fastened. Hence the two rows of buttons still seen today.

JACKET AND TROUSERS

Like the double-breasted dinner jacket, the tailcoat has peaked lapels, usually in grosgrain. The coat fronts should just cover the waistband of the trousers and the tails should reach the back of the knee. White-tie trousers differ from black-tie trousers in two respects. First, they are cut to be worn at the natural waist. This is because the white waistcoat must cover the trousers' waistband without extending below the coat fronts worn over it. Second, by tradition, the trousers have two, rather than one, silk braid stripes running down the outside seam of each leg.

SHIRT, WAISTCOAT AND BOW TIE

The shirt is made of marcella or, less commonly, plain broadcloth and is starched stiff at the front and cuffs. A cleverly designed shirt has a loop which attaches to the fly of the trousers to keep the shirt from billowing. A stiff wing collar is essential, and this means it must be detachable – it is very hard to make an attached collar stiff. The collar should be at least 1¾ inches high, despite the preponderance of shorter specimens. Like the shirt, the waistcoat is cut from white marcella and is worn stiff. It has a deep opening and only closes at the base, with studs. It may have a back, usually in satin, or attach behind with only an adjustable band. Cufflinks and studs for the shirt and waistcoat are traditionally gold or mother of pearl, with precious stones also seen. The marcella bow is tied like any other bow tie.

ET CETERA

Shoes are patent leather, either lace-ups or (less commonly) court pumps with a ribbed satin bow. Socks are now black and handkerchiefs off-white, although some colour can be displayed by a man who knows the rules. It is not ostentatious to wear a pocket watch, the fob (chain) being attached to a purpose-made hole in the waistcoat. The wristwatch is removed if a pocket watch is worn, and arguably even if one isn't. Decorations are worn in the presence of a member of the royal family or if they are indicated on the invitation, as in 'Evening dress – decorations'.

❦ UNDERWEAR

There are three types of men's underwear. Briefs, called Y-fronts in the UK, cover the groin and have elastic edges around the thighs; they are usually white. Boxers shorts, sometimes called boxers or shorts, are loose fitting and extend partially down the thigh. Boxer briefs, a more recent innovation, are a hybrid between the two – briefs with snug legs. The history of all three is not long, as Hardy Amies (p 175) explains:

> It is important to remember that all undergarments were used to protect the suit from contact with the body, not just the loins. Suits were objects of value and by the poor considered heirlooms to be handed down to the next generation. They were not washable and, of course, there was no dry-cleaning. So there were no 'briefs' or shorts until well into the [20th] century. By the 1920s the modern lounge suit required the abandonment of 'long johns' – certainly in the summer. Also of one piece underwear known as 'combinations'.

BOXERS VERSUS BRIEFS

A perennial men's question is whether boxers or briefs are best. From a fashion point of view, the biggest difference between them is that briefs are more revealing. Is this more attractive? Bear in mind that men's dress, unlike women's, has never sought to attract by exposing the flesh: shorts are not sexier than trousers. The interest in briefs seems, in part, to derive from a false analogy with women's underwear, where less is usually more.

The most common argument in favour of briefs is that they offer 'support'. However, it is not clear that this is what Nature intended. It is well known that men's testicles are designed to function at a lower temperature than the rest of the body. Do briefs interfere with temperature regulation by keeping the testicles in proximity with the groin? A scientific investigation into the question was conducted by R. Munkelwitz and B. R. Gilbert ('Are boxer shorts really better? A critical analysis of the role of underwear type in male subfertility', *The Journal of Urology*, **160**, 1337 (1998)). The authors find:

> Mean scrotal temperature plus or minus standard deviation was 33.8 +/– 0.8 °C and 33.6 +/– 1.1 °C in the boxer and brief group, respectively [body temperature is 37.0°C]. There were no significant temperature differences between the groups. Differential temperatures comparing core to scrotal temperature and semen parameters also were not significantly different… It is unlikely that underwear type has a significant effect on male fertility.

❦ TIES

Like most elements of Western men's dress, the tie has its origins in England. 'If we, the Brits, cannot claim to have invented the modern tie', argues Hardy Amies, 'no other nation can either.' The earliest record of the tie in its modern form is in 1850s England, where it was worn by young men as sporting attire. The style became fashionable at once, eclipsing the cravats and stocks popular at the time. Much has been said about the demise of the tie, and throughout the last hundred years its death has been repeatedly prophesied. It should be borne in mind, however, that knotted neckcloths have been standard attire for men for 350 years, and if the tie does vanish something knotted around the neck will almost certainly replace it.

Essential ties

We will not talk about the colour or pattern of ties here, apart from saying that two ties are essential in any man's wardrobe: a solid navy tie in woven silk; and a solid black tie in woven or knitted silk. A navy tie never goes amiss, whether it is worn with a morning suit, blazer or a pair of jeans. Black ties, despite their relatively recent exclusive association with funerals, have long been a favourite of James Bond and Italians.

Tie size

The ideal width of a tie is 3–3½ inches, which is in natural proportion with the typical man's suit. While most ties available today are wider than this, the best tie makers, such as Hermès and many of the shops along London's Jermyn Street, have consistently produced ties of the ideal width. Once tied, the length should be such that the tip of the wide blade ends anywhere within 1 inch above or below the waistband. If the thin blade descends below the wide blade, there are a number of ways to address it. One is to choose a bigger knot (see Tie Knots, p 64); another is to tuck the thin blade into the shirt between the second and third buttons down; a third is described in Label, opposite.

Dimple

'When the fabric of the tie permits (if it is silk twill or a supple Jacquard silk, for example), a beautiful effect can be obtained by using the index finger to press a slight convex cavity into the tie just below the knot. The French call this little hollow a *cuillère*, which means spoon or scoop,' explains François Chaille in *The Book of Ties*. This hollow is called a dimple in English, and it is best suited to ties that are wide at the neck (just below the knot). But while one dimple is smart, two is affected and conveys all the sartorial elegance of a handkerchief carefully folded to show four points.

Label

On the back of the wide blade a small horizontal band can be found, usually a label with the name of the maker or, on better-made ties, a band of the same material as the tie itself. While most men slip the thin blade through this band to secure it, it is arguably smarter to leave it free to flow. If the thin blade is too long, slip it through the label from the opposite direction, with the excess falling over and down.

Tie handkerchief

If you can't make up your mind as to whether to wear a tie, you can keep the option open and put the tie in the breast pocket of your jacket, where it doubles as a handkerchief. This looks best with solid-coloured ties, with the tie folded in half three times over.

Tie belt

A truly worn-out or unwanted tie can be turned into a belt. It is simple to make. You cut off the wide blade such that the tie is 6 inches longer than the circumference of your waist, and sew the cut end around two identical metal rings, about 1½ inches 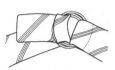 in diameter and ⅛ inch thick. The belt is 'buckled' by weaving the opposite end through the rings as shown. Pulling the end tightens the belt.

Storage

Tie experts are divided over the best way to store a tie. Some say that a tie should be rolled up in a coil when not in use, starting from the thin end. Others suggest simply hanging it from the middle over a hanger or bar. In either case a tie should never be left knotted when not in use, which tends to leave heavy creases. It is possible, of course, to tie a tie once and never untie it, but this comes at the expense of wearing the same knot, tied with the same execution, whatever the occasion, collar or mood.

Cleaning

It is often said that ties should never be dry-cleaned, but this is not quite true. It is not the cleaning but the inevitable pressing afterwards which most harms a tie, and the latter can be avoided if a cleaner is warned beforehand. Nonetheless a tie should not be cleaned unless it shows visible marks or stains. The death of a much-loved tie invariably results from the fraying of the wide blade's bottom edges, which usually happens long before any other part of the tie wears out. The solution is to have the tie shortened by half an inch, which many alterations tailors will do if asked. It is a somewhat delicate operation but, if done with care, it can double a tie's life.

❦ TIE KNOTS

In *The 85 Ways to Tie a Tie* (see Books, p 175), Thomas Fink and Yong Mao proved that there are 85 different knots which can be tied with a conventional necktie. Of these, the 15 knots below are of particular interest.

Oriental	Nicky	Half-Windsor	Cavendish	Grantchester
Four-in-hand	Pratt	St Andrew	Christensen	Hanover
Kelvin	Victoria	Plattsburgh	Windsor	Balthus

The four most popular are described here. For an explanation of the sequence notation, see the author's homepage (Colophon, p 213).

FOUR-IN-HAND

Number: 2   *Size*: 4 moves   *Sequence*: Li Ro Li Co T

The four-in-hand is today the most frequently worn tie knot of all. It was introduced simultaneously with the tie in the 1850s. Tied in an ordinary silk tie, it is a small knot with a characteristic elongated, asymmetric shape. In thicker ties, the four-in-hand can look deceptively large (see the Windsor knot, right). 'Four-in-hand' refers not only to the knot described here, but also to the modern necktie itself. There are a number of possible explanations of the name: drivers of the four-in-hand carriage tied their scarves with the knot; the reigns of the carriage were tied in the same way; it was worn by members of the now-defunct Four-in-Hand Club. In any case, the name of the knot is not derived from the four moves needed to tie it.

NICKY

Number: 4   *Size*: 5 moves   *Sequence*: Lo Ci Ro Li Co T

The Nicky is between the four-in-hand and half-Windsor in size and has a compact, symmetric shape. It is a natural choice for those seeking a symmetric knot of modest volume. Unlike the three other knots described here, the Nicky begins with the tie inside-out around the neck. The odd number of moves ensures that the wide blade emerges outside-out.

HALF-WINDSOR

Number: 7   *Size*: 6 moves   *Sequence*: Li Ro Ci Lo Ri Co T

This symmetrical knot is medium-sized and shaped like an equilateral triangle. Its origin remains mysterious. Although its name suggests that it was derived from the Windsor, there is little evidence for this claim. The half-Windsor is not half the size of the Windsor, but rather three-quarters (six moves versus eight), and the two sequences of moves seem altogether unrelated. Like the Nicky, it is a versatile knot, and can satisfactorily be worn with collars of most sizes and spreads.

WINDSOR

Number: 31   *Size*: 8 moves   *Sequence*: Li Co Ri Lo Ci Ro Li Co T

The Windsor is a large, bulbous, triangular knot, sometimes erroneously referred to as a double-Windsor. In Ian Fleming's novels, James Bond (p 181) thinks the Windsor knot is 'the mark of a cad'. Today it is the knot of choice of (once) communist leaders and dictators: Hugo Chávez, Vladimir Putin and the Chinese leaders Jiang Zemin and Hu Jintao are all fans (but so is Arnold Schwarzenegger). Despite the knot's name, it was not invented by the Duke of Windsor, as is commonly held. In *A Family Album* (see Books, p 172), the duke explains that it was his specially made thick ties, rather than a complicated knot, that produced the effect:

> The so-called 'Windsor knot' in the tie was adopted in America at a later date. It was I believe regulation wear for GIs during the war, when American college boys adopted it too. But in fact I was in no way responsible for this. The knot to which Americans gave my name was a double knot in a narrow tie – a 'slim Jim' as it is sometimes called. It is true that I myself have always preferred a large knot, as looking better than a small one, so during the 1920s I devised, in conclave with Mr Sandford, a tie always of the broad variety which was reinforced by an extra thickness of material to produce this effect. As far as I know this particular fashion has never been followed in America or elsewhere.

❦ BOW TIES, ETC.

BOW TIE

Despite its longer lineage than the necktie, today the bow tie is worn almost exclusively with formal clothes. Some men persist in wearing a bow tie with a jacket or suit, but at a cost: against the backdrop of modern men's dress, bow ties appear studied or eccentric. They confer a diminished impression of authority. A man's dress is made remarkable only by its absence of defect. Conspicuous inconspicuousness is the rule, and the bow tie does nothing if not draw attention. 'If you insist on wearing a bow tie to business – and bow tie wearers are a stubborn lot – I suggest you wear it with the proper accessories', writes John Molloy in *Dress for Success*. 'A red nose and a beanie cap with a propeller.'

Bow ties worn with a dinner jacket or tailcoat are made of black silk or white cotton, and can be found in three shapes: the butterfly, the batswing and the one-hander (left to right). All are tied the same way.

TYING A BOW TIE

Unlike a necktie, both ends of a bow tie can be manipulated to form a knot, making bow tie knots potentially much more complicated than tie knots. The only known knot which can be tied with conventional bow ties is the usual reef bow, below. The granny bow (p 92) causes the tied bow to sit vertically rather than horizontally. Alternative knots may exist, but have yet to be discovered. The author welcomes candidates for new knots – or a proof

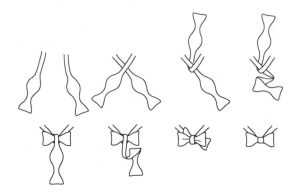

of their impossibility. Of course, bow ties should be self-tied rather than ready-tied. '[The bow tie] and the stiff wing collar are the direct descendants of Beau Brummell's starched cravats. He had trouble tying these. How could the rising middle classes cope?…I cannot blame men for buying "made-up" ties, sin though it is to wear one,' writes Hardy Amies.

The tied bow has four layers of cloth emanating from each side of the knot, three of which form the bow (shown top-down below) and one of which goes around the neck. Pulling on the three bow layers produces different effects, essential to optimizing all but the most expertly tied knots.

A Pulling here increases one side while decreasing the other half as much.
B Pulling here increases one side while tightening the knot.
C Pulling here increases one side while decreasing the other twice as much.

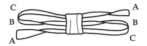

CRAVAT AND ASCOT

The modern cravat is a long, rectangular neckcloth, pleated in the centre to form a neckband. It is made of silk, usually in a print of polka dot, paisley or foulard. Despite being a direct descendant of the plain white linen neckcloths of Beau Brummell, it is rarely found in plain colours. Continentals often wear it casually around the neck and tucked under an open-collared shirt, a practice which has not caught on in Britain, where cravats are limited to weddings with a morning suit (p 56). Cravats are tied as follows:

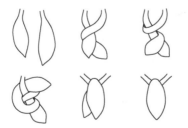

Apart from its narrower blades, the Ascot differs from the cravat most noticeably in the knot used to tie it. It is tied in a reef knot (p 92) with the descending blades of equal length, one carefully folded over the other and fixed with a pin. It is mostly worn with morning dress at weddings and the eponymous race meeting.

❦ ACCESSORIES

HANDKERCHIEFS

Contrary to popular belief, the purpose of the handkerchief is not aesthetics but utility. It has for centuries been a practical accessory: to catch a sneeze, open a bottle or dry up tears. During the First World War, the handkerchief was kept tucked into the jacket sleeve because the uniform pockets buttoned down. It has since returned to the breast pocket, and whether it is on display or not, that is where it belongs. 'The most important [rule] is that it must look as though you use it; and you must. To have a handkerchief showing in the breast pocket and another one for use is to provide the most "naff" gesture a man can make', writes Hardy Amies in *The Englishman's Suit*. The second rule is that it must not look like a piece of origami; tricorns, shells and bird bases should be avoided. If a handkerchief is to be arranged it must be done so with studied indifference, like Prince Charles', or simply folded, like his father's.

Apart from being square and having rolled edges, a handkerchief can be made from just about anything: silk, linen, even cotton, the backs of old shirts proving a thrifty source. It should of course not match the tie but rather in its lustre oppose it: linen or cotton for satin ties, silk for matt or wool ties. 'Of course it's extravagant to blow your nose in a silk handkerchief, but we are talking about style and not economics', writes Amies. 'There are now quite beautiful coloured cotton handkerchiefs…of the bandanna type… Very good to add a touch of the country squire.'

BUTTONHOLES

Like most details of the men's suit, the buttonhole on the left lapel is not fanciful. Originally it was a true button hole – an artefact of the high-fastening lapels of the 18th century. Buttoning descended but the button holes did not. Putting the buttonhole to unintended use is not new: in the early 18th century the ends of the lace cravats popular at the time were pulled through it, a style known as the Steinkerk. Today the buttonhole is used to hold a flower, though a sprig of ivy would not be out of place. Well-tailored suits have a loop inside the lapel to hold the stem. It is incorrect to pin a flower to a lapel without a buttonhole. A hole can easily be added by a tailor, the only exception being the shawl-collared dinner jacket, whose lapel never fastened. The buttonhole flower itself should look as though it came from the neighbour's garden, not arranged by a florist. Small carnations and thistles are smart. Orchids are camp. In England a rose is worn on St George's Day and paper poppies in the runup to Remembrance Sunday. In America wearing miniature flags is a recent custom among politicians.

BELTS AND BRACES

Men, unlike women, do not have pronounced hips, and thus their trousers must be fixed at the waist. This is done by a belt, braces or side fasteners.

Belts are the most common, but also the most recent and informal. With a suit they are acceptable but discouraged; with formal dress they are a solecism. Men's belts are threaded through the belt loops in a counterclockwise fashion, unlike women's, which are threaded clockwise. If the belt is leather, it should match the shoes: black belts with black shoes, tan belts with tan shoes, and so on. Informal belts can also be made of cotton or silk; instructions for making a tie belt are given on p 63. At a pinch, the end of a leather belt can be used as a shoehorn.

Braces, called suspenders in America, keep the trousers fixed but not snug. They attach to the trousers' waistband at the front left, front right and centre back. They should always be attached by buttons, sewn on to the inside or outside waistband, never clips. Braces are sometimes worn with a suit and especially with formal clothes. The most popular and handsome variety are plain and coloured and made of felt.

Side fasteners are adjustable bands on both sides of the trousers which can be used to vary the size of the waist by about 1 inch. They are customary on better suits. If present, there should be no belt loops.

BANDANNAS

The word 'bandanna' is derived from the Hindi word *badhnu*, an Indian method of selectively dyeing cloth by tying it in knots. It now refers to the cotton and sometimes silk squares printed with simple patterns of paisley or polka dots. Bandannas are bigger than handkerchiefs, typically 22 inches square as opposed to 16. They are worn in the breast or front trouser pockets; beware of using the back pocket unless you are familiar with the camp semiotics of the 'hanky code'.

Bandanna uses: babushka · bandage · bandanna doll · Barbie parachute · belt (two tied together) · bib · blindfold · bottle apron · cat cape · cheesecloth · coffee filter · cold compress · cravat · dish cloth · dog kerchief · dust mask · gag · gang allegiance · garotte · gift wrap · glasses cleaner · handcuffs · handkerchief · headband · hobo pack · kindling (for fire) · lunch box · muffler · napkin · nappy · neckerchief · origami · picnic cloth · pillow cover · pirate costume · placemat · polish rag · pot holder · poultice · scarf · shoe shine cloth · shoo away bugs · sit upon · sling · smokescreen mask · splint · strainer · sweat band · tie ponytail · towel · touch football (American) · tourniquet · washcloth · whip · Wild West costume · wrap breakables

❦ JEWELLERY

A man's jewellery, like his clothes, should be plain, masculine and conspicuously inconspicuous. It should be limited to a few functional items, either explicitly useful, like a watch or cufflinks, or as a mark of specific status, like a wedding band. The use of jewellery to adorn – and this includes necklaces, bracelets, earrings and piercings – is an essentially feminine concept.

RINGS

Wedding rings Although the association of rings and marriage is ancient, before the Second World War only women wore wedding rings. Married soldiers away from home took to the idea of wearing a band as a symbol of their fidelity. Today the wearing of men's weddings bands varies from country to country. In America most men wear them, in Britain just under half, and in Europe somewhere in between. The ring itself, which should be a plain gold band, is worn on the same finger as the women's, that is, the third finger of the left or right hand, depending on the country.

Signet rings These are traditionally worn by men whose family has its own coat of arms. The arms are engraved on the ring in metal or semiprecious stone, originally used to authenticate documents. Signet rings are usually worn on the small finger of the left or right hand, depending on country.

WATCHES

Men's watches are unusual in being the only article of dress that men, as opposed to women, wear because of brand recognition. A man's suit, by contrast, never outwardly advertises its maker; it must be judged by its merits: cloth, cut and fit. For this reason there is something slightly effete about paying large sums for famous watches. It is not expensive to produce a handsome, accurate, robust timepiece. Therefore it remains in the best taste to wear one of whatever make. As regards design, thinner watches tend to be smarter than thick ones, leather bands than metal, black bands than brown, minimal movement than complex. While most watches must occasionally be removed, there is something to be said for one which can be worn without concern during a spontaneous splash or climb in a tree.

HARDWARE

Men's dress, especially formal dress, makes use of an array of links, pins and fasteners – collectively called hardware – which is summarized below.

Cufflinks join double cuffs, sometimes called French cuffs. Their popularity varies considerably between countries. In Britain they are popular at work with a suit or jacket, and are occasionally seen with a pair of jeans. In America they can look flamboyant. Brown wears them daily, Sarkozy more often than not and Bush only at his more important meetings. One of the simplest types of cufflinks, and also the smartest, is two silver or gold metal ovals joined by a chain. Silk knots in all colours are an inexpensive and handsome alternative. There are countless other varieties, some of which have ingenious designs. But there is a fine line between the smart and the naff, and the inexperienced are advised to stick to the plainest designs. Double-sided links tend to be more formal than single-sided ones. In all cases it is acceptable to detach the link from one side of the cuff and roll up the sleeves.

A *tie bar* is used to restrain the necktie, usually for the sake of safety or formality. It is a hairpin-shaped piece of metal or other material which slides over the shirt and tie, keeping the tie immobilized.

Tie clips are similar to tie bars but spring-loaded. Both are hopelessly dated.

Tie tacks on the other hand, when worn with a morning coat (p 56), are rather fashionable. They are made of a circular metal disk with a pin on it which passes through the tie and attaches to a base secured to a button hole.

A *collar pin* or *collar bar* is a sturdy metal safety pin or rod which clasps both sides of the collar. Pins pierce the collar, bars pass through holes in specially made collars and are secured with screw-on ends. Both pass under the tie, forcing the knot forward and causing the tie to billow slightly away from the chest.

Collar bones or *collar stiffeners* are inserted into the collars of shirts with purpose built slots sewn in to keep the points of the collar from curling. These are typically plastic, sometimes metal, best of all bone.

Studs close the front of formal shirts in place of buttons. They resemble miniature dumbbells and can only be worn with shirts with button holes on both sides. When worn with black tie (p 58), they are silver or silver and black (onyx); with white tie (p 60), gold or gold and white (mother-of-pearl). Studs for white tie waistcoats are plain mother-of-pearl.

Collar studs attach detachable collars to the shirt. Like studs, they have a dumbbell shape, but with one end small and the other broad and flat. Two collar studs are used to attach a collar: a short one for the back, and a long one for the front, which also takes the place of the top shirt button.

❦ PELHAM'S MAXIMS

Edward Bulwer-Lytton's novel *Pelham; or, The Adventures of a Gentleman*, first published in 1828, contains in it a collection of rules on dress usually known as Pelham's maxims (volume ii, chapter vii):

Never in your dress altogether desert that taste which is general. The world considers eccentricity in great things genius; in small things folly.

Always remember that you dress to fascinate others, not yourself.

To win the affection of your mistress appear negligent in your costume – to preserve it, assiduous: the first is a sign of the passion of love; the second of its respect.

Is the great man whom you would conciliate a coxcomb? – go to him in a waistcoat like his own. 'Imitation', says the author of Lacon, 'is the sincerest flattery'.

The handsome may be showy in dress, the plain should study to be unexceptionable; just as in great men we look for something to admire – in ordinary men we ask for nothing to forgive.

There is a study of dress for the aged, as well as for the young. Inattention is no less indecorous in one than in the other; we may distinguish the taste appropriate to each by the reflection that youth is made to be loved – age, to be respected.

The most graceful principle of dress is neatness – the most vulgar is preciseness.

Avoid many colours; and seek, by some one prevalent and quiet tint, to sober down the others. Apelles used only four colours, and always subdued those which were more florid, by a darkening varnish.

A very benevolent man will never shock the feelings of others, by an excess either of inattention or display; you may doubt, therefore, the philanthropy both of a sloven and a fop.

Inventions in dressing should resemble Addison's definition of fine writing and consist of 'refinements which are natural, without being obvious'.

He who esteems trifles for themselves is a trifler – he who esteems them for the conclusions to be drawn from them, or the advantage to which they can be put, is a philosopher.

TOWN

Oscar Wilde · It is better to have a permanent income than to be fascinating. (*The Model Millionaire*, 1904)

E. M. Forster · All men are equal – all men, that is to say, who possess umbrellas. (*Howards End*, 1910)

Samuel Johnson · There are few ways in which a man can be more innocently employed than in making money. (Boswell, *Life of Johnson*, 1791)

Gore Vidal · It is not enough to succeed. Others must fail.

Peter Ackroyd · [London] contains every wish or word ever spoken, every action or gesture ever made, every harsh or noble statement ever expressed. It is illimitable. (*London: The Biography*, 2000)

Gordon Gekko · The point is, ladies and gentlemen, that greed, for lack of a better word, is good. Greed is right. Greed works. (*Wall Street*, 1987)

Samuel Johnson · Whoever thinks of going to bed before twelve o'clock …is a scoundrel. (Hawkins, *The Life of Samuel Johnson*, 1787)

Naff places to live

St John's Wood	Putney
Surrey	Chiswick
Essex	Guildford
Mayfair	Weybridge
Cheam	Chobham
Sunningdale	Jersey
Kingston	Canada
Barnes	

(*The Complete Naff Guide*, 1983)

Benjamin Franklin · Those who are fear'd, are hated. ❧ Nothing but money is sweeter than honey. ❧ Beware of the young doctor and the old barber. ❧ There are three faithful friends – an old wife, an old dog and ready money. ❧ Drive thy business, or it will drive thee. ❧ Let thy discontents be thy secrets – if the world knows them 'twill despise thee and increase them. (*Poor Richard's Almanack*, 1732–1757)

❦LONDON CLUBS

A gentlemen's club* is a private members' club for the idling, dining, drinking, smoking, combination and conversation of like-minded men. It is a home away from home – and usually away from women; until recently women were not allowed into most clubs, and even today the best clubs prohibit women's use. This is, of course, part of their *raison d'être*: a club is a place where men do what they do in the absence of women. Like the paradox of Schrödinger's cat, when a women observes a gentlemen's club it ceases to be one.

It is an undisputed truth that the best collection of gentlemen's clubs in the world is to be found in London. George Augustus Sala offers the following explanation:

> The English are the only clubbable people on the face of the earth. The proper club for the Frenchman is his cafe, for without women to admire him, or to admire, your Monsieur cannot exist.The Russian has more of the clubbable element in him, but the clubs will never flourish in Muscovy till a man can be morally certain that the anecdote he is telling his neighbour will not be carried…to the Grand Master of Police.

Below is a list of the traditional gentleman's clubs of London, along with a list of other more specialized or egalitarian associations.

*In America and Japan, a gentlemen's club is also a euphemism for a high-end strip club or go-go bar. However, being open to the fee-paying public, they cannot strictly be said to be clubs at all.

GENTLEMEN'S CLUBS

Club	Address (London)	☎ (020)	Since	
Army & Navy	36 Pall Mall, sw1	7930 9721	1837	♀
Arts	40 Dover St, w1	7499 8581	1863	♀
Athenaeum	107 Pall Mall, sw1	7930 4843	1824	♀
Authors'	40 Dover St, w1	7499 8581	1891	♀
Beefsteak	9 Irving St, wc2	7930 5722	1876	♀
Boodle's	28 St James's St, sw1	7930 7166	1762	–
Brooks's	St James's St, sw1	7493 4411	1764	♀
Buck's	18 Clifford St, w1	7734 2337	1919	♀
Caledonian	9 Halkin St, sw1	7235 5162	1891	♀
Canning	4 St James's Sq., sw1	7827 5757	1910	♀
Carlton	69 St James's St, sw1	7493 1164	1832	♀

Cavalry & Guards	127 Piccadilly, W1	7499 1261	1893	♀
East India	16 St James's Sq., SW1	7930 1000	1849	♀
Garrick	15 Garrick St, WC2	7379 6478	1831	–
Junior Carlton	69 St James's St, SW1	7493 1164	1832	♀
Lansdowne	9 Fitzmaurice Place, W1	7629 7200	1935	♀
National Liberal	Whitehall Place, SW1	7930 9871	1883	♀
Naval	38 Hill St, W1	7493 7672	1919	♀
Naval & Military	4 St James's Sq., SW1	7827 5757	1862	♀
Oriental	11 Stratford Place, W1	7629 5126	1824	♀
Oxford & Cambridge	71–77 Pall Mall, SW1	7930 5151	1821	♀
Pratt's	14 Park Place, SW1	7493 0397	1857	♀
RAC	89 Pall Mall, SW1	7930 2345	1897	♀
RAF	128 Piccadilly, W1	7499 3456	1922	♀
Reform	104 Pall Mall, SW1	7930 9374	1841	♀
St James's	728 Park Place, SW1	7629 7688	1857	♀
St Stephen's	34 Queen Anne's Gate, SW1	7222 1382	1870	♀
Savage	1 Whitehall Place, SW1	7930 8118	1857	–
Savile	69 Brook St, W1	7629 5462	1868	♀
Travellers'	106 Pall Mall, SW1	7930 8688	1819	–
Turf	5 Carlton House Terrace, SW1	7930 8555	1861	♀
White's	37 St James's St, SW1	7493 6671	1693	–

OTHER CLUBS

Club	*Address (London)*	☎ (020)	*Since*	♀
Alpine	55 Charlotte Rd, EC2	7613 0755	1857	♀
Anglo-Belgian	60 Knightsbridge, SW1	7235 2121	1942	♀
City of London	19 Old Broad St, EC2	7588 7991	1832	♀
City University	50 Cornhill, EC3	7626 8571	1895	♀
Groucho	45 Dean St, W1	7439 4685	1984	♀
Hurlingham	Ranelagh Gardens, SW6	7736 8411	1869	♀
MCC	St John's Wood Rd, NW8	7289 1611	1787	♀
New Cavendish	44 Great Cumberland Place, W1	7723 0391	1909	♀
Portland	69 Brook St, W1	7499 1523	1816	♀
Roehampton	Roehampton Lane, SW15	8480 4205	1901	♀
Royal Thames Yacht	60 Knightsbridge, SW1	7235 2121	1775	♀

KEY   Women have: ♀ = full use   ♀ = limited use   – = no entry

Athenaeum More a club for dons than wits, but many people think the intellectual climate is less impressive than it once was. Little club atmosphere, but food and wine have greatly improved in recent years.

Beefsteak Terrible food at a single table where members sit where they are placed, but the best company and conversation. 'The Beefsteak is a pleasant little club. The only qualification is that you have to be a peer who has learned to read and write or a journalist who has learned table manners' (The Earl of Kintore).

Boodle's Churchill was a member, as was Ian Fleming, who preferred it to White's because 'they gas too much'. In Fleming's James Bond novels, M.'s club, Blades, is modelled on Boodle's. 'M looked like any member of any of the clubs in St James's Street. Dark grey suit, stiff white collar, the favourite dark blue bow tie with white spots, rather loosely tied…the keen sailor's face, with the clear, sharp sailor's eyes' (Ian Fleming, *Moonraker*).

Brooks's The most handsome of the remaining Regency clubs, in its early days it was a Whig outpost. Trevelyan described it as 'the most famous political club that will ever have existed in London'.

Buck's By his own account, the closest thing to P. G. Wodehouse's idea of the Drones Club. It invented the drink Buck's Fizz: 1 part orange juice and 1 part champagne.

Caledonian A traditional club, principally for Scots, where members are required to have 'at least one Scottish parent or grandparent or to have a close association with Scotland'.

Carlton Once a virtual Conservative Central Office, it remains deeply Tory. In *The Gentlemen's Clubs of London*, Anthony Lejeune writes that it is 'certainly the most famous political club of modern times, and for a while was perhaps even more directly influential than Brooks's had been in the politics of an earlier period'.

East India Having amalgamated with the Devonshire, the Sports and the Public Schools Clubs, the East India has a diverse membership. It is popular among the young as a first club to join.

Garrick Once known for theatrical talent, now stuffed full of lawyers, the Garrick offers lively conversation and a questionable club tie, of which some members are unaccountably proud. The waiting list is presently more than five years. 'In 1861 I became a member of the Garrick Club. Having up to that time lived very little among men, having hitherto known nothing of clubs, having even as a boy been banished from social gatherings, I enjoyed infinitely at first the gaiety of the Garrick. It was a festival for me to dine there – which I did indeed but seldom' (Anthony Trollope).

Groucho Founded as an antidote to the traditional club, it is consciously non-grand and has excellent food and drink. Mainly media members.

Hurlingham More an American country club than anything else, it helped introduce polo to the Western world. Very much in demand, largely for its spacious grounds and fine sports facilities.

Lansdowne Here women have long been on an equal footing with men. The club welcomes families and married couples, and has, as a result, less club atmosphere than others. A swimming pool and gym are on the premises, and lately well-attended balls for young people have been regularly organized there.

Oxford & Cambridge Housed in a fine building, it has a nondescript membership but remains a convenient first club to join. In 1996 it voted to admit women as full members.

Pratt's An intimate club which, like the Beefsteak, has a single dining table. You can dine late on straightforward, hearty fare. Until recently it had the longest waiting list of any club.

RAC Sir John Betjeman said that the great thing about the RAC is that you could sit there the whole afternoon and never see a single gentleman. It has a superb Turkish bath and a swimming pool.

Reform Originally a hotbed of progressives, the Reform now houses Old Turks, fabled liberals and civil servants. Phileas Fogg used the magnificent building to launch his 80-day trip around the world.

Savage Founded by the Victorian journalist George Augustus Sala and his literary circle, the Savage is a mix of gentility and Bohemia, one of the more warm-hearted clubs in London.

Travellers' Graced for years by permanent resident Monsignor Alfred Gilbey, who converted a cupboard into a tiny chapel, which still remains. Attracts many young fogeys, some of indeterminate sex. 'There is a fine library…an excellent fire, billiards, cards, coffee, a thousand ways of dining badly for twelve francs, etc. I do not eat there…but I arrive with a serious expression [and] take off my hat in the English manner – that is to say with a bad grace as if someone is dragging it off me' (Louis de Vignet).

White's From the days when Beau Brummell passed judgement from its famous bow window to the present, White's has remained the grandest club in the world, an 'oasis of civilization in a desert of democracy'. 'I knew I could not be a knight of the garter, or a member of White's – the only two things an Englishman cannot command' (Benjamin Disraeli).

❦POLISHING SHOES

There are three domestic arts a man should know: how to polish shoes, how to iron a shirt (see p 79) and how to carve a joint (see p 142). All other chores can in principle be delegated, but these three will prove necessary at some point in a man's life.

POLISHING SHOES

Polishing shoes requires perseverance. It is not a single shine that determines a shoe's appearance but frequent polishing over a long period. The trick is to polish lightly but often, which eventually levels the pores and irregular surface of the leather. Black shoes, having no colour of their own, should reflect light and therefore be highly polished. Black toecap shoes are sometimes polished to a moderate shine, with the toecaps themselves polished excessively (spit shine). With brown shoes it is not gloss but patina that should be emphasized, and this can only be achieved with time and regular polish in a colour just lighter than the shoe itself. The combination of polish and wear produces a complex patchwork of colours and tones.

Smooth leather shoes should be polished with a wax-based polish, such as Kiwi (suede and nubuck shoes are brushed, not polished). Only a few colours are ever necessary: black, brown, various shades of tan (light, mid and dark) and cordovan (a burgundy-brown colour used for penny loafers). There are two main methods of polishing.

Standard shine This is described on the back of the Kiwi tin: 'Apply polish with a cloth or brush. Let dry for one to two minutes, then brush to a bright shine. For heightened gloss, apply another light coat, sprinkle with water and buff with a soft cloth.' A cloth applies polish more evenly than a brush and is disposable, whereas a brush is quicker and reaches into crevices but must be cleaned immediately after with soap and water. The brush used to give lustre to the dried polish should be a separate, larger brush made of horse hair. The gloss can be enhanced by a final buff with a nylon stocking.

Spit shine A more laborious technique, known as a spit shine or sweating, is used to obtain the mirror-like finish especially prized on black shoes. The finish is much more handsome than patent leather, whose gloss comes from a plastic coating. The method involves no brushes, but is entirely done with a cloth wrapped around the fingers and kept moist with a few drops of water. Using the cloth, rub a small amount of polish vigorously but lightly into a small area of the shoe until it is no longer cloudy. Repeat this process many dozens of times until the leather begins to resemble a black mirror.

⚡ IRONING A SHIRT

Ironing well is less about doing it correctly (many methods give the same result) than doing it quickly and sufficiently. The first thing to consider is that different fibres burn at different temperatures. The standard recommended ironing temperatures, listed on most irons, are:

110 °C	230 °F	acetate, acrylic, modacrylic, nylon, spandex
150 °C	302 °F	polyester, rayon, silk, triacetate, wool
200 °C	392 °F	cotton, linen

FIVE-MINUTE METHOD

With a steam iron and some practice, a shirt can be ironed in five minutes. If the iron doesn't make steam, a spray bottle can be used to keep the shirt damp as ironing proceeds, but this is more time consuming. Bear in mind that dark fabrics should be ironed on the wrong side to avoid a shine.

Collar (25 sec.) Keep the collar flat – there is no need to iron in a crease where it turns down. Iron the underside first, then the outside. Move from the collar tips to the centre to prevent creasing at the edges.

Cuffs (45 sec.) Iron the non-showing side first, then the showing side, being sure to iron from the edges inwards. Double cuffs should be ironed flat – again there is no need to iron in a crease.

Yoke (25 sec.) This part of the shirt covers the shoulders, and is the trickiest part to get to. Use the narrow end of the ironing board.

Sleeves (90 sec.) Start from the shoulder and finish near the cuff, ironing in the gauntlet pleats leading into it. Most sleeves are creased, but there is no consensus as to whether they should be. (Creases are avoided with the aid of a specialized narrow board inserted into the sleeve.)

Back (45 sec.) This large but uninterrupted piece of cloth is one of the fastest to iron. Since the bottom half will be tucked in, it need not be ironed.

Front (70 sec.) Again, disregard the bottom half. Ironing around the buttons need not be perfect since, done up, the inside placket will not show.

If time is short and a jumper or jacket is to be worn, the time can be reduced to two minutes by ironing the collar, cuffs and front only.

A stiff shirt is worn with evening dress (p 60) and, by some, a dinner jacket. The stiffness comes from starch, which is usually applied by a drycleaner. At a pinch it can be done at home by repeated applications of spray starch, after each of which the shirt is ironed on the wrong side to avoid yellowing. Only the front, collar and cuffs are starched. DIY starching of detachable collars is hopeless and they should always be done professionally.

❧CHARACTER

Here are four famous guides to character from the last four centuries.

TWELVE GOOD RULES

King Charles I, king of England from 1625 to 1649, is credited with composing these rules of conduct. At 41 words in length, the 12 maxims remain one of the most concise and elegant codes of behaviour.

Urge no healths	Maintain no ill opinions
Profane no divine ordinances	Keep no bad company
Touch no state matters	Encourage no vice
Reveal no secrets	Make no long meals
Pick no quarrels	Repent no grievances
Make no comparisons	Lay no wagers

FRANKLIN'S VIRTUES

Benjamin Franklin, 18th-century American statesman, businessman, scientist and author of *Poor Richard's Almanack*, composed this list of 13 virtues and their descriptions as a personal guide in the 1720s.

Temperance Eat not to dullness. Drink not to elevation.

Silence Speak not but what may benefit others or yourself. Avoid trifling conversation.

Order Let all your things have their places. Let each part of your business have its time.

Resolution Resolve to perform what you ought. Perform without fail what you resolve.

Frugality Make no expense but to do good to others or yourself: i.e., waste nothing.

Industry Lose no time. Be always employed in something useful. Cut off all unnecessary actions.

Sincerity Use no hurtful deceit. Think innocently and justly; and if you speak, speak accordingly.

Justice Wrong none, by doing injuries or omitting the benefits that are your duty.

Moderation Avoid extremes. Forbear resenting injuries so much as you think they deserve.

Cleanliness Tolerate no uncleanliness in body, clothes, or habitation.

Tranquility Be not disturbed at trifles, or at accidents common or unavoidable.

Chastity Rarely use venery but for health or offspring; never to dullness, weakness, or the injury of your own or another's peace or reputation.

Humility Imitate Jesus and Socrates.

RULES OF CIVILITY

George Washington transcribed the *Rules of Civility and Decent Behavior* in the mid-1740s as a schoolboy, and ever since Americans have revisited them as a means of self-improvement. The collection of rules is largely derived from a 16th-century French Jesuit etiquette manual. Many of the rules go into arcane details; the more concise are listed here.

When in company, put not your hands to any part of the body not usually discovered.

Put not off your clothes in the presence of others, nor go out of your chamber half dressed.

When you sit down, keep your feet firm and even, without putting one on the other or crossing them.

Shift not yourself in the sight of others, nor gnaw your nails.

Let your countenance be pleasant but in serious matters somewhat grave.

Show not yourself glad at the misfortune of another though he were your enemy.

Let your discourse with men of business be short and comprehensive.

Strive not with your superior in argument, but always submit your judgment to others with modesty.

Undertake not to teach your equal in the art himself professes; it savours of arrogancy.

When a man does all he can, though it succeed not well, blame not him that did it.

Wherein you reprove another be unblameable yourself, for example is more prevalent than precepts.

Use no reproachful language against any one; neither curse nor revile.

Eat not in the streets, nor in the house, out of season.

Detract not from others, neither be excessive in commanding.

Reprehend not the imperfections of others, for that belongs to parents, masters and superiors.

Treat with men at fit times about business and whisper not in the company of others.

Be not tedious in discourse or in reading unless you find the company pleased therewith.

Be not curious to know the affairs of others, neither approach those that speak in private.

Undertake not what you cannot perform but be careful to keep your promise.

Be not tedious in discourse, make not many digressions, nor repeat often the same manner of discourse.

Speak not evil of the absent, for it is unjust.

Take no salt or cut bread with your knife greasy.

Drink not nor talk with your mouth full; neither gaze about you while you are drinking.

If others talk at table be attentive, but talk not with meat in your mouth.

Let your recreations be manful not sinful.

Labour to keep alive in your breast that little spark of celestial fire called conscience.

IDEA OF A GENTLEMAN

In *The Idea of a University* (1854), Cardinal John Henry Newman wrote:

Hence it is that it is almost a definition of a gentleman to say he is one who never inflicts pain. This description is both refined and, as far as it goes, accurate. He is mainly occupied in merely removing the obstacles which hinder the free and unembarrassed action of those about him; and he concurs with their movements rather than takes the initiative himself… The true gentleman in like manner carefully avoids whatever may cause a jar or a jolt in the minds of those with whom he is cast – all clashing of opinion, or collision of feeling, all restraint, or suspicion, or gloom or resentment; his great concern being to make every one at his ease and at home. He has his eyes on all his company; he is tender towards the bashful, gentle towards the distant and merciful towards the absurd; he can recollect to whom he is speaking; he guards against unseasonable allusions or topics which may irritate; he is seldom prominent in conversation and never wearisome. He makes light of favours while he does them, and seems to be receiving when he is conferring… He never speaks of himself except when compelled, never defends himself by a mere retort; he has no ears for slander or gossip, is scrupulous in imputing motives to those who interfere with him, and interprets everything for the best… From a long-sighted prudence, he observes the maxim of the ancient sage, that we should ever conduct ourselves towards our enemy as if he were one day to be our friend. He has too much good sense to be affronted at insults, he is too well employed to remember injuries and too indolent to bear malice. He is patient, forbearing and resigned, on philosophical principles; he submits to pain because it is inevitable, to bereavement because it is irreparable, and to death because it is his destiny.

If he engages in controversy of any kind, his disciplined intellect preserves him from the blundering discourtesy of better, perhaps, but less educated minds, who, like blunt weapons, tear and hack instead of cutting clean, who mistake the point in argument…and leave the question more involved than they find it. He may be right or wrong in his opinion, but he is too clear-headed to be unjust; he is as simple as he is forcible, and as brief as he is decisive. Nowhere shall we find greater candour, consideration, indulgence: he throws himself into the minds of his opponents, he accounts for their mistakes. He knows the weakness of human reason as well as its strength, its province and its limits.

If he be an unbeliever, he will be too profound and large-minded to ridicule religion or to act against it; he is too wise to be a dogmatist or fanatic in his infidelity. He respects piety and devotion; he even supports institutions as venerable, beautiful or useful, to which he does not assent; he honours the ministers of religion, and it contents him to decline its mysteries without assailing or denouncing them. He is a friend of religious toleration, and that, not only because his philosophy has taught him to look on all forms of faith with an impartial eye, but also from the gentleness and effeminacy of feeling, which is the attendant on civilization.

❦UMBRELLAS

Two types of umbrellas are carried by men: a short, collapsible umbrella; and a long (36-inch) one with a curved handle. Both are black. A short umbrella is stored away in a pocket or briefcase when not in use, whereas a long umbrella is swung.

FOUR-STEP UMBRELLA RHYTHM

The chief umbrella rhythm repeats every four steps. With the umbrella carried in the right hand, it touches the ground with the first left step, rises just before the first right, stays high on the second left, and begins to fall just after the second right. (A step is the instant when the foot is fully planted on the ground.) The curved handle slides through the hand on the way down. It is ideal for getting around town.

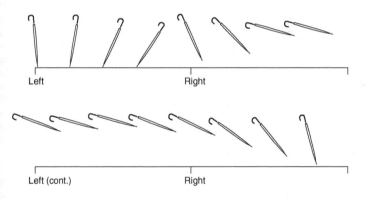

Left   Right

Left (cont.)   Right

TWO-STEP UMBRELLA RHYTHM

Less known is an umbrella rhythm which repeats with twice the frequency of the rhythm above. With the umbrella in the right hand, it follows the motions of the left leg but with a small delay. Ideal for slower strolls and walking over uneven ground, where the umbrella doubles as a walking stick.

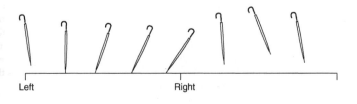

Left   Right

❦ SHIRTMAKERS

The shirt market has become markedly international over the last decade, with English, Italian, American and even French shirts available in major cities across the world. As a whole, Britain take shirts more seriously than any other country. The shirtmakers' Mecca is Jermyn (pronounced German) St in London, which has the highest concentration of shops selling shirts, ties and general men's kit in the world. The good news is that you no longer need to visit London – or Milan or New York for that matter – to buy the world's best shirts.

Here is a guide to the world's leading shirtmakers. The prices below are likely to change, and do not take into account frequent sales and reductions; many shirts can be found for half the listed price. Nevertheless they offer a fair indication of relative expense.

POPULAR AND NOTABLE SHIRTMAKERS

KEY   R = ready made   ✄ = bespoke   – = not applicable

Shirtmaker	Website (or address if none)	Since	R (£)	✄(£)
Alexander Kabbaz	www.customshirt1.com	1937	–	375
Algernon Moncrieff	www.algernon-moncrieff.com	2006	69	–
Brooks Brothers	www.brooksbrothers.com	1818	59	139
Budd	1A Piccadilly Arcade, London SW1	1910	65	135
Charles Tyrwhitt	www.ctshirts.co.uk	1986	55	–
Charvet	28 Place Vendôme, Paris 75001	1838	100	230
Coles	www.coles-shirtmakers.com	1878	50	110
Cordings	www.cordings.com	1839	55	–
Duchamp	www.duchamp.co.uk	1988	105	–
Ede & Ravenscoft	www.edeandravenscroft.co.uk	1689	95	175
Emma Willis	www.emmawillis.com	1987	120	190
Emmett Shirts	www.emmettlondon.com	1992	79	125
Ermenegildo Zegna	www.zegna.com	1910	125	–
Frank Foster	40 Pall Mall, London SW1	1959	–	135
Gieves & Hawkes	www.gievesandhawkes.com	c. 1785	80	–
Hackett	www.hackett.com	1983	79	110
Hardy Amies	www.hardyamies.com	1946	89	149
Harvie & Hudson	www.harvieandhudson.com	1946	40	165
Hawes & Curtis	www.hawesandcurtis.com	1913	59	–
Hilditch & Key	www.hilditchandkey.co.uk	1899	70	160
J. Press	www.jpressonline.com	1902	50	–

Lands End	www.landsend.co.uk	1962	29	–
Marks & Spencer	www.marksandspencer.com	1884	29	–
New & Lingwood	www.newandlingwood.com	1865	80	165
Paul Smith	www.paulsmith.co.uk	1970	120	200
Racing Green	www.racinggreen.co.uk	1990	40	–
Ralph Lauren	www.ralphlauren.co.uk	1967	65	–
Stephen Lachter	16 Savile Row, London w1	1986	–	130
Thomas Pink	www.thomaspink.co.uk	1984	65	160
Thresher & Glenny	50 Gresham St, London ec2	*c.* 1780	60	115
T. M. Lewin	www.tmlewin.co.uk	1898	75	–
Tommy Hilfiger	www.shoptommy.co.uk	1984	60	–
Turnbull & Asser	www.turnbullandasser.co.uk	1885	70	165
Van Heusen	www.van-heusen.co.uk	*c.* 1919	32	–

SELECTED NOTES

Alexander Kabbaz Many believe New York-based Kabbaz is the world's leading custom shirtmaker. 'I have a different philosophy than most', he writes. 'A truly bespoke – or "custom" – shirt is exactly what my client wants it to be... It is the client's own individual pattern draughted completely from scratch...and fitted until absolutely correct.'

Algernon Moncrieff This new online label offers particularly fitted shirts, a welcome innovation when so many other shirtmakers are producing shirts with loose-cut sleeves and body. Attention to detail includes a horizontally cut last buttonhole for ease of dressing in the dark.

Brooks Brothers Once the definitive and most influential men's store in the US, Brooks Brothers invented and popularized the button-down collar.

Budd That Budd does not have a website is the first sign that this famous shirtmaker has an anachronistic streak. These cramped quarters house some of the most traditionally made shirts in the world. Budd also offers the most comprehensive range of shirts and accessories for dinner jackets and tail coats.

Charles Tyrwhitt Tyrwhitt (pronounced 'tirrit') is the UK's largest internet and mail order shirtmaker. It recently set up shops in the UK as well as in New York and Paris, where it provides good standard shirts at bargain prices.

Coles Once a familiar sight on Jermyn St, Coles packed up after 'more and more discount shirt businesses sought to establish shops in Jermyn Street hoping to gain credibility by association'. The company now operates largely online. It offers fine fit and cutaway collars, if limited breadth of patterns.

Emma Willis Smart, clean-cut shirts from 'one of the few women to be making waves in the traditionally male-dominated tailoring world' (*Time Out*).

Ermenegildo Zegna 'British style is something the Americans have been stealing for years, the French have been nicking constantly and the Italians just take and sell back to us', observes designer Jeff Banks. One of the best of the Italian designers, Zegna makes fine shirts. But pound for pound, the only men's clothes the Italians do better than the British are trousers.

Hackett 'Hackett is the only London firm with the savvy and taste to revive the true classics of old England without making them appear either showy or retrospective', writes Alan Flusser. They design some of the most handsome patterns, stripes and checks.

Harvie & Hudson Especially known for their colourful and bold stripes.

Hawes & Curtis Once shirtmakers to the Duke of Windsor, it also claims to be the creator of the Windsor knot.

Hilditch & Key Along with Turnbull & Asser and Budd, this is one of the top three traditional British shirtmakers. Their ready-made shirts were ranked best by *The Times* of London.

J. Press With branches scattered around New England, this is the true guardian of the Ivy League look. 'The store reeks of pipes and porkpies, bow ties and fraternities, repp ties and raccoon coats' writes Alan Flusser.

New & Lingwood Originally founded as outfitters to Eton College, this very English company has been selling shirts to 'gentlemen of refinement and quiet good taste from all over the world'.

Paul Smith With several hundred shops in the UK and abroad, Paul Smith's clothes combine traditional English tailoring and cut with eclectic fabrics and patterns. Look under the double cuffs for pin-up girls and other surprises.

Thomas Pink Pink must be lauded for contributing to the revival of interest in English shirtmaking. Despite their polished image, they have a flair for unusual colours and patterns.

T. M. Lewin Despite its lengthy history, Lewin today operates in volume. With constant half-price bargains, they have contributed to the sometimes fierce price war among British shirtmakers. They offer a wide variety of fabrics and colours and three collar styles.

Turnbull & Asser This shirtmaker to the Prince of Wales is always listed among the world's best. Their array of colours, stripes and checks are enough to make Daisy cry stormily.

Van Heusen Since 2000 the number-one-selling shirtmaker in the world.

COUNTRY

Izaak Walton · No man is born an Artist nor an Angler. (*The Compleat Angler*, 1653)

Chuck Noland · Aha! Look what I've created! I have made fire! (*Castaway*, 2000)

Roger Scruton · My life divides into three parts. In the first I was wretched; in the second ill at ease; in the third hunting. (*On Hunting*, 1998)

Ed: Look, what is it that you require of us? *Mountain man*: Well we, uh, re-quire' that you get your[selves] up in them woods! (*Deliverance*, 1972)

Ernest Shackleton · Men wanted for hazardous journey. Low wages, bitter cold, long hours of complete darkness. Safe return doubtful. Honour and recognition in event of success. (Supposed newspaper advertisement for Shackleton's South Pole expedition. It has never been verified.)

Samuel Johnson · Knotting ought to be reckoned, in the scale of insignificance, next to mere idleness. (*Dictionary*, 1755)

Capital City Fly Fishers · Piscator non solum piscatur (There is more to fishing than catching fish, motto)

Ernest Hemingway · To me heaven would be a big bull ring with me holding two barrera seats and a trout stream outside that no one else was allowed to fish in… (letter to F. Scott Fitzgerald, 1925)

Sir Robert Baden-Powell · No man can be really good, if he doesn't believe in God and he doesn't follow His laws. This is why all Scouts must have a religion. (*Scouting for Boys*, 1908)

Robert De Niro · You have to think about one shot. One shot is what it's all about. A deer's gotta be taken with one shot. (*The Deer Hunter*, 1978)

❦ SURVIVAL

KNIFE

The most essential survival tool is a knife. With it you can construct numerous other tools for obtaining food, building shelter and making fire. It is considered so vital that it is usually omitted from lists of survival tools. A knife is used foremost to carve wood; second to prepare food; and third as a tool for miscellaneous tasks. Two knives are ideal: a folding pocket knife with one or two strong blades for the bulk of carving and cutting; and a multi-tool knife for more specific tasks. The best multi-tools are made by Victorinox, Wenger (acquired by Victorinox), Gerber and Leatherman.

SURVIVAL TOOLS

Whether camping, hiking or lost, the difference between an agreeable or arduous time in the wilderness comes down to a handful of key tools. In the *SAS Survival Handbook* (see Books, p 173), John Wiseman lists the following 12 essential items. The total weight need not exceed 8 ounces.

Matches	Needles and thread	Snare wire
Candle	Fish hooks and line	Flexible saw
Flint	Compass	Medical kit
Magnifying glass	Beta light	Surgical blades

NOTES

Matches The ability to create fire is the most important survival skill, and the first four items in this list are aids to firestarting. Matches should be kept in a watertight container. Their heads can be dipped in candle wax as a means of making them water resistant, to be scratched off when needed.

Candle In the *Complete Book of Camping*, Leonard Miracle makes a strong case for a candle: 'Lighted with a match, it will burn long enough to dry out and ignite the most stubborn campfire fuel. It will light the inside of a tent…[and], propped under a can or a pan, a thick candle will cook food or boil coffee water when no other fuel is available. The same thick candle burning inside a tin can is a tiny heater that will substantially raise the inside temperature of a small tent. Melted candle wax rubbed into the fabric will stop a minor tent leak or seal the seams of a leather hunting boot.'

Flint Virtually everlasting, a flint (meaning artificial flint, not flintstone) is used to make sparks by striking it with steel. The sparks are longer lasting and more substantial than those produced by flintstone, offering a reasonable chance of igniting common tinder.

Magnifying glass Used to start a fire by concentrating the sun's rays on to dark tinder (see Fire, p 90). It is also an aid to removing splinters and stings.

Needles and thread Thin nylon thread is better than cotton. Include several sizes of needles and a large one for sewing coarse objects with fishing line.

Fish hooks and line You are more likely to catch small fish than big ones, so include small-sized hooks. Braided nylon line (25 lb test) is preferable to monofilament because it is less susceptible to damage and can double as binding material for tent and rucksack repairs and lashing together sticks.

Compass Floating compasses are generally superior to dry ones. Make sure it has luminous markers so that it can be read in the dark.

Beta light Also known as self-powered lighting or radioluminescence, a beta light will emit light for over 10 years (the half-life is 12.3 years). The light is caused by the beta decay of the unstable hydrogen isotope tritium.

Snare wire A snare is a wire noose used to trap passing animals by the neck or leg. Struggling causes the wire to tighten, thus securing the prey. Although included here as an aid to catching animals, it is also useful as an all-purpose fastener. Setting effective snares is a science and requires considerable knowledge.

Flexible saw There are two types: wire saws and chain saws. Both have handles at the endpoints. A wire saw is a piece of wire with an abrasive finish, whereas a chain saw is a chain with teeth attached to the links, similar to that found on a motorized chainsaw but lighter. At 5 ounces, chain saws are the heavier of the two, but offer much greater cutting efficiency.

Medical kit 'What you include depends upon your own skill in using it', advises Wiseman. He suggests the following: analgesic, intestinal sedative, antibiotic, antihistamine, water sterilizing tablets, antimalaria tablets, potassium permanganate, butterfly sutures and plasters. In addition to sterilizing water and wounds, potassium permanganate is combustible when combined with sugar (one part to two) and struck by a rock.

Surgical blades While these are meant to fit special metal handles, they can be attached to improvised wooden handles if necessary.

❦ FIRE

FIRE STARTING

Primitive methods of starting a fire, such as the bow and drill or striking rocks, are attractive in principle but require considerable effort and optimization. Literally weeks of practice and experimentation are needed to ignite tinder from sparks thrown off by striking flint. Some more practicable and ingenious methods are described below.

Compact OED One of the easiest ways of starting a fire is by using a magnifying glass. A well-suited specimen is conveniently included with the compact edition of the *Oxford English Dictionary*. Held a couple of inches above the ground, it concentrates the parallel rays of the sun into a sharp focus capable of igniting most dark tinder (see Firewood, opposite).

Cling film If the *OED* is not at hand, a simple but effective lens can be constructed from water and cling film. With the four corners held together, fill a 12-inch-square piece of film with water and twist the corners so as to create an approximate sphere. With some manipulation, the sun's rays can be concentrated into a point sufficiently tight to ignite tinder (see opposite).

Coke can In principle the sun's rays can be concentrated by a number of hand mirrors, each reflecting the rays on to the same spot. The continuum limit of such a collection of small nearby mirrors is a parabolic mirror. True parabolic mirrors, sometimes found in telescopes, can be hard to come by. Much more common, and just as effective once modified, is the bottom of a Coke (or other aluminium) can. The concave bottom already has the right shape, but its dull, machined outer surface must be polished. This is best done in steps, starting with an abrasive polish, such as coffee grinds or steel wool, then finishing with a finer paste like chocolate or toothpaste. Apply the polish with a small cloth or toothbrush, finishing with just the cloth itself. The choice of polishes is not crucial, so long as the final polish is fine.

Magnesium This lightweight metal is extremely flammable (though not explosive) as a powder or in the form of shavings, but resistant to combustion in bulk. A small block of the metal, along with a flint for making sparks, can be bought as an extreme-weather fire starter. Form a pile of shavings, at least ½ inch in diameter, by scraping the soft metal with a knife. Strike the back of the knife against the flint to cast sparks on to the shavings. Once ignited, the magnesium will burn with an intensely hot white flame. It should immediately be covered with tinder.

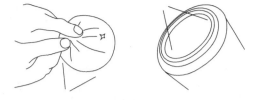

FIREWOOD

Easily combustible material for the purpose of starting a wood fire is called tinder – any dry paper or leaves, or finely prepared bark or wood, will work. When starting a fire using concentrated light, it is important to use dark tinder, which absorbs light, rather than fair, which reflects it. In the case of the Coke-can mirror, the tinder must be suspended by a thin stick so as not to obstruct the sun's rays.

Once a fire is started, additional tinder and kindling should be added stage-wise to keep the fire going. After a base of coals has collected, just about any wood can be used to keep the fire going indefinitely, even green or wet wood which, if placed close by, will quickly dry. Nevertheless, some trees make better firewood than others. The chief desired properties are high heat production and low smoke emissions and ash deposits. The energy output of firewood is measured in British thermal units (BTUs). A BTU is the amount of energy necessary to heat one pound of water one degree Fahrenheit; it will light a 60-watt lamp for 18 seconds. A cord is the standard unit for measuring firewood: it is a stack of parallel logs 8ft × 4ft × 4ft, or the equivalent volume. The energy output per cord in millions of BTU for different species of trees is listed below. A good guide is the weight of the wood – energy output is almost directly proportional to density. Slow-growing trees, such as oak and most fruit trees, tend to be the densest.

BEST TREES FOR FIREWOOD

Species	MBtu/cord				
Oak, Live	35	Douglas Fir	25	Fir, White	20
Eucalyptus	33	Juniper, Western	25	Pine, Ponderosa	20
Locust, Black	30	Walnut, Black	25	Alder	19
Beech	29	Cherry	23	Cedar, Incense	19
Dogwood	29	Elm	23	Fir, Red	19
Birch	27	Hemlock, Western	23	Redwood, Coast	19
Oak, White	27	Magnolia	23	Pine, Sugar	18
Tanoak	27	Sycamore	23	Willow, Black	18
Ash	25	Maple, Big Leaf	22	Aspen	17
		Sweetgum	21	Cottonwood	16

❦ KNOTS

In their broadest sense, knots comprise all practically useful or decorative complications in cordage, though not periodic ones, which are known as weaves. Most practical knots can be assorted into three categories: knots, which are any conformation tied into a single line itself; hitches, which are used to attach a line to an object; and bends, which are used to join two lines.

The simplest knot is the overhand, which is the first half of a reef knot. When tied around an object, it is called a half-hitch. While the reef is probably the most familiar of all knots, it is often confused with the practically useless granny knot. The bowline, sometimes called the king of knots, offers a simple, strong fixed loop in the end of a line. A more foolproof and very dependable alternative is the figure-of-eight knot, used in rock climbing.

Some of the knots below are used in a man's daily rituals. A half-hitch is used to tie a jumper around the waist. An Ascot (see p 67) is tied with a reef knot before pinning the overlapping ends. The usual four-in-hand necktie knot (see p 64) is the buntline hitch. The seemingly complicated bow tie knot (see p 66) is just the reef bow, which is also the knot used to tie shoelaces. When a bow tie or shoelace knot is offset by 90 degrees, it has been tied with a granny bow rather than a reef bow.

ESSENTIAL KNOTS

Knots	*Any conformation in a single rope*
Reef or square knot	Common knot for tying packages, bandages, etc
Granny knot	Common, useless result of a mistied reef knot
Reef bow	Easily untied knot used for shoelaces, gifts and bows
Surgeon's knot	Less likely to slip while tying than the reef knot
Bowline	Essential knot for a fixed loop at the end of a rope
Figure-of-eight loop	Easily remembered fixed loop for critical situations
Butterfly knot	A fixed loop along a rope. Useful as a handle
Spanish bowline	Two adjustable fixed loops along a rope
Sheepshank	Reduces excess length in a rope without using the ends

Hitches	*For attaching a rope to an object*
Timber hitch	Useful under constant tension, e.g., when hauling logs
Clove hitch	Used for attaching line to round posts or sticks
Constrictor hitch	A surprisingly secure knot around trees or posts
Buntline hitch	A sturdy slip knot that will resist jerking
Tautline hitch	Easily adjusted to keep line taut. Useful for tents
Clinch or half-blood knot	Joins monofilament line to a hook or swivel

Bends   *For joining two ropes*
Sheet bend   If one rope is thicker, it should be the one on the right.
Carrick bend   For ropes of equal width, especially heavy ones.

Reef knot

Granny knot

Reef bow

Surgeon's knot

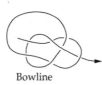

Bowline

Figure-of-eight loop

Butterfly knot

Spanish bowline

Constrictor hitch

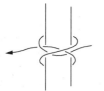

Clove hitch

Buntline hitch

Tautline hitch

Sheet bend

Carrick bend

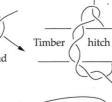

Timber hitch

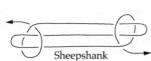

Sheepshank

Clinch

93

❦ SCOUTS

The Boy Scouts was founded in England by Sir Robert Baden-Powell (B-P) in 1907. Scouting can now be found in nearly every country, with a world-wide population of 25 million boys and young men. It is by far the largest youth organization in the world.

SCOUT HISTORY

Scouting has its origins in B-P's military training manual, *Aids to Scouting for NCOs and Men*, published in 1899. When B-P shot to fame with his legendary defence of the town of Mafeking during the Second Boer War, his manual was widely adopted by youth organizations throughout Britain. Encouraged to adapt it for a younger audience, B-P wrote *Scouting for Boys* (see Books, p 172), the basis of what is today called the *Boy Scout Handbook* in America. B-P put his ideas into practice at a camp he organized for 22 boys on Brownsea Island in 1907. Scouting was spontaneously taken up by adolescents throughout the country and the British Empire at an extraordinary rate. On the advice of the King, B-P retired from the army in 1910 to devote his energy to the organization, which 12 years later numbered one million worldwide.

Knowing his days were numbered, B-P wrote his 'Last message to Scouts', which was found among his possessions after his death in 1941. It ended:

> I have had a most happy life and I want each one of you to have as happy a life too. I believe that God put us in this jolly world to be happy and enjoy life. Happiness doesn't come from being rich, nor merely from being successful in your career, nor by self-indulgence. One step towards happiness is to make yourself healthy and strong while you are a boy, so that you can be useful and so can enjoy life when you are a man.
>
> Nature study will show you how full of beautiful and wonderful things God has made the world for you to enjoy. Be contented with what you have got and make the best of it. Look on the bright side of things instead of the gloomy one.
>
> But the real way to get happiness is by giving out happiness to other people. Try and leave this world a little better than you found it and when your turn comes to die, you can die happy in feeling that at any rate you have not wasted your time but have done your best. 'Be Prepared' in this way, to live happy and to die happy – stick to your Scout promise always – even after you have ceased to be a boy – and God help you to do it.
>
> Your Friend Baden-Powell

SCOUT METHOD

Central to Scouting is the so-called Scout Method, a philosophy of education based on learning by doing, the formation of small groups and the stage-wise completion of activities. Considerable attention is given to Scoutcraft, a collection of skills for proficiency out of doors. They include such things as chivalry, edible wild plants, fire building, first aid, nature lore, patriotism, physical fitness, signalling, swimming, tracking, tying knots and using an axe. Advancement in these and related skills is marked by earning badges (see p 96), a key aspect of day-to-day Scout activity.

MOTTO AND 10 ESSENTIALS

Be Prepared, after B-P's initials, which means 'you are always in a state of readiness in mind and body to do your duty', wrote B-P in *Scouting for Boys*.

Water bottle · Extra clothing · First aid kit · Map and compass · Matches and fire starter · Pocket knife · Rain gear · Sun protection · Torch · Trail food

PROMISE AND LAW (UK)

On my honour, I promise that I will do my best, to do my duty to God and to the Queen, to help other people and to keep the Scout Law.

A Scout is to be trusted.
A Scout is loyal.
A Scout is friendly and considerate.
A Scout belongs to the worldwide family of Scouts.
A Scout has courage in all difficulties.
A Scout makes good use of time and is careful of possessions and property.
A Scout has self-respect and respect for others.

SCOUT SECTIONS (UK)

There are five Scout sections, organized by age. It is not necessary to have been active in one section to join the next.

Section	Ages	Meet in
Beaver Scouts	6–8	Colonies
Cub Scouts	8–10½	Packs
Scouts	10½–14	Troops
Explorer Scouts	14–18	Units
Scout Network	18–25	largely autonomous

SCOUT BADGES (UK)

Scouts wear cloth badges on their uniforms to signify membership, achievment and awards. The assorted badges vary from section to section, apart from Staged Activity Badges and Group Awards, which apply to all sections. A primary focus of Scouting is learning new skills and performing new activities, and these are marked by a wide variety of Activity Badges. There are 12 Activity Badges for Beaver Scouts, 34 for Cub Scouts, 71 for Scouts and 28 for Explorer Scouts.

Badges for all sections

★ *Staged Activity Badges*
Emergency Aid
Hikes Away
Information Technology

Musician
Nights Away
Swimmer
★ *Group Awards*

Environment Award
Faith Award
International Friendship
    Award

Beaver Scouts

★ *General Badges*
Beaver Scout
    Membership Award
Chief Scout's
    Bronze Award
Joining In Awards
Moving-On Award
★ *Challenge Badges*

Discovery
Friendship
Outdoor
★ *Activity Badges*
Adventure
Air Activities
Animal Friend
Creative

Experiment
Explore
Faith
Health and Fitness
Healthy Eating
Hobbies
Imagination
Safety

Cub Scouts

★ *General Badges*
Chief Scout's
    Silver Award
Cub Scout
    Membership Award
Joining In Awards
Moving-On Award
★ *Challenge Badges*
Caring
Creative
Fitness
Global
Outdoor
★ *Activity Badges*
Adventure
Air Activities

Animal Carer
Artist
Astronomer
Athlete
Athlete Plus
Book Reader
Camper
Chef
Collector
Communicator
Cyclist
DIY
Entertainer
Equestrian
Global Conservation
Hobbies

Home Help
Home Safety
Local Knowledge
Map Reader
Martial Arts
My Faith
Naturalist
Navigator
Personal Safety
Physical Recreation
Road Safety
Scientist
Skater
Sports Enthusiast
Water Activities
World Faiths

Scouts

★ *General Badges*
Chief Scout's
 Gold Award
Moving-On Award
Participation Awards
Scout Membership Award
★ *Challenge Badges*
Adventure
Community
Creative
Expedition
Fitness
Global
Outdoor
Outdoor Plus
★ *Activity Badges*
Administrator
Aeronautics
Air Researcher
Air Spotter
Angler
Artist
Arts Enthusiast
Astronautics
Astronomer
Athlete
Basic Aviation Skills
Aviation Skills
Advanced Aviation Skills

Camp Cook
Camper
Campsite Service
Canoeist
Caver
Chef
Circus Skills
Climber
Communicator
Craft
Cyclist
Dinghy Sailor
DIY
Dragon Boating
Electronics
Entertainer
Equestrian
Fire Safety
Forester
Global Conservation
Guide
Heritage
Hiker
Hill Walker
Hobbies
Interpreter
Librarian
Lifesaver
Martial Arts

Master at Arms
Mechanic
Meteorologist
Model Maker
My Faith
Naturalist
Basic Nautical Skills
Nautical Skills
Advanced Nautical Skills
Navigator
Orienteer
Parascending
Photographer
Physical Recreation
Pioneer
Power Coxswain
Public Relations
Pulling
Quartermaster
Smallholder
Snowsports
Sports Enthusiast
Street Sports
Survival Skills
Water Sports
World Faiths
Writer
Activity PLUS
Instructor badges

Explorer Scouts

★ *General Badges*
Chief Scout's
 Diamond Award
Chief Scout's
 Platinum Award
Explorer Belt
Explorer Scout
 Membership Award
Moving-On Award
Queen's Scout Award
★ *Activity Badges*
Activity Centre Service
Air Activities

Athlete
Aviation Skills
Advanced Aviation Skills
Canoeing
Caving
Climbing
Community
Creative Arts
Hill Walking
Lifesaver
Motor sports
Mountain Biking
Nautical Skills

Advanced Nautical Skills
Navigation
Performing Arts
Physical Recreation
Public Relations
Quartermaster
Racquet Sports
Science and Technology
Scouting Skills
Skiing
Snowboarding
Street Sports
Water Activities

❦ TREEHOUSES

Despite the fascination with treehouses innate in all men, few understand the principles of constructing a stable, comfortable living space in a tree. The secret to treehouses, in a word, is bolts – of which, more later. We first begin with some planning considerations.

Obstacles

There are two potential external obstacles to bear in mind: planning permission and neighbours. First, planning permission is not generally required in the UK and most other countries if (i) a treehouse does not overlook an adjoining property and (ii) it can be classified as a temporary structure. For the sake of (ii), electricity and plumbing are not advised – an electrical lead to the tree can serve most power needs. Second, a treehouse will most likely be visible from a distance, and unhappy neighbours are likely to complain. The best approach is to involve potentially difficult neighbours from the start – it is harder to complain about something you have known about for a long time. It is also wise to make the treehouse as handsome as possible. Any material other than natural wood finishes, such as paint or plastic, looks conspicuous in a tree and should not be used.

Foundation

Building a treehouse is little different from building any other outdoor shelter apart from the foundation, which poses three concerns. First, a tree is a living thing, and the points of treehouse support must be strong but not injurious. Second, the foundation must rest on a limited number of contact points. Contrary to intuition, it is best to keep the number of support points as small as possible, usually three or four. Third, trees move, mostly owing to swaying in the wind rather than growth, so the contact points must not be vulnerable to a relative shift in the trunks or branches. Once the foundation has been built, further work on the walls and roof can be done in a conventional fashion. Many of the grandest treehouses have stairs or a bridge leading to them, but this seems to go against their spirit, which is one of elevation and exclusion of the outside world. A simple rope ladder is the best way to access the house. Once in, you can pull it up behind you.

Bolts

To understand how best to attach the treehouse to the tree, a cursory knowledge of tree biology is helpful. The living part of a tree is the bark and outermost layers (the outer ½–2 inches, depending on species and size) which carry resources to the branches and foliage. The interior, called heartwood, is dead but remains strong. Accordingly, the most damaging injury is one which disrupts a significant fraction of the bark along a circumference; the least harmful is a hole perpendicular to the surface, such as a bolt. A cable tied around a tree will eventually cut off its supply line, literally strangling it. Screws and nails, while individually safe, are not suitable for treehouse construction for two reasons: they do not penetrate deep enough to hold fast; and too many minor wounds in a cluster can lead to compart-mentalization, in which the tree blocks off the damaged region and lets it decay. Heavy bolts are the best solution, at least ¾ inch thick. These are threaded and screwed into pre-drilled holes. Purpose-built bolts, called Garnier Limbs (available online), are 1¼ inch thick and are rated at 8,000 lb.

Tree movement

The distance that a tree sways increases with height, while the force it can exert decreases with height. In other words, a tree acts as a lever, with small but powerful motions near the base. Relative movement of 1 inch during a storm can snap the strongest bolt. Tree growth, on the other hand, is not normally a concern. Growth in height takes place at the tips of the branches, not in the trunk or branches themselves. Growth in girth, which occurs throughout and gives rise to annual rings in the wood, is a much slower process. There are three approaches to minimizing the effects of tree motion. The first is to build on a single trunk. The second is to build close enough to the ground for the amount of motion between trees or branches to be negligible. The third, and preferable, method is to incorporate floating con-tacts on the bolts, described below.

Contact points

Choosing which trees or limbs to build on is something of an art. Conifer-ous (needle-bearing) trees tend to have long, vertical trunks with few sturdy or accessible branches, and treehouses built on them use either a single trunk or multiple trunks close together. Deciduous (seasonal leaf-bearing) trees allow more imaginative possibilities. A forked branch can act as a con-venient floating support point. The three foundation configurations below make use of one, three and four trunks or branches. Note that the first re-quires four bolts and diagonal supports. The frames are made of 2 × 6-inch beams. The regions of the beams where they rest on the bolts should be covered with steel brackets or sheet metal. If the bolt ends do not already protrude, nuts can be welded to them to keep the supports from sliding off.

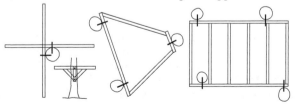

❦ TOOLS

Here are the 50 most useful tools for domestic repairs and building projects.

ESSENTIAL TOOLS

Adjustable wrench Perhaps the most elegant tool of them all, it can fill in for countless wrenches and sockets.

Chisels A small set of wood chisels (¼, ½, ¾ inch) is indispensable. Ideally hit with a carpenter's wooden mallet, not a hammer.

Drill While a hand-held drill may be convenient for small jobs, it cannot compete with the efficiency of a cordless electric drill.

Hammer There are several kinds: claw, ball peen, tack. A 16-ounce claw hammer with a hickory or fibreglass handle is the most versatile.

Hand saw There are many kinds of saw, but for quick results and cutting long straight lines a hand saw is the best one.

Measuring tape (25 foot) At least 1 inch wide and marked with imperial and metric units. Wider tapes remain extended at greater distances.

Screwdriver Flathead and Phillips in a few sizes each. Keep similar bits for the cordless drill.

Slip-joint pliers Of the many varieties of pliers available, these are the most versatile for everyday use.

Spirit level Of the torpedo sort. Determines true horizontal, vertical and 45-degree angles, for jobs from hanging pictures to framing a house.

Utility knife As well as cutting cardboard, insulation and carpet, its sharp edge is useful for scoring wood. Best with breakable blades.

BASIC TOOLS

Allen keys	cold chisel	plumb bob
awl	compass	random orbital sander
bar-clamps	drill bit set	reciprocating saw
bench vice	electrical tape	sandpaper, various
bevel gauge	files (wood and metal)	socket set (imperial
bullnose nippers	glass cutter	and metric)
carpenter's pencil	hacksaw	staple gun
carpenter's square	hand plane	surform
cat's-paw (prybar)	interchangeable tip	tin snips
caulking gun	screwdriver	tool belt
C-clamps	locking pliers	tool box
chalk line (100 foot)	nail set	whetstone
channel-lock pliers	needle-nose pliers	wire-stripper
circular saw	pipe wrench	wooden mallet

DRINKING

George Best · I spent 90% of my money on women, drink and fast cars. The rest I wasted.

Richard Braunstein · The hard part about being a bartender is figuring out who is drunk and who is just stupid.

Samuel Johnson · A man who exposes himself when he is intoxicated has not the art of getting drunk. (Boswell, *Life of Johnson*, 1791)

Christopher Howse · Real ale fans are just like train-spotters, only drunk.

Ernest Hemingway · An intelligent man is sometimes forced to be drunk to spend time with his friends.

Abraham Lincoln · I believe, if we take habitual drunkards as a class, their heads and their hearts will bear an advantageous comparison with those of any other class. There seems ever to have been a prone-ness in the brilliant and warm-blooded to fall into this vice. (Address to the Washingtonian Temperance Society, 1842)

Peter the Great of Russia · Of all wine, Irish wine is the best.

The Massachusetts Spy · The cordial drop, the morning dram, I sing, / The mid-day toddy, and the evening sling.

Frank Sinatra · I feel sorry for people who don't drink. When they wake up in the morning, that's as good as they're going to feel all day.

Pablo Picasso · Drink to me. (last words)

Benjamin Franklin · He that drinks fast, pays slow. ✒ Never praise your cyder or your horse. ✒ There's more old drunkards, than old doctors. ✒ Beer is proof that God loves us and wants us to be happy. (*Poor Richard's Almanack*, 1732–1757)

❦ BEER

Beer is the alcoholic beverage made from fermented grain. Drinks fermented from other sources have other names: fermented honey is called mead; apple juice, cider; grape juice, wine; and pear juice, perry. The ingredients of beer are generally limited to water, malted barley, hops and yeast. Barley is a grain, like wheat, and it is malted by allowing it to germinate (sprout). This releases enzymes which convert its starches to sugars. Hops are the seed vessels of a vine-like plant, and they impart flavour and bitterness. Yeast causes fermentation – the conversion of sugar to alcohol – of which carbonation is a natural by-product.

Beer can be classified by the kind of yeast used in fermentation. Wild, naturally occurring yeast is used to make *lambics*. Much more often the yeast is cultivated, and if it is top-fermenting the beer is called *ale*; if bottom-fermenting, *lager*.

LAMBICS

Lambics are neither top- nor bottom-fermented, but instead rely on wild yeast native to the area they are brewed in, usually around Brussels. This is one of the oldest styles of brewing, and lambics have a complex, yeasty, tart, dry taste. ❧ *Fruit beers* are made from lambics by the addition of fruit, the sugars of which lead to a refermentation. ❧ *Kriek* and *Framboise* are made by adding cherries and raspberries, respectively.

LAGERS

Bottom-fermentation is a more recent innovation than top, and consequently the styles of lager are not as broad as they are for ales. Tell-tale signs of lager are a translucent colour and a clean, crisp taste.

Pilsners Often referred to simply as lagers, these have a light-gold colour and pronounced hop flavour. Ideally, Pilsners should be 5% alcohol by volume, or just under.

Pale lagers These have minimal malt or hop character and are light-gold to straw-coloured. Sometimes called session beers, their chief advantage is that they can be drunk in large volumes without significant taste or intoxication. They are aggressively marketed and their parent companies often leverage bars to sell them at the exclusion of finer, more distinctive beers.

Bocks These are a strong, dark variety of lager with minimal hop flavour which originated in the German town of Einbeck. Their robust character makes them popular from autumn to early spring. ❧ *Doppelbock* and *Eisbock* are stronger varieties still, the latter being strengthened by freezing and removing the ice (water freezes before alcohol).

ALES

Ale, which is top-fermented, is a much older style of beer than lager, with complex roasted and fruity flavours. There is an enormous range of varieties, some of which evade easy classification.

Anglo-American ales *Bitter* refers to a lightly carbonated, pale-ale-style beer, usually served on draught, and accounts for a large fraction of the ale sold in Britain. ❧ *Old Ale* is stronger with a malty taste and is often sweet. ❧ *India pale ale* (IPA) was originally made for export to India, with a strong presence of hops as a preservative for the long voyage. ❧ *Barley wine* usually refers to a brewer's most potent ale, typically 8% or higher. ❧ *Winter Warmer* is sometimes used to describe similar, slightly weaker versions.

Porter and stout These are made from dark-roasted malt or barley and are dark-brown to black. ❧ *Porter* is the lighter-bodied of the two, and it has had a revival after a period of decline. ❧ *Stout*, which is more complex and filling, can be further divided into *dry stouts* and *sweet stouts*.

Belgian-style ales Sometimes called Belgian speciality beers, this is a diverse category of ales produced in and around Belgium. They tend to have distinctive flavours and include many of the most highly esteemed beers in the world. Some better-known breweries are Leffe, Rodenbach and Duvel. ❧ *Abbey ales* are made by breweries associated with a monastery or imitative of that style, such as L'Abbaye des Rocs and Karmeliet. ❧ *Trappist ales* are brewed within the walls of a Trappist monastery under the complete control of the resident monks and are internationally renowned. At present only seven abbeys are allowed to carry the 'Authentic Trappist Product' logo: Achelse Kluis, Chimay, De Koningshoeven (La Trappe), Orval, Rochefort, Westmalle and Westvleteren. ❧ *Dubbels* are double-fermented and are strong (over 6.5%) and dark with a malty, fruity taste. ❧ *Tripels* are stronger yet and tend to be pale with a substantial hoppy character.

Wheat beers Beer made from wheat in addition to barley is called wheat beer or white beer. They are fair and opaque and are often flavoured with orange peel or coriander. One of the most refreshing styles of beer, they are popular in warm weather, sometimes with a slice of lemon.

POPULAR AND NOTABLE BEERS

Lambic	Variety	Origin	ABV
Cantillon Gueuze-Lambic	Lambic	Belgium	5.0
Kriek Girardin	Kriek	Belgium	5.0
Lindemans Cuvée René	Lambic	Belgium	5.0

Lager	Variety	Origin	ABV
Amstel Herfstbock	Bock	The Netherlands	7.0
Bitburger Premium Pils	Pilsner	Germany	10.0
Budweiser (Anheuser-Busch)	Pale lager	Missouri, USA	5.0
Budweiser Budvar	Pilsner	Czech Republic	5.0
Carlsberg	Pale lager	Denmark	5.0
Cobra	Pale lager	India (now UK)	5.0
Corona Extra	Pale lager	Mexico	4.6
Heineken	Pale lager	The Netherlands	5.0
Paulaner Salvator	Double bock	Germany	7.5
Peroni Nastro Azzurro	Pale lager	Italy	5.2
Pilsner Urquell	Pilsner	Czech Republic	4.4
Samuel Adams Boston Lager	Lager	Mass., USA	4.9
Tsingtao	Pilsner	China	4.2

Ale	Variety	Origin	ABV
Adnams Broadside	Old ale	England	6.3
Alaskan Smoked Porter	Porter	Alaska, USA	6.1
Bass No. 1	Barley wine	England	10.5
Beamish Irish Stout	Dry stout	Rep. of Ireland	4.0
Brains SA	Bitter	Wales	4.2
Burton Bridge Porter	Porter	England	4.5
Chimay Blue	Trappist ale	Belgium	9.0
De Koningshoeven (La Trappe)	Trappist ale	The Netherlands	6.5
Duvel	Belgian-style ale	Belgium	8.5
Fuller's 1845	Winter warmer	England	6.3
Fuller's London Pride	Bitter	England	4.7
Guinness Extra Stout	Dry stout	Rep. of Ireland	4.2
Hoegaarden Witbier	Wheat beer	Belgium	5.0
Leffe Brune	Abbey ale	Belgium	6.5
Murphy's Irish Stout	Dry stout	Rep. of Ireland	4.0
Orval	Trappist ale	Belgium	6.2
Sierra Nevada IPA	IPA	California, USA	6.9
Theakston Old Peculier	Old ale	England	5.6
Westvleteren 8	Trappist ale	Belgium	8.0
Young's Bitter	Bitter	England	3.7

♥WINE

The simplest classification of wines is by the variety of grapes used to produce them. Some are made from a single grape, others are blended from two or more varieties. Traditionally, six dominant grapes, called noble grapes, were used to make the best wines in the world: the white grapes Sauvignon Blanc, Riesling and Chardonnay; and the black grapes Pinot Noir, Cabernet Sauvignon and Merlot. Today the list of top grapes is longer, due especially to innovative winemaking in the New World.

WHITE WINE GRAPES

Chardonnay This is the basis of the burgundy white wines Chablis, Côte d'Or and Mâcon. It is blended with Pinot Noir and Pinot Meunier to make champagne. When only Chardonnay is used, champagne is called blancs de blancs.

Gewürztraminer Produces wine with a distinct spicy, aromatic taste which makes it suitable for stronger foods. It is largely grown in cool climates.

Muscat Possibly the oldest variety of all, from which all others have descended. The grapes can be black or white, and are used to make a wide array of wines, all of which exhibit a common distinct taste.

Pinot Noir In addition to its use in reds, it is blended to make champagne.

Riesling The premier grape of Germany, and the chief grape used for fine wine production in that country.

Sauvignon Blanc With Sémillon, used to make Graves and Sauternes.

Sémillon Rarely used to make wine on its own, it is mostly blended with Sauvignon Blanc to make Sauternes and other dessert wines and dry wines of varying quality.

RED WINE GRAPES

Cabernet Franc Mostly grown in France, where it is blended to make red bordeaux.

Cabernet Sauvignon One of the most widely planted grapes, it is the basis of red bordeaux, where it is blended with Cabernet Franc and Merlot, and of much Californian red wine.

Gamay Notable only as the grape of the light red wine Beaujolais.

Merlot The basis of the red wines Pomerol and St-Emilion.

Pinot Noir This is the basis of red burgundy. The grape is grown extensively outside France but with less consistent results.

Syrah Also known as Shiraz in Australia and South Africa. Used to make the Rhône wines Côte Rôtie and Hermitage, and also blended with other grapes because of its strong, smoky taste.

Tempranillo Used to make Rioja and other Spanish reds, it is the premier red grape of Spain but is little grown outside that country.

Zinfandel Largely produced in California, where it is used to make reds and pale rosé.

BOTTLE SIZES

Wine is sometimes sold in larger or smaller volumes than the usual 750 ml bottle. Champagne normally undergoes secondary fermentation in standard bottles and magnums, which are decanted into the different bottles below. An exception is Drappier Champagne, where the final bottle is used throughout the process. Drappier is one of the few producers to sell most of the sizes below – all but the Rehoboam.

Bottles	Litres	Champagne	Bordeaux	Port
¼	0.188	Split	–	–
½	0.375	Half-bottle	Fillette	–
1	0.75	Bottle	Bottle	Bottle
2	1.5	Magnum	Magnum	Magnum
3	2.25	–	Marie-Jeanne (approximately)	Tappit Hen
4	3	Jeroboam	Double Magnum	Jeroboam
6	4.5	Rehoboam	Jeroboam	–
8	6	Methuselah	Imperial	–
12	9	Salmanazar	–	–
16	12	Balthazar	–	–
20	15	Nebuchadnezzar	–	–
24	18	Solomon or Melchior	–	–
36	27	Primat	–	–

WINE CUSTOMS

Opening a bottle

This is one of the most satisfying of all drinking rituals. The best corkscrew is the simplest: a metal spiral attached to a perpendicular wooden handle. See that you get one that is solid like a drill bit rather than wire twisted into a spiral. A spiral corkscrew offers no leverage but depends solely on strength. The usual technique is to place the bottle between the legs, just above the knees, and hold the neck with the one hand while pulling the corkscrew with the other. If your shoulders are not up to strength, a regime of upright rows (p 22) will help. In the absence of a corkscrew, pushing the cork *in* with a blunt tool works surprisingly well. Depress it slowly to avoid spraying wine when it gives way. Pouring the first glass is awkward because the cork gets in the way, but subsequent glasses are easy.

Opening a champagne bottle

The pressure in champagne and sparkling wine bottles increases with temperature and agitation, so very cold bottles handled carefully release their corks with the least force. First, remove the foil to expose the wire cage. While this is untwisted, keep the thumb over the cork to prevent its spontaneous expulsion. The trick to removing the cork quietly is to hold it with the one hand, with the thumb on top of it, while with the other slowly turning the bottle. Alternatively, to project the cork as far as possible across a room or away from a picnic, keep the bottle still and gently massage the cork with the thumb and forefinger wrapped around its base. In both cases keep a glass nearby for any overflow.

Pouring wine

An ordinary-sized wine glass should be filled to two-thirds full and refilled when below one-third full. When serving sparkling wine, it is best to tilt the glass so as to minimize the loss of gas.

Order of wines

The *Larousse Encyclopedia of Wine* gives the following conventions: 'White wine before red, young before old, light before heavy, dry before sweet, minor before fine or rare. White wines accompany the first courses in a meal, red ones the main or later courses.' Exceptions are champagne and white dessert wines, which are sometimes served with pudding. Sherry makes a fine pre-prandial drink, enhanced as it is by smoking. If multiple wines are on offer at dessert, they rotate clockwise in the order of their fineness: port first, then claret or other red wine, then dessert wine.

Decanters

These are sometimes used as attractive replacement vessels for bottled wine and are essential for wines that throw a deposit, such as vintage ports and many old reds. Decanters for wine are round and uncut so that the wine can be seen. Port decanters are round and sometimes cut. Decanters for spirits are generally square and cut.

❦ SPIRITS

Spirits are the result of the distillation of wine or other fermented (alcohol-containing) liquids. Distillation is a method of separating two liquids that are mixed together on the basis of their different volatilities: alcohol is more volatile than water, and when the mixture is heated the alcohol will vaporize more readily. When the vapor is condensed back into a liquid, it will have a higher alcohol content than the original mixture.

Spirits can be divided into families according to the source of the mash which is fermented: grape, fruit, grain or sugar. Some spirits, such as vodka, are so highly distilled that the choice of mash has little effect on the end product. Most spirits are bottled at 40–50% ABV, which is 80–100 proof, though some are much stronger than this. It is difficult to give specific indications of strengths because they vary from spirit to spirit and producer to producer.

GRAPE SPIRITS

Spirits distilled from fermented grape juice are called brandy. Other fermented fruit juices, once distilled, are called fruit brandies; hence apples yield apple brandy, pears pear brandy and so on. The more popular brandies have specific appellations: Cognac and Armagnac are the best known. Cognac is produced around the small French town of Cognac and Armagnac is produced in the Gascony region. Occasionally brandy bottles are marked VS, VSO or VSOP, which mean Very Special, Very Special Old and Very Superior Old Pale. These marks, however, are not backed up by an industry standard and cannot be considered serious indications of quality or age. Like all high-proof liquors, brandy, once bottled, ceases to develop.

The greatest by-product of the wine-making process is pomace, the leftover skins, stems and seeds of the pressed grapes. These remains are used to make pomace brandy, a spirit with a long reputation for being a harsh drink. Today, many distinctive, subtle versions are produced. Pomace brandy made in Italy is called grappa; that made in France is called marc; and that made in Portugal is call Bagaleira.

FRUIT SPIRITS

A broad spectrum of spirits is made from fruits and succulent plants, of which apple and agave are the most popular. Applejack is the traditional American name for apple brandy distilled from cider, potent if not always palatable. In the UK this is called cider brandy. Calvados, a more refined drink, is made directly from fermented apple or apple and pear juice and aged in oak casks before bottling. Tequila and mezcal both come from the fermented juice of the agave family of succulents, tequila from the blue agave and mezcal from the maguey plant. Despite their similar origin, the two spirits have different methods of production and are markedly different in taste. It is mezcal, not tequila, which sometimes comes with a worm in the bottle, the 'worm' in fact being a moth larva.

GRAIN SPIRITS

The most widely drunk spirits are distilled from grains, such as barley, corn and rye. The purest of these is vodka, which can in principle be made from anything containing starch or sugar. In practice grain or potatoes are most often used. Poteen is similar to vodka, but more flavourful and, until recently at least, harsher. It is made in Ireland, usually from potatoes or grain. Despite being made privately for centuries, poteen could not be legally produced in Ireland until 1989, nor sold domestically until 1997. Gin, by which is meant London dry gin, is simply neutral grain spirit flavoured chiefly with juniper and redistilled. Sloe gin is not a spirit but a liqueur, made by infusing sloe berries, a small wild plum, in gin and sugar. Aquavit, sometimes called schnapps, is made like gin: neutral grain spirit is infused with caraway seeds and other spices and redistilled. It is traditionally drunk neat and cold. Malt whisky, described in detail on p 114, is made exclusively from barley, yeast and water. The mash used in bourbon (p 117) must include 51% corn; the mash in rye whiskey, 51% rye.

SUGAR SPIRITS

Of the spirits made from sugar, rum is the best known. It is produced from sugar cane or, more often, molasses: the dark, viscous fluid that remains after sugar is crystallized out of sugar cane juice. Whether rum is light or dark depends on how long it is aged in the barrel and how much caramel is added. The taste of dark rum is much more robust than light rum, and the two cannot be used interchangeably. Cachaça (pronounced ka-shah-sa) is made directly from sugar cane juice rather than molasses and has a flavour distinct from rum. It is the best-selling spirit in Brazil and is the basis of the excellent – some would say world's finest – cocktail, the caipirinha (p 120).

NOTABLE GRAPE SPIRITS

Spirit	Source	Origin
Armagnac	white grapes	Gascony (France)
Brandy	grapes	France

Bagaleira	grape pomace	Portugal
Cognac	white grapes	southwest France
Grappa	grape pomace	Italy
Marc	grape pomace	France
Metaxa	grapes	Greece
Pisco	Muscat and other grapes	Peru, Chile

NOTABLE FRUIT SPIRITS

Applejack	cider	New England (USA)
Arrack	coconut sap	South-East Asia
Calvados	apples (or apples & pears)	Normandy (France)
Cider brandy	cider	England
Kirsch	cherries	Alsace (France), Germany, Switzerland
Kislav	watermelons	Russia
Mezcal	maguey plant	Mexico
Mirabelle	yellow plums	Alsace–Lorraine (France)
Palinka	plums, apples, apricots	Austria, Hungary, Romania
Quetsch	purple plums	Central Europe
Raki	grapes, figs, plums	Turkey
Slivovitz	plums	Balkan countries
Tequila	blue agave	Mexico

NOTABLE GRAIN SPIRITS

Aquavit	grain, potatoes (with caraway seeds)	Scandinavia
Bourbon	corn	southern USA
Gin	grain (with juniper)	The Netherlands
Jenever	rye, wheat, malted barley	The Netherlands, Belgium
Malt whisky	barley	Scotland
Poteen	grain or potatoes	Ireland
Rye whiskey	rye	USA
Schnapps	grain, fruit	Austria, Germany
Shochu	rice, grain, potatoes	Japan
Vodka	grain, potatoes	Russia, Poland

NOTABLE SUGAR SPIRITS

Batavia arrack	sugar cane	Indonesia
Cachaça	sugar cane	Brazil
Rum	molasses	Caribbean

❦ LIQUEURS

A liqueur is a spirit flavoured with fruit, herbs or spices – collectively called botanicals – to which sugar is added. This final distinction is important: modern gin, which is grain spirit flavoured with juniper, is not a liqueur, but 18th-century gin, which was sweet, is. To be called a liqueur the product must, by European law, contain not less 100 grams of sugar per litre and be at least 15% ABV. Most liqueurs are 25–40% ABV, but some are considerably stronger: Elixir Végétal de la Grande-Chartreuse is 71%, although in France it is considered a pharmaceutical product rather than an alcoholic drink.

Liqueurs are drunk in one of three ways. First, they are an essential ingredient in countless cocktails (see Cocktails, p 118), where they are used to add sweetness and flavour to the drink. Second, they are drunk neat, usually from a cordial or shot glass, occasionally from an old-fashioned glass over ice. Third, they are diluted with water and ice to make a refreshing long drink, especially the anise-flavoured liqueurs, which turn white on dilution.

PRODUCTION

There are several ways by which flavouring can be added to a base spirit. Maceration is the combination of cold spirits and botanicals left to blend over a period of time. Infusion is the mixture of warm spirits and botanicals; as with tea, the higher temperature accelerates and enhances the process of extraction. Alternatively, the mixture of alcohol and flavourings can itself be distilled – a process simply called distillation. In this case only the essential oils and other volatile flavourings from the botanicals remain in the resulting spirit. In all three cases, the liquor is sweetened by adding sugar.

CLASSIFICATION

Liqueurs may be divided into those that are flavoured with fruit, including cocoa and coffee beans, and those that are flavoured with herbs and spices, such as apricot kernels, attar of roses, vanilla and mint. In practice, many liqueurs are a mixture of the two. Because liqueurs are often flavoured with dozens of different botanicals, they can have complex, subtle tastes which are not easily described. The ingredients themselves are usually heavily guarded secrets, in some cases known by only a handful of people at any one time.

The best liqueurs are the longstanding proprietary brands, many of which have remained more or less unchanged for centuries. The two most famous, and arguably the oldest, liqueurs are Benedictine and Chartreuse.

BENEDICTINE

Benedictine originates from an elixir made during the Renaissance by the Benedictine monk Dom Bernardo Vincelli at Fécamp Abbey in France. Production of the popular drink had ceased by the time of the French Revolution. However, in 1863, Alexandre Le Grand discovered instructions for making the liqueur in a 16th-century manuscript, and he began marketing a modified version of the drink. Benedictine is still produced in Fécamp today, although no longer by the monks themselves, unlike Chartreuse (below). The letters DOM, inscribed on every bottle, stand for *Deo Optimo Maximo*: 'To God, Most good, Most great'. According to the company, Benedictine is made from 27 plants and spices, including angelica, hyssop, juniper, myrrh, saffron, aloe, arnica and cinnamon.

CHARTREUSE

Elixir Végétal de la Grande-Chartreuse, the original drink made by the Carthusian monks at the eponymous monastery in France, was first made in 1737. While this concentrated elixir was intended as a medicine, it was increasingly consumed as a drink, and in 1764 the monks began producing the weaker – though at 55% ABV still very strong – liqueur known as Chartreuse Verte. A sweeter and milder variation on this recipe, Chartreuse Jaune (40% ABV), was created in 1838.

Chartreuese Verte is the best known of the various drinks produced by the monks. To make it, according to the company, 'some 130 herbs, plants, roots, leaves and other natural bits of vegetation are soaked in alcohol for an unknown length of time, then distilled and mixed with distilled honey and sugar syrup before being put into large oaken casks...for maturation'. In Waugh's *Brideshead Revisited* (Books, p 172), Anthony Blanche offers the pale-green liqueur to Charles Ryder: 'Real G-g-green Chartreuse made before the expulsion of the monks. There are five distinct tastes as it trickles over the tongue. It is like swallowing a sp-spectrum.' Chartreuse is also the name given to the colour of the pale green-liqueur, specifically the colour with hexadecimal triplet 7F FF 00.

NOTABLE HERB LIQUEURS

Name	*Tasting notes*	ABV
Chartreuse Elixir Végétal	medicinal, aromatic	71
Absinthe (La Fée)	aniseed, mint, lemon	68
Chartreuse Verte	aromatic, herbs, liquorice	55
Pastis (Ricard)	star anise, liquorice, black pepper	45

Benedictine	mixed spices, honey, citrus, cognac-based	40
Benedictine B & B	a mix of Benedictine and brandy	40
Chartreuse Jaune	honey, aromatic	40
Danzig Goldwasser	orange peel, anise, caraway seed	40
Drambuie	honey, orange, aromatic, malt whisky-based	40
Sambuca (Molinari)	aniseed, black liquorice	40
Strega	mint, fennel, aniseed	40
Ouzo (12)	anise, cinnamon	38
Glayva	honey, spices, whisky-based	35
Irish Mist	Irish whiskey, honey, heather	35
Galliano	spice, aniseed, citrus, vanilla	30
Royal Mint Chocolate	after dinner mints	28.5
Amaretto (Disaronno)	apricot kernels, almonds, baked cake	28
Parfait Amour	rosewater, orange, vanilla	25
Pimm's No. 1 Cup	citrus, spices, gin-based	25
Frangelico	hazelnut, caramel, butter	24
Advocaat (Warninks)	custard, brandy- & egg-yolk-based	17.2

NOTABLE FRUIT LIQUEURS

Name	*Tasting notes*	ABV
Cointreau	sweet oranges, bitter orange peel	40
Grand Marnier	burnt oranges, orange peel, cognac-based	40
Southern Comfort	caramel, citrus	40
Triple Sec	oranges, orange peel	30–40
Mandarine Napoleon	candied orange peel, bitter marmalade	38
Jägermeister	mixed spices, liquorice, medicinal	35
Limoncello (Villa Massa)	lemon drops, lemon peel	30
Kahlúa	coffee, dark chocolate, vanilla, sharp then sweet	26.5
Tia Maria	Jamaican coffee, milk chocolate	26.5
Sloe gin (Plymouth)	raspberries, forest fruits, gin-based	26
Campari	bitter orange peel, honey	25
Cherry brandy (Heering)	ripe cherries, almonds, brandy-based	24.7
Peach schnapps (Archers)	sweet peach flesh	23
Malibu	sweetened coconut, rum-based	21
Pisang Ambon	banana split, overripe bananas	21
Midori	honeydew melon	20
Passoã	passion fruit, citrus	20
Baileys	Irish whiskey, cream, dark chocolate	17
Tequila Rose	strawberries, tequila-based	17
Chambord	raspberries, honey, jam	16.5

❦ WHISKY

To be called a single malt Scotch, a whisky (spelled whiskey in America and Ireland) must satisfy three conditions:

Single It must be produced at a single distillery, although it may be mixed from separately aged casks.

Malt It must be made entirely from malted (sprouted) barley, to which only yeast and water can be added. Other whiskies and bourbons may contain additional grains, such as corn or rye.

Scotch It must be distilled and aged in Scotland. There are curiously few single malt distilleries elsewhere in the world; Michael Jackson (Books, p 173) names six, located in Australia, Ireland, Japan, New Zealand and Pakistan.

Unlike wine or other spirits, the world of single malt Scotch is small and can be approached with a view to comprehensive familiarity.

There are 119 distilleries which now produce or have recently produced single malt Scotch whisky. Each brand of spirit has a distinctive, characteristic taste. Some of the distilleries, such as Rosebank, are closed but previous production is still being aged and is available on the market. For each distillery the following information is listed:

Name If the distillery has changed name, the most recent name is given.
District One of nine regions of Scotland in which the distillery is located.
Classification (Cls) One of 12 similarity classes to which each whisky was assigned (p 116). If omitted (–), the whisky was not studied.

Distillery	Region	Cls
Aberfeldy	Midlands	A
Aberlour	Speyside	B
Allt-á-Bhainne	Speyside	–
Ardberg	Islay	I
Ardmore	Speyside	C
Arran	Island	–
Auchentoshan	Lowlands	D
Aultmore	Speyside	F
Balblair	N Highlands	E
Balmenach	Speyside	K
Balvenie	Speyside	B
Banff	Speyside	L
Ben Nevis	W Highlands	D
Benriach	Speyside	F
Benrinnes	Speyside	B
Benromach	Speyside	F
Bladnoch	Lowlands	E
Blair Athol	Midlands	C
Bowmore	Islay	I
Brackla	Speyside	K
Braeval	Speyside	–
Bruichladdich	Islay	H
Bunnahabhain	Islay	F
Caol Ila	Islay	E
Caperdonich	Speyside	L
Cardhu	Speyside	F
Clynelish	N Highlands	C
Cnoc	Speyside	–
Coleburn	Speyside	D
Convalmore	Speyside	K
Cragganmore	Speyside	G
Craigellachie	Speyside	K
Dailuaine	Speyside	K

Dallas Dhu	Speyside	K	Inchmurrin	W Highlands	E
Dalmore	N Highlands	B	Inverleven	Lowlands	E
Dalwhinnie	Speyside	F	Jura	Island	I
Deanston	Midlands	H	Kinclaith	Lowlands	E
Drumguish	Speyside	–	Knockando	Speyside	F
Dufftown	Speyside	I	Knockdhu	Speyside	K
Edradour	Midlands	E	Ladyburn	Lowlands	H
Fettercairn	E Highlands	H	Lagavulin	Islay	I
Glen Albyn	Speyside	J	Laphroaig	Islay	A
Glenallachie	Speyside	F	Linkwood	Speyside	J
Glenburgie	Speyside	E	Littlemill	Lowlands	E
Glencadam	E Highlands	L	Loch Lomond	W Highlands	–
Glen Deveron	Speyside	F	Lochnagar	E Highlands	L
Glendronach	Speyside	K	Lochside	E Highlands	B
Glendullan	Speyside	B	Longmorn	Speyside	G
Glen Elgin	Speyside	L	Longrow	Campbeltown	I
Glenesk	E Highlands	K	Macallan	Speyside	B
Glenfarclas	Speyside	I	Mannochmore	Speyside	–
Glenfiddich	Speyside	H	Millburn	Speyside	B
Glen Flagler	Lowlands	–	Miltonduff	Speyside	F
Glen Garioch	E Highlands	L	Mortlach	Speyside	K
Glenglassaugh	Speyside	G	North Port	E Highlands	J
Glengoyne	W Highlands	J	Oban	W Highlands	B
Glen Grant	Speyside	J	Pittyvaich	Speyside	–
Glen Keith	Speyside	K	Port Ellen	Islay	C
Glenkinchie	Lowlands	F	Pulteney	N Highlands	E
Glenlivet	Speyside	B	Rosebank	Lowlands	G
Glenlochy	W Highlands	I	St Magdalene	Lowlands	J
Glenlossie	Speyside	J	Scapa	Island	A
Glen Mhor	Speyside	H	Singleton	Speyside	B
Glenmorangie	N Highlands	C	Speyburn	Speyside	D
Glen Moray	Speyside	G	Springbank	Campbeltown	F
Glen Ord	N Highlands	K	Strathisla	Speyside	B
Glenrothes	Speyside	K	Strathmill	Speyside	–
Glen Scotia	Campbeltown	F	Talisker	Island	C
Glen Spey	Speyside	H	Tamdhu	Speyside	J
Glentauchers	Speyside	H	Tamnavulin	Speyside	G
Glenturret	Midlands	B	Teaninich	N Highlands	L
Glenugie	E Highlands	A	Tobermory	Island	H
Glenury Royal	E Highlands	I	Tomatin	Speyside	K
Highland Park	Island	B	Tomintoul	Speyside	G
Imperial	Speyside	L	Tormore	Speyside	K
Inchgower	Speyside	F	Tullibardine	Midlands	F

WHISKY CLASSIFICATION

Below is a classification of 109 distilleries producing single malt Scotch whisky, based on a mathematical study of Jackson's 1989 tasting notes. (At the time of their analysis, the authors had information on only 109 of the 119 distilleries listed on pp 114–115.) The dendrogram is best considered as a tree, viewed from above. The trunk is the centre point from which the branches emanate. Two whiskies (leaves) which join near the outer edge are similar in taste: for example, Glenlivet and Glendullan at four o'clock. The closer to the centre a path between two whiskies travels, the less similar they are.

The two main branches from the centre divide the spirits into two classes: 69 'full-gold-coloured, dry-bodied and smoky' whiskies (A–H) and 40 'amber, aromatic, light-bodied, smooth palate and fruity finish' whiskies (I–L). Further out, 12 sub-branches are labelled A–L; these are the 12 similarity classes overleaf. Redrawn from F.-J. Lapointe and P. Legendre, 'A classification of pure malt Scotch whiskies', *Applied Statistics* **43**, 237 (1994).

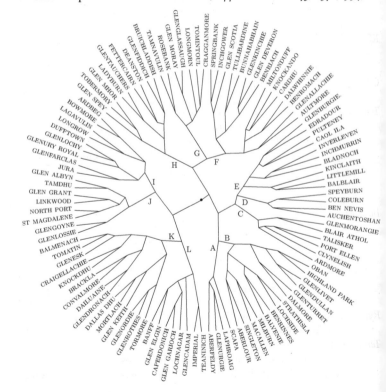

❦ BOURBON

The word 'bourbon' is often used as an all-inclusive term for American whiskey. However, there are a number of different types, each with a distinct method of production protected by law. Here is an introduction.

TYPES OF AMERICAN WHISKEY

Bourbon Bourbon was defined as America's 'native spirit' by an Act of Congress in 1964. To be called bourbon, a whiskey must be made from between 51% and 80% corn, be aged in new charred oak barrels and be at least 40% ABV when bottled. While bourbon can be produced in any American state, only Kentucky can put its name on the label. An essential step in making bourbon is the addition of sour mash, which is the leftover mash used to make the previous batch of whiskey. The taste of bourbon is distinct from Scotch whisky, which tends to be more flavourful. It is bourbon, rather than Scotch, which is called for in most whiskey-based cocktails.

Rye whiskey This type of whiskey must be made from at least 51% rye (a type of grain like wheat and barley). Rye whiskey tends to be heavier than bourbon, comparable to Irish whiskey or, some say, Islay.

Corn whiskey This little-produced spirit must be made from at least 80% corn. Receiving little or no ageing, it is not normally a subtle drink.

Tennessee whiskey This is a whiskey, made from 51% of any one grain, which has undergone the so-called Lincoln County Process, whereby the whiskey is filtered through charcoal. The charcoal is typically made from maple wood, broken into pellets and packed into a column.

NOTABLE AMERICAN WHISKEYS

Bourbon	State of production	ABV
Buffalo Trace	Kentucky	45
Four Roses Yellow Label	Kentucky	40
Jim Beam White/Black Label	Kentucky	40/43
Maker's Mark	Kentucky	45
Old Forester	Kentucky	43
Wild Turkey	Kentucky	50.5
Rye whiskey		
Wild Turkey Rye	Kentucky	50.5
Tennessee whiskey		
Jack Daniels Old Number 7	Tennessee	40–50
George Dickel No. 8/12	Tennessee	40/45

❦ COCKTAILS

A cocktail is an iced spirit modified by juices, liqueurs, sugar, aromatic wines and bitters, which may or may not be diluted by a sparkling beverage or water. David Embury, the author of the most influential book on cocktails (see Books, p 174), defines a cocktail axiomatically:

1 It must whet the appetite, not dull it;
2 It should stimulate the mind;
3 It must be pleasing to the palate;
4 It must be pleasing to the eye;
5 It must have sufficient alcoholic flavour;
6 Finally it must be well iced.

From these axioms a number of properties of cocktails can be deduced. Axioms five and six tell us what a cocktail is not, namely, anything made without spirits or warm. Thus a kir (white wine and cassis) is not a cocktail, nor is an Irish coffee, which is hot. However desirable a cocktail may be after dinner, it must function as an aperitif before (axiom 1). The variety of cocktail glasses is partly explained by axiom 4, each type of drink being most tempting in its own shape of glass.

CLASSIFICATION

Cocktails fall into three categories: short drinks, which are undiluted; long drinks, which are diluted with soda water or other carbonated drink; and punches, which are diluted with water. Of course, in practice all cocktails are to some extent diluted by adding ice, and are the better for it, but this implicit dilution is not considered in their definition.

Short drinks should be at least 50% spirit by volume, which is about as strong as port or sherry. Consequently, they are served in smaller portions, usually in martini or old-fashioned glasses. They may be further divided into sours and aromatics. Sours, which do not in general taste sour because sugar is added, have as a modifying agent lemon or lime juice. With aromatics the principal modifying agent is one of the bitters, such as Angostura or Peychaud, or an aromatic wine, such as vermouth.

Long drinks differs from short drinks by the addition of a neutral background beverage, generally soda water, but sometimes tonic water, ginger ale or Coke. If it is made without citrus juice, it is a highball; with lemon juice, a collins; and with lime juice, a rickey.

Punches, which have the longest lineage, are correctly diluted with still water, although in many recipes this has been replaced by soda water or lemonade. Punches are typically served from a bowl containing a block of ice; ice is not added to each glass.

Quality over quantity

Most books on cocktails contain far too many recipes, many of them un-palatable. In fact there are not more than two dozen drinks from which nearly all others can be derived. Start, for example, with the Gimlet: it is made of four parts gin, two parts lime juice and one part sugar syrup. If the gin is replaced with light rum, it is a Daiquiri. Add some crushed mint leaves and soda water and it becomes a Mojito. Substitute bourbon for rum and drop the soda and lime for a Mint Julep. Replace the mint with lemon and it is a Whiskey Sour. Indeed, a thorough understanding of which flavours mix with others, and in what proportions, makes cocktail recipes altogether redundant.

Stirring versus shaking

The debate over stirring versus shaking should be laid to rest, as there is lit-tle difference between the two: shaking involves slightly less dilution if the ice is much colder than 0 °C (32 °F). The exception is drinks that froth, such as those made with egg whites, where shaking is essential. More important is whether to strain (keeping the ice out of the drink) or pour (leaving it in). Pouring is more common with long drinks. In all cases drinks should be as cold as possible, and to this end they are sometimes served in chilled glasses.

Muddling

This is the mashing of ingredients in the base of an old-fashioned or high-ball glass with a 1 inch thick wooden rod, called a muddler. It is usually done to citrus fruit, sometimes with sugar, with the remains left in the glass. Bruising, as the name suggests, is a very light muddling.

Making many drinks

Apart from bartenders, most mixers need to make not one drink at a time but two or four or six. All of the drinks listed overleaf are given in terms of relative, rather than absolute, measures. This means that a cocktail can be made in as large a quantity as desired by changing the volume of a single part. As a rule of thumb, the typical amount of spirits (40% ABV) in a cock-tail is 43 ml (see Bartenders' Bible, p 123). For larger gatherings, it is often impractical to shake drinks in small batches, and mass mixing is a must. The best method is to combine in a jug or large bowl all the ingredients ex-cept ice, sparkling beverages and pieces of fruit which, if called for, are added one glass at a time.

INGREDIENTS

What are cocktails made from? The most useful ingredients must be those that come up most frequently in cocktail recipes. An analysis of the 100 most popular cocktails yields a total of 94 different ingredients, distributed as follows (only the top 12 ingredients in each column are listed):

Spirits	%	Other alcohol	%	Non-alcohol	%
vodka	30	Angostura	14	ice	98
gin	18	Cointreau	12	sugar syrup	46
light rum	10	framboise	8	lime juice	28
tequila	8	champagne	6	lemon juice	22
bourbon	7	dry vermouth	5	soda water	12
cognac	7	sweet vermouth	5	orange juice	10
dark rum	6	blackberry liqueur	4	cranberry juice	8
Scotch whisky	4	cassis	4	apple juice	7
cachaça	3	Kahlúa	4	egg white	6
gold rum	2	peach schnapps	4	ginger beer	6
Pisco	2	Baileys	3	pineapple juice	6
Irish whiskey	1	Grand Marnier	3	Rose's lime cordial	5

The distribution of glasses is also of interest. The same 100 cocktails are served in these glasses (see Glasses, p 124):

Glass	%				
martini	33	old-fashioned	21	hurricane	3
highball	27	flute	6	shot	2
		pilsner	4	other	4

A DOZEN COCKTAILS FOR LIFE

These 12 classic drinks have stood the test of time. Proportions can and should be adjusted to suit individual tastes. The glass and garnish for each cocktail are labelled Y and ᗅ, respectively.

Caipirinha
8 parts Cachaça
¾ lime per glass
3 parts sugar syrup
Y old-fashioned, straw
Muddle sliced lime in glass. Add rest and crushed ice and stir.

Cosmopolitan
6 parts vodka
3 parts Cointreau
6 parts cranberry juice
1 part lime juice
Y martini, ᗅ orange peel
Shake with crushed ice and strain into glasses.

Gimlet

4 parts gin
2 parts lime juice
1 part sugar syrup
Y martini, ○ lime slice

Shake with crushed ice and strain into glasses.

Manhattan

5 parts bourbon
1 part dry vermouth
2 dashes Angostura per glass
Y martini, ○ orange peel

Shake with crushed ice and strain into glasses.

Margarita

2 parts tequila
1 part Cointreau
1 part lime juice
Y martini, ○ lime slice

First salt glass rims. Shake with crushed ice and strain into glasses.

Martini

7 parts gin
1 part dry vermouth
Y martini, ○ lemon peel

Shake with crushed ice and strain into glasses.

Mint Julep

3 parts bourbon
1 part sugar syrup
10 mint leaves per glass
1 dash Angostura per glass
Y highball, straw

Bruise mint leaves with bourbon. Add rest and crushed ice and stir.

Mojito

4 parts light rum
4 parts soda water
½ lime per glass
10 mint leaves per glass
1 part sugar syrup
Y highball, straw

Muddle sliced lime and mint in glass. Add rest and crushed ice; stir.

Old-fashioned

5 parts bourbon
1 part sugar syrup
2 dashes Angostura per glass
Y old-fashioned, ○ orange slice

Shake with crushed ice and pour (with ice) into ice-filled glasses.

Sidecar

2 parts Cognac
1 part lemon juice
1 part Cointreau
Y martini, ○ lemon peel

Shake with crushed ice and strain into glasses.

Singapore Sling

8 parts gin
4 parts cherry brandy
2 parts lemon juice
1 part sugar syrup
1 dash Angostura per glass
Y highball, straw, ○ cherry

Shake with crushed ice, pour (w. ice) into glasses and top with soda water.

Whiskey Sour

2 parts bourbon
1 part lemon juice
1 part sugar syrup
2 dashes Angostura per glass
Y old-fashioned, ○ lemon slice

Shake with crushed ice and pour (with ice) into glasses.

❦ BARTENDERS' BIBLE

ESSENTIAL DRINKS CABINET

What should be stocked in a man's drinks cabinet? Two bottles each of red and white wine, and a sparkling wine, are essential, as is your preferred lager and ale. The principal masculine drink is bourbon or whisky, and a bottle of each, along with ice and soda water for mixing, come next. From the point of view of making cocktails, gin, vodka and rum come to mind, all of which mix well with many flavours. Of the liqueurs, the oldest two (Chartreuse and Benedictine) should be stocked for drinking neat, along with a triple sec (Cointreau) for mixing. The aromatics vermouth and Angostura are useful for cocktails, along with tonic water, sugar and lemons.

Beer and wine	*Spirits*	*Other alcohol*	*Non-alcohol*
2 bottles red wine	whisky	Chartreuse Verte	ice
2 bottles white wine	bourbon	Benedictine	soda water
1 bottle sparkling wine	vodka	Cointreau	tonic water
6 bottles lager	gin	dry vermouth	sugar syrup
6 bottles ale	light rum	Angostura bitters	lemons

SERVING SIZE

Typical drinks servings are listed below. Interestingly, a pint of UK beer contains only slightly less alcohol than a shot of absinthe. A unit of alcohol, intended to allow comparison of alcohol by volume between drinks, is defined (somewhat arbitrarily) to be 10.0 ml ethanol by the UK government, which likes to quantify these sorts of things. The government's recommended weekly intake of alcohol for men is 21 units, or 210 ml ethanol, equivalent to 2.3 bottles of wine or 7.4 pints of beer.

Measure	ABV	*Proof*	*Drinks/ bottle*	*Vol/ drink (ml)*	*Ethanol/ drink (ml)*
250 ml glass of UK beer	5%	10	–	250	12.5
12 oz can of US beer	4%	8	–	355	14.2
pint of UK beer	5%	10	–	568	28.4
glass of wine	12%	24	6	125	15.0
glass of port or sherry	20%	40	10	75	15.0
shot of spirits	40%	80	16.4	42.6	17.0
shot of cask-strength whisky	60%	120	16.4	42.6	25.6
shot of absinthe	70%	140	16.4	42.6	29.8
shot of Everclear	95%	190	16.4	42.6	40.5

MEASURING DRINKS

Measures for drinks have a complex history, and different conventions exist in different places. In Europe and most of the rest of the world, volume is specified in millilitres (ml). In Britain and America, where many popular drinks originate, imperial units are more common, but these definitions are almost all different between the two countries. The most common measure for mixed drinks is the shot. Despite the recent preponderance of 40 ml, the more historically correct (and generous) definition is 1½ ounce, which is 42.6 ml in the UK. This matters little when cocktail recipes (p 119) are given in relative terms (so many parts of this and that, as is the case in this book), rather than absolute ones.

	UK definition		US definition	
	fl. oz (UK)	ml	fl. oz (US)	ml
dash	⅟₄₈	0.592	⅟₄₈	0.616
teaspoon (tsp)	⅛	3.55	⅙	4.93
tablespoon (tbsp)	½	14.2	½	14.8
fluid ounce or pony	1	28.4	1	29.6
shot, jigger or bar glass	1½	42.6	1½	44.4
gill	5	142	4	118
cup	10	284	8	237
can Coke	11.6	330	11.2	330
pint	20	568	16	473
bottle spirits	24.6	700	23.7	700
bottle wine	26.4	750	25.4	750

PROOF

The association of the word 'proof' with alcoholic strength derives from an ingenious test of whether or not a spirit is stronger than a certain threshold, namely, 57.15% alcohol by volume. This is the concentration of spirit above which a gunpowder paste made with it will still ignite, thus proving its potency. Today three methods are used to quantify alcoholic strength:

Alcohol by volume (ABV)	millilitres ethanol per 100 millilitres solution
Proof	twice the alcohol by volume times a hundred
British proof	approximately ⅞ proof; rarely used now

Thus a bottle of whisky at 40% ABV is 80 proof or 70 British proof. The strongest spirit that can be produced using conventional distillation is 95% (190 proof), available in America under the name Everclear.

❦ GLASSES

Different drinks require different glasses, not only by tradition but also be
cause of variations in serving size, serving temperature and volatility. Al
glasses should be made of clear glass or crystal. Crystal is cut lead glass
that is, glass with 12–30% lead oxide by weight, which gives the glass a
higher refractive index and makes it sparkle. The different kinds of glasses
shown opposite, are not numerous, and can be divided into three categories

STEMLESS GLASSES

Stemless glasses are cylindrical or have a slightly inverted conical shape
with flat bottoms. The largest is the *pint glass*, which is mostly used for serv
ing beer on draught. It is standardized to hold a pint of beer (568 ml), plu
room for the head. In the UK underfilling a pint glass is heavily frowne
upon – selling pints 10% short can lead to prosecution. The *pilsner* is use
to serve many bottled beers, and has a circular foot attached to the base fo
added stability. The *beer mug* is thick-walled and sturdy and comes in var
ious sizes. The *highball* and *collins* are used for water, juice and long cock
tails, the only difference being that a highball has parallel sides and a collin
sloping sides. The *old-fashioned* is stockier and sturdier with a heavy glas
base; it is used for neat spirits and short cocktails. Smallest of all is the *sho
glass*, in which neat spirits and shooters are served without ice.

STEMMED GLASSES FOR WINE

There are many varieties of wine glass, but only a few are necessary to drin
any given wine at its best. The spherical *red wine glass* in various sizes is th
most familiar, and is sometimes used as a general-purpose vessel for othe
types of wine. The *white wine glass* is cylindrical near the top; because it i
intended to keep the wine cold, large examples are rarely seen. The *cham
pagne flute*, designed to stay cold and minimize carbonation loss, has a sma
circumference at the top, unlike the largely obsolete champagne bowl wit
its shallow sides. The *sherry glass* is used for the fortified wines sherry an
port which, being stronger, require smaller vessels. Finally, the *tasting glas
is medium-sized and has a small opening to concentrate a wine's aroma

STEMMED GLASSES FOR SPIRITS AND LIQUEURS

Of the stemmed glasses used for spirits, liqueurs and cocktails, the *brand
snifter* is the largest, though it is never filled anywhere near capacity. Its con
tents are warmed by the hand on which the bowl rests. The familiar V

shaped glass is known as a *martini* or *cocktail* glass. It is used for short cock-tails served without ice (with ice, use an old-fashioned). Liqueurs are served in a *cordial*, a small stemmed vessel similar in volume to a shot glass. A *hurricane* is a curvaceous glass used to serve cocktails made with lots of crushed ice. Finally, a *toddy* is for hot drinks, such as Irish coffee. It is in the shape of a tall mug attached to a stem and base, designed to keep the drink warm.

Pint glass   Pilsner   Beer mug   Highball

Collins   Old-fashioned   Shot glass   Red wine glass

White wine glass   Champagne flute   Sherry glass   Tasting glass

Brandy snifter   Martini or cocktail glass   Cordial   Hurricane   Toddy

❦HANGOVERS

A hangover, in medicine called veisalgia, refers to the nausea, headache and weakness that follows excessive alcohol consumption and lasts from several to 36 hours. The pathology of hangovers is not well understood.

HANGOVER PREVENTION

The simplest way to prevent hangovers, apart from reducing alcoholic intake, is to combine your drinks carefully. In Evelyn Waugh's *Brideshead Revisited*, after Sebastian is sick on Charles' floor, Sebastian's friend apologizes on his behalf: 'The wines were too various,' he said. 'It was neither the quality nor the quantity that was at fault. It was the mixture. Grasp that and you have the root of the matter.' The following alcoholic commutation rhymes advise which drinks to drink before others:

Beer before wine, you're fine;   Beer before liquor, never sicker.
   Wine before beer, oh dear.   Whisky before beer, never fear;
Liquor before beer, in the clear;   Beer before whisky, kind of risky.

While some of these maxims are at odds, it is widely held that grain followed by grape is preferable to the alternative, and that champagne should not follow anything – it is best had to start the evening. For a clear head the next day, neat grain spirit, such as whisky, throughout the evening is ideal.

HANGOVER CURE

There is no shortage of remedies that are supposed to alleviate or cure a hangover, most of which are meant to amuse as much as perform. In a study of the leading treatments published in the *British Medical Journal* (M. H. Pittler, J. C. Verster and E. Ernst, 'Interventions for preventing or treating alcohol hangover', **331**, 1515 (2005)), the authors concluded that 'no compelling evidence exists to suggest that any complementary or conventional intervention is effective for treating or preventing the alcohol hangover'. (The agents tested were propranolol, tropisetron, tolfenamic acid, fructose or glucose, borage, artichoke, prickly pear and a yeast-based preparation.)

Nevertheless, many drinkers swear by a favourite remedy. Those which have a large following include drinking water before going to bed, drinking Coca-Cola after waking up and the so-called hair of the dog (that bit you): treating a hangover with another drink. According to *Brewer's Dictionary of Phrase and Fable*, the term alludes to 'the old notion that the burned hair of a dog is an antidote to its bite', an application of 'like cures like'.

SMOKING

Arnold Schwarzenegger • I have inhaled, exhaled everything.

Klinger • A good cigar is like a beautiful chick with a great body who also knows the American League box scores. (*M*A*S*H*)

Winston Churchill • My rule of life prescribed as an absolutely sacred rite smoking cigars and also the drinking of alcohol before, after, and if need be during all meals and in the intervals between them. (*Triumph and Tragedy,* 1953)

Anonymous • Thus dost thou every taste and genius hit, / In smoke thou'rt wisdom; and in snuff thou'rt wit.

Joseph Cullman (head of Philip Morris) • Some women would prefer having smaller babies. (*Face the Nation* interview, 1971)

A. A. Gill • When on occasion I'm asked by groups of aspiring writers what they should do to get on, my advice is always, emphatically, smoke… It's a little known, indeed little researched, fact of literature and journalism that no nonsmoker is worth reading. (*Sunday Times,* 1999)

Cigarette slogans
Benson & Hedges The length you go to for pleasure
Camel I'd walk a mile for a Camel
Carlton If you smoke, please smoke Carlton
Chesterfield Blow some my way
L & M Just what the doctor ordered
Lucky Strike Reach for a Lucky instead of a sweet
Marlboro Come to where the flavour is
Newport Alive with pleasure
Pall Mall Wherever particular people congregate
Salem Springtime…it happens every Salem
Virginia Slims You've come a long way, baby
Winston Tastes like a cigarette should

❧SMOKING ETIQUETTE

The introduction of indoor smoking bans in countries around the world is changing the way men smoke. There is more smoking in private residences and out of doors, and the much-persecuted community of smokers is voicing solidarity. Here is a guide to smokers' rights and wrongs. Throughout this section, 'smoking' refers to the use of cigarettes, cigars and pipes, but not snuff and chewing tobacco, which are permissible everywhere.

INDOOR SMOKING

First, is it acceptable to ban guests from smoking in your house? James Leavey, editor of the *FOREST Guide to Smoking in London*, advises:

> There are those who will not permit any smoking in their home. It is their prerogative but of course their smoking guests may consider this anti-social. It is very unkind to confront a heavy smoker in your home with the fact that he or she will have to suffer a smoke-free evening. Better to warn your guests when you invite them, so they can decide whether or not to turn down your invitation.

John Morgan, in *Debrett's New Guide to Etiquette and Modern Manners*, concurs. 'If you as the host hate the habit, you can quite legitimately never invite smokers to your table. However, it is not appropriate to forbid a guest to smoke in your house once he or she is there.'

Second, when is it acceptable to light up in someone else's house? In an ideal world, if you are known to be a regular smoker and have been invited, you are welcome to smoke. In reality, you have to be on the watch for context clues. The presence of ashtrays is a sure sign that smoking is allowed. The possession of a personal portable ashtray, on the other hand, does not confer a licence to smoke anywhere. If you cannot see an ashtray, an unabashed 'May we smoke?' is often answered in the affirmative. Smoking while others at your table are eating is bad manners, although a cigarette between courses is perfectly acceptable. Children are known to enjoy being in the presence of all forms of fire and smoke.

OUTDOOR SMOKING

More and more smokers are forced to smoke outside bars and restaurants in Europe and the US, and certain special rules apply to this community in exile. The usual social reservation between strangers is lifted: striking up conversation with a stranger is to be encouraged, and asking him for a cigarette is perfectly acceptable. At work, dedicated smokers should coordinate their outdoor smoking breaks, and the same applies to restaurants.

DEALING WITH NON-SMOKERS

What is the correct response to hostile or disapproving non-smokers in places where smoking is permitted? A gentle smoker would like, on the one hand, to avoid causing pain (in the words of Newman, p 82). On the other, he has a moral duty to resist non-smoking bullies. With regard to the first, he will realize when his habit is not welcome and adjust his behaviour accordingly – standing near an open window, for example. With regard to the second, he will nip intolerance in the bud with a smug smoke ring or firm puff in the direction of the complainer. As host, if one guest shows annoyance at another's smoking, the easiest solution is to isolate not the smoker but the complaining guest: 'Let's step outside for a chat on the balcony while John finishes his cigarette.'

A less considered problem is the *apparent* non-smoker who persistently leeches off the secondhand smoke of others. While this may be unintentional, ultimately it means that there is less secondhand smoke to go round. Like a man at the pub who never buys his round, a repeat offender should be encouraged to leave or light up himself.

ASHES, BUTTS AND DOTTLE

The question of where you can dispose of ash, butts and dottle is a tricky one (dottle is the burnt and partially burnt tobacco left in the bowl of a pipe). Certainly it is acceptable to flick your ash on to the ground or pavement out of doors. Dropping butts and dottle is an unattractive habit but there are occasions when this is the only option. If there is no ashtray or bin nearby, it is acceptable in public, though not private, outdoor spaces. Indoors the policy is similar, but more stringent by one degree. When necessary, ash can be dropped on public, though not private, hard floors; butts and dottle must be properly disposed of. Carpets require special care – it is hugely annoying to find cigarette burns the morning after a drinks party.

LIGHTING UP

When the occasion arises, a man should light a woman's cigarette directly, but should offer the lighter to a man for him to light his own. The exception is when both men are lighting up simultaneously; in this case you light the other's first, then your own. Lighting cigars (p 135) and pipes (p 136) is a comparatively complex ritual and is always executed by the smoker himself.

❦HOW TO START SMOKING

Everyone knows how to quit smoking and the advantages it offers, but there is very little information available on how to start smoking. Most apparent pro-smoking pamphlets and websites are either tricks – they contain anti-smoking propaganda in disguise – or spoofs – they are meant to be funny rather than useful. The result is that first-time smokers have to learn how to smoke through trial and error. Here are some pointers on why and how to pick up the habit.

ADVANTAGES OF SMOKING

At a time when smoking bans are being put into effect around the world, it is tempting to think that there is no worse time to start than now. In truth it may be as good a time as ever. As is often the case, when a morally neutral act is banned, more people turn to it than would have otherwise; a classic example of this is foxhunting in Britain. Moreover, like underage (under 21) drinking in America, illicit activities are more likely to be perceived as fashionable. A persecuted minority mixes more freely among itself, and a ban does nothing if not add to the social fluidity between smokers (see Smoking Etiquette, p 128).

There are a number of benefits associated with smoking which may well offset the known disadvantages. Smoking can be an effective method of weight control, as Lucky Strike put into profitable effect with their famous slogan 'Reach for a Lucky instead of a sweet'. Smoking satisfies man's innate fascination with fire, particularly in the case of cigars and pipes, which offer little in the form of a chemical kick. Smoking is manly, notwithstanding its popularity with women relatively recently in its long history. Finally, for many smoking is an essential means of relaxation. It brings reflection, and with reflection more considered judgement, if not wisdom. A Bushongo man, having learnt to smoke on a journey away, said this of smoking on his return:

> When you have a quarrel with your brother, in your fury you may wish to slay him: sit down and smoke a pipe. When the pipe is finished you will think that perhaps death is too great a punishment for your brother's offences, and you will decide to let him off with a thrashing. Relight your pipe and smoke on. As the smoke curls upwards you will come to the conclusion that a few hard words might take the place of blows. Light up your pipe once more, and when it is smoked through you will go to your brother and ask him to forget the past.
>
> M. W. Hilton-Simpson, *Land and Peoples of the Masai*, 1911

GETTING STARTED

The first step towards habitual smoking is to decide which kind to take up: cigarettes, cigars, pipes and snuff (see pp 132–138) suit some personalities more than others. While cigarettes are the most popular, cigars and pipes are not inhaled and are consequently much safer, despite the stark health warnings they may carry. Most first-time cigarette users find inhaling the most difficult aspect of smoking. The first couple of packs are likely to be accompanied by a slew of coughing, but this reaction should disappear soon after.

A new smoker must at all times be in possession of his tools of the trade. Depending on his choice of tobacco, this may include a pack of cigarettes, a pack, tube or case of cigars, a pipe and bag of tobacco, a lighter or matches, a cigar cutter and a pipe tool. It is frustrating to be separated from your essential smoking kit, so get into the habit of putting everything you need in the same pocket and always check it as you leave the door.

You will invariably receive pressure from others to either not take up smoking or refrain from smoking in their presence, particularly at dinners and parties. The best response to this is a defensive one: surround yourself with other smokers, which makes taking up smoking much more enjoyable. Two or three smokers together at a party are a social attraction; walk up to them and light up and you will be sure to be taken in with open arms.

Early on try different brands of cigarettes to find which one most suits your taste; old smoking habits die hard. If you are smoking cigars, start with an inexpensive brand, as most beginners will appreciate an ordinary cigar no less than an expensive Cuban. It is also wise to begin with a small ring gauge – a cigarillo or a panatella, for example – and work your way up to bigger cigars with experience, if at all. Like big game hunters, men who smoke big cigars should have learned the ropes with smaller ones.

SMOKING WITH CONFIDENCE

Like most things in life, confident smoking comes with experience, but there are a few things to bear in mind from the beginning. Choose an un-affected hold that suits you, as an awkward grip is the easiest way to spot a novice (see Cigarettes, p 133). Pack the cigarettes by firmly rapping the box on to the palm of your hand; this compresses the tobacco for a supposedly better smoke and gives the impression of a man who knows what he is doing. Compared to lighting a cigar or a pipe, lighting a cigarette looks easy. But there is a certain knack to inhaling at just the right moment from the right part of the flame to light up with a swift and elegant motion. The beginner lingers too long, burning too much of his cigarette in the process.

❦ CIGARETTES

Although there are many brands of cigarettes available, smokers are a loyal bunch and rarely try other makes. So it is useful to be reminded what the alternatives are. Below are the most popular brands in the UK and the US.

TOP-SELLING CIGARETTE BRANDS

UK market share, by brand/type		*US market share, by brand*	
Lambert & Butler KS	13.5%	Marlboro	35.4%
Benson & Hedges Gold	7.3%	Doral	6.3%
Mayfair King Size	7.1%	Newport	6.2%
Richmond Superkings	6.6%	Camel	5.3%
Richmond King Size	4.9%	Winston	5.2%
Marlboro Gold King Size	4.4%	Basic	4.9%
Regal KS	3.5%	GPC	4.7%
Royals King Size Red	3.4%	Kool	3.3%
Superkings	3.3%	Salem	3.2%
Silk Cut Purple	3.2%	Virginia Slims	2.6%
SOURCE www.ash.org.uk		SOURCE www.tobacco.org	

THE PROS AND CONS OF SMOKING

By law, cigarette packets must include conspicuous warnings of the health risks associated with smoking. For those who are already familiar with the risks, FakeFags (Websites, p 177) offers alternative messages in the form of stickers which are applied directly to the cigarette box.

Government warning	*FakeFags sticker*
Smoking kills	You could get hit by a bus tomorrow
Smokers die younger	My gran smokes 40 a day and she's 93
Smoking causes fatal lung cancer	Live fast, die young
Smoking causes ageing of the skin	You will get fat if you stop smoking
Smoking is highly addictive, don't start	At least I don't smoke crack
Smoking when pregnant harms your baby	It's OK, I'm not pregnant
Smoking can cause a slow and painful death	You've got to die of something
Smoking seriously harms you and others around you	Non-smokers may cause irritation
Smoking can damage the sperm and decreases fertility	Smoking makes you look sexy
Stopping smoking reduces the risk of fatal heart and lung diseases	Nobody likes a quitter

CIGARETTE HOLDS

One's first impression of a smoker depends not so much on his choice of cigarette as on the way he holds it. Here is a catalogue of good grips.

Classic cigarette This standard hold for cigarettes will not draw attention as being too negligent or too much studied.

Gentry A variation on the classic grip that conveys gravitas and authority. It need only be used momentarily to produce the desired effect.

Twee This affected hold is a quick giveaway of (i) a new smoker hoping to impress or (ii) a man who bats for the wrong side.

Comfort This ingenious hold can be used for cigarettes and cigars. The middle finger acts as a natural rest for one's heavier smokes.

Classic cigar Used by the majority of cigar smokers, this natural grip can handle anything from cigarillos to the highest of ring gauges.

Chap What this hold suffers from in functionality it makes up for in aesthetics. Note that the cigarette must not be held too close to the butt.

Bounder Apart from damaging the cigarette, this unusual hold enables any smoking ruffian to throw a punch at a moment's notice.

Stealth At a distance, this clever hold conceals a cigarette from smoking-ban vigilantes. At closer proximity the smoke may prove incriminating.

Woman's Continental women frequently use cigarettes as a fashion accessory, and this elegant hold is bound to attract a few catcalls.

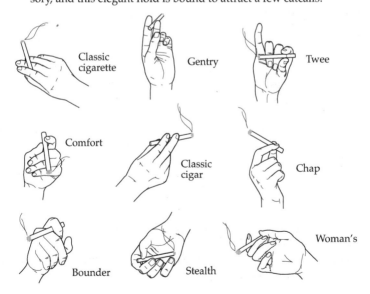

Classic cigarette

Gentry

Twee

Comfort

Classic cigar

Chap

Bounder

Stealth

Woman's

❦CIGARS

CIGAR SIZE

The first thing to consider when smoking a cigar is not the brand but the size. Size effects the intensity of flavour, prescribes the occasion and determines the duration: a typical cigarillo can be smoked in under 10 minutes, while a giant may last more than two hours. The length of a cigar is measured in inches and the diameter, or ring gauge, in 64ths of an inch. Although there is no prescription as to which cigars should be smoked by whom, it is loosely accepted that 'the ring gauge should match your age'. Thus a 24-year-old man might smoke a ⅜-inch cigarillo, a 32-year-old a ½-inch panatella and a 48-year-old a ¾-inch Churchill. The smallest cigarillos tend to have ring gauges in the low 20s, which is probably the earliest age to be seen smoking cigars.

SIZE CHART

There is a longstanding tradition of associating names with certain cigar sizes, and some names have specific meaning in the cigar industry. But there is no set convention, and some names conflict or are redundant. Below is an attempt to rationally divide the entire size range, taking into account present usage. Measurements between sizes belong to the larger size.

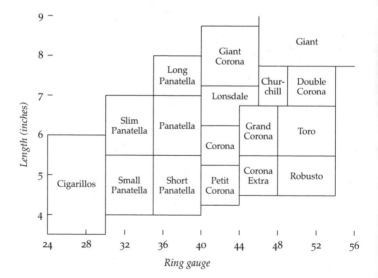

Typical dimensions of each size are as follows:

Cigarillo	4 × 26	Giant Corona	7.5 × 44
Small Panatella	5 × 32	Corona Extra	5.5 × 46
Slim Panatella	6 × 34	Grand Corona	6.5 × 46
Short Panatella	5 × 38	Robusto	5 × 50
Panatella	6 × 38	Toro	6 × 50
Long Panatella	7.5 × 38	Churchill	7 × 48
Petit Corona	5 × 42	Double Corona	7.5 × 50
Corona	5.5 × 42	Giant	8.5 × 52
Lonsdale	6.5 × 42		

CIGAR CUSTOMS

Storage Left in the open air, a cigar will dry out, making the wrapper brittle and liable to crack and the cigar itself smoke hot and fast. The best way to circumvent this is to store cigars in a humidor, which is any softwood-lined box with a wet sponge or a small pot of water inside. A cheap hygrometer, which measures humidity, is found in many commercial humidors, but this is unnecessary so long as the sponge is kept wet, or pot filled.

Grip The most common mistake of a cigar novice is to hold a cigar as if it were a cigarette – between the middle and index finger. Instead it should be held between both the middle and index fingers and the thumb (p 133).

Ash The ash on a cigar is much sturdier than the ash on a cigarette, and it is not necessary to flick it in an ashtray nearly as often. With better cigars the ash is robust enough to extend an inch or more. Knowing just when the ash is about to fall, and flicking it off beforehand, is an acquired skill.

Extinguishing Whereas a cigarette will burn continuously whether it is smoked or not, a cigar will die in several minutes when it is left unattended. For this reason it is not necessary to snub out a cigar when you have finished smoking it, which is considered inelegant; instead, leave it to die.

Removing the band There is no consensus as to whether the paper band at the base of the cigar should be removed. In general it is not necessary because a cigar is not normally smoked to the end, which has a bitter taste.

Lighting To ensure that the cigar is evenly lit, hold it at a 45-degree angle an inch above a flame while rotating it until the edge begins to smoke, and then light it in the usual way by inhaling from the flame.

❦ PIPES

The attraction to pipe smoking is not based on nicotine – like cigars, pipes are not inhaled – but association and ritual: the routine filling of the bowl; the warmth of the briar; the subconscious fascination with fire. Pipe smoke itself is more instinctively pleasant than the smoke from rolled tobacco. Cigars are typically smoked in company, pipes in solitude.

Pipes can be made from briar, meerschaum, clay, corncob or calabash (gourd). Of these, briar is by far the most popular. It is the hardened root burl of the Mediterranean heath tree. The most distinctive feature of a pipe is whether the stem is bent or straight. Bent stems are easier to hold in the mouth (they exert less torque on the teeth) while straight are presently smarter. The style of stem does not determine the shape of the bowl, which comes in many varieties. Pipe authority Richard Carleton Hacker (see Books, p 173) classifies bowls into eight types, as follows.

TYPES OF PIPE

Apple   An elegant, spherical, comparatively squat bowl.

Billiard   Classic shape; height of bowl equals length of shank.

Bulldog   A bevelled top with carved ridge and diamond-shaped stem.

Canadian   A long shank and short bit, thus more difficult to make.

Dublin   Wider at the top than base, with a flat or concave rear.

Freehand   A freeform style inspired by the individual briar stock.

Pot   The shortest and broadest of the bowls, with a rounded bottom.

Poker   A flat-bottomed, clean-cut, cylindrical bowl.

INSTRUCTIONS FOR LIGHTING A PIPE

The main skill in smoking a pipe is knowing how to fill and light it. This determines how easily the pipe draws, how long the tobacco lasts and how much dottle (ash and partially burnt tobacco) remains at the end. Bear in mind that pipes, like cigars, go out from time to time and must be relit. Here are instructions for filling and lighting:

1 Fill the bowl of the pipe until it slightly overflows by dropping in loose strands of tobacco, taking care to disentangle clumps.
2 Using a pipe tool or the head of a nail, tamp down the tobacco with light force until it has been reduced to about half its volume.

3 Again, drop loose tobacco into the bowl until it overflows.

4 Tamp the tobacco until it is just below the surface of the bowl.

5 Light the pipe, ideally with a horizontal match, and take in several short puffs of smoke. Stop and wait for the coals to die out. This is known as the charring light.

6 Tamp down once more, creating a layer of charred tobacco. This essential step ensures that the bowl of tobacco lights evenly.

7 Light the pipe a second time, as before, and continue to draw.

BREAKING IN A NEW PIPE

A well-used briar pipe will have accumulated over time a thick layer of charred soot and resin on the inside of the bowl. This coating, or cake as it is often called, is crucial to the normal function of the pipe: it insulates the wood from the heat of the burning tobacco and, like a bed of coals, stores heat, ensuring a more even burn. New pipes do not have the benefit of this protective layer, and much care should be taken when breaking them in, as smoking such a pipe too hot can burn deep into the briar. Some experts suggest applying a thin layer of honey to the inside of a new bowl, which will carbonize and encourage the development of a cake. After smoking half a dozen pipefuls, a thin cake will have emerged, which will continue to accumulate over time.

CLEANING A PIPE

Ideally, a pipe should be cleaned after every one or two smokes, although in practice it is common to move on to other pipes and then clean them all in parallel. Two things are essential for cleaning a pipe: a pipe tool and pipe cleaners. Pipe tools come in a variety of designs; a typical and inexpensive one is a folding multi-tool with a circular tamper, a spoon and a thin rod for picking. Pipe cleaners are long, thin wire brushes.

The first step in cleaning is to use the spoon to scrape out any dottle and residue from the bowl, taking care not to remove much, if any, of the insulating cake described above. Knowing just how firmly to scrape, and therefore how much of the cake to remove, is learnt with experience;

The second step is cleaning the air hole. To do so, first separate the stem from the bowl by gently twisting the stem out; this should never be done before the pipe has cooled completely, because the wood tends to expand with heat. Then fully insert a pipe cleaner into the air hole of each half. Repeat this process, each time with a new pipe cleaner, until the cleaner emerges without any residue, which may take four cleaners for the stem and six for the bowl. Soiled pipe cleaners have a tendency to make a whole room reek, so they should be immediately disposed of, ideally in a fire.

❦ S N U F F

The introduction of indoor smoking bans throughout the world is of course cause for smokers' sorrow. But even this dark cloud brings with it some cause for hope: snuff. With the exception of fire, the smokeless tobacco offers all of the attractions of smoking: the kick, the kit, the ceremony and the camaraderie. The clampdown on smoking might bring snuff use back to levels not seen since it was taken up by the 19th-century gentility and 20th-century coal miners. The motto of Wilson of Sharrow, snuff producers in England since 1737, is timely: 'Smoke when you can, snuff when you can't.'

Snuff is finely powdered tobacco leaf and stalk which is not ignited but sniffed directly into the nose. It comes in many varieties, falling roughly into three classes: natural, perfumed and medicated. Perfumed snuff is scented with the essential oils of fruits or flowers; medicated, with menthol or eucalyptus or aniseed. First-time users might have a tendency to sneeze, but this dies off with experience. Snuff is stored in a snuffbox, a small lidded container with any one of a number of (preferably airtight) closing mechanisms. While snuff boxes of some value are available, an experienced snuff taker uses a sober metal or wooden box which can be lost without regret.

There are two ways of taking snuff. The first is executed by placing a pinch of snuff in the depression on the back of the left hand, between the forefinger and outstretched thumb. From here it is sniffed into both nostrils or one nostril at a time. In the case of the latter it is helpful, if inelegant, to close the other nostril with the right hand. Note that to sniff is not to snort: unlike other powdered substances, snuff is not meant to reach the sinuses. The second technique is described in a mid-19th-century snuff pamphlet:

INSTRUCTIONS FOR TAKING SNUFF

1 Take the snuff box in the right hand.
2 Pass it to the left hand.
3 Rap the snuff box.
4 Open the box and inspect the contents.
5 Present box to surrounding company with a courteous bow.
6 Receive it back with the left hand.
7 Gather up the snuff by striking the box side with middle and forefinger.
8 Take a pinch with the right hand.
9 Hold the snuff for a second or two between fingers before taking.
10 Carry the pinch to the nose.
11 Snuff with precision by both nostrils and without grimaces or distortion of the features.
12 Close snuff box with a flourish.

COOKING

The Simpsons · Lisa: Do you have any food that wasn't brutally slaughtered? Homer: Well, I think the veal might've died of loneliness. (Faith Off, episode BABF06, 2000)

Byron · All human history attests / That happiness for man – the hungry sinner! – / Since Eve ate apples, much depends on dinner. (Don Juan, canto xiii)

National Cattlemen's Beef Association · Beef: It's what's for dinner. (American advertising campaign)

Esquire · The average woman, to this day, can't make a good cup of coffee. It must be that, basically, coffee is a man's drink. (*Esquire's Handbook for Hosts*, 1949)

Jonathan Swift · For this is every cook's opinion, / No savoury dish without an onion; / But, lest your kissing should be spoiled, / Your onions must be thoroughly boiled (Market Women's Cries)

Pink Floyd · If you don't eat your meat, you can't have any pudding. How can you have any pudding if you don't eat your meat? (*The Wall*, 1979)

Paul Erdős · A mathematician is a device for turning coffee into theorems. (Attributed; more likely by Alfréd Rényi)

Charles Pierce · The perfect lover is one who turns into a pizza at 4:00 a.m.

Gordon Ramsay · Parents of obese children should be fined. (*Daily Mail*, 2007)

Benjamin Franklin · Never spare the parson's wine, nor baker's pudding. ઢ Three good meals a day is bad living. ઢ After fish, milk do not wish. ઢ Beware of meat twice boil'd, and an old foe reconcil'd. ઢ He that would travel much should eat little. ઢ Many dishes, many diseases. (*Poor Richard's Almanack*, 1732–1757)

❦KITCHEN BASICS

A bachelor's kitchen needn't be crowded with gadgets to produce impressive dishes. The 30 most necessary utensils are listed below, which can also be used to improvise anything missing.

ESSENTIAL UTENSILS

Chopping board A large wooden chopping board is better for knives, better to look at and better at killing bacteria than plastic.

Coffee-maker There are many ways of mixing ground coffee and hot water. See p 144 for a discussion.

Colander Essential for pasta, rice and washing salad. Plastic is preferable to wire mesh, which can trap rice and some pastas in its holes.

Frying pans One non-stick and one cast iron. The latter is the traditional man's choice: it is indestructible and offers uniform heat owing to its high heat capacity. If wiped clean with little or no soap, it will build a carbonized layer which is excellent for frying on.

Kettle Putting a pot on the stove is impractical, and putting a flask in the microwave inelegant. For boiling water quickly, an electric cordless kettle is best.

Knives Three good knives is better than the usual hoard found in most kitchens: a 4-inch (10-cm) paring knife, a 6-inch (15-cm) chef's knife and a long serrated knife for cutting bread, cakes and tomatoes.

Measuring cup and spoons These invaluable devices are often overlooked. They help make cooking a science as much as an art.

Roasting pan The pan should have 2-inch (5-cm) sides.

Saucepans Ideally three, with lids: a small one for sauces and soups; a medium one for chilli; and a large one for pasta, rice and vegetables.

Spatula Its worth is only realized when you can't find one. Keep two: one plastic and one straight bamboo.

BASIC UTENSILS

bottle opener	knife sharpener	teapot
can opener	long fork	toaster
corkscrew (see p 106)	(for roasts)	vegetable brush
double boiler	meat thermometer	vegetable peeler
earthenware casserole	mixing bowls	wire whisk
funnel	peppermill	wooden spoon and
grater (four-sided)	salad bowl	fork
kitchen scissors	(wooden)	

BASIC PROVISIONS

Apart from whatever ingredients are necessary for a particular dish, a sensible chef will always have the items below in store.

Dry goods	*Perishables*	*Herbs and spices*
biscuits (cookies)	balsamic vinegar	basil
bread	butter	bay leaf
cheese biscuits	garlic	chilli powder
coffee	lemons	crushed chillis
flour	milk	cumin
nuts	mustard	curry powder
pasta	olive oil	oregano
rice	onions	paprika
sugar	Parmesan cheese	peppercorns
tea	stock cubes	salt

COOKING PRIMER

Cooking means to prepare food with heat, but there are many variations. Here is a summary.

Boiling is cooking in water at the boiling point, 100°C (212°F).

Broiling is cooking with high heat not in direct contact with the food, usually from a source above (thermal radiation).

Deep frying is frying in enough oil or fat to submerge the food.

Frying is cooking in oil or fat at a temperature over 100°C (212°F).

Grilling is cooking on a rack over an open flame or heat source whereby the food does not cook in its own juices.

Simmering is cooking in water just below boiling, 85°C–95°C (185°F–203°F).

Sautéing is frying at high heat with a small amount of oil, usually with the intention of browning it.

Steaming is cooking with the steam from water boiling but not in contact with the food.

Stewing is slow cooking at low temperature in a small amount of liquid.

❦ CARVING

Confident carving has long been an essential skill for men. Here are some guidelines from *Esquire's Handbook for Hosts* (p 174), written just after WWII.

MEAT

Meat should always be cut across the grain, the one exception to this rule being the saddle of mutton which is always carved…parallel with the fibres or grain… Ham and beef should be cut in very thin slices, and lamb, mutton and pork in fairly thick ones.

[Beef]

A round of beef, or ribs rolled, are not so easy to carve as some joints. A thin-bladed knife is recommended. First, cut a thick slice off the outside of the joint at its top, so as to leave the surface smooth, then thin and even slices should be carved.

Veal

Breast of veal consists of two parts: the rib bones and the gristly brisket. These two parts should be separated: then the rib bones may be detached separately and served.

Mutton

Leg of mutton is comparatively simple to carve. The knife should be carried sharply down and slices taken from either side, as the guests may desire. ❧ The saddle of mutton is a fine old English dish: it consists of two loins connected by the spinal bone. The meat is generally carved across the ribs in slices running parallel with the backbone and the grain of the meat, and with each portion is usually served a small piece of fat cut from the bottom of the ribs… ❧ In carving a shoulder of mutton the joint should be raised from the dish and as many slices cut away as can be managed. After this the meat lying on either side of the blade bone should be served by carving it from the knuckle end. The joint can then be turned and slices taken off along its whole length.

Pork

A leg of pork is carved as a leg of mutton: the knife should be carried sharply down to the bone right through to the crackling. A loin of pork, if it is properly prepared at the butcher's, may be divided into neat and even chops and presents no particular carving problems.

Ham

Here the carver must be guided by whether he desires to practise economy or to serve immediately from the best part. Under the first supposition, he will commence at the knuckle and cut thin slices toward the thick part of the ham. If he prefers to serve the finest part first, he will cut across and down to the bone at the centre of the ham.

Lamb

A leg or shoulder of lamb is carved as a leg or shoulder of mutton.

BIRDS

[*Turkey*]

First sink the fork at a spot a couple of inches behind the point of the breast bone with one prong on either side of the bone; there is a special place for it...and you will find it readily. Now slip the point of the knife under the far wing and make an upward cut for the joint that holds the wing to the turkey, a straight cut well towards the neck so as not to undershoot the joint. If the wing doesn't drop off, get the knife into the joint and break it if necessary. The leg or drumstick and the second joint should be removed in one piece. Make a straight cut for the joint that holds it to the turkey. Cut an inch or two above the 'Pope's nose', going as far as you can; then slip the knife behind the joint and cut to the juncture again. This should separate the whole business from the body of the fowl. Once it is off, put the fork in the second joint and cut for the juncture of the drum stick and the second joint. Now one side of the bird is stripped of its appendages and you are ready to carve the breast. Put the fork in the same position in which you originally inserted it into the bird, and lay the bird on its side, legless side up, so that the slices of breast, as you carve them, will remain in position until you lift them off. If you permit the bird to remain upright, the slices would fall off to the side and...be difficult and unappetizing to handle... Cut the slices with firm, even strokes. Slices should not be thick.

Duck

Duck or duckling is carved in a similar manner to chicken or turkey. First, the wings are removed and then the breast is either sliced or, if it be a small bird, it is removed in one piece. Next the leg and second joint are removed, divided or served in one piece if it is small.

Goose

Remember that the breast of a goose, more than that of any other bird, is most highly esteemed, and the carver may not have to give much attention to any other part, though some people find the legs excellent.

Fowl

Roast and broiled fowl (chickens, capon, etc.) are cut in a manner similar to roast turkey.

Pheasant

The choicest parts of the pheasant are the breast and the wings, as is true of most fowl. Pheasant is carved exactly as turkey.

Partridge

The usual method is to cut the bird along the top of the breast bone and divide it into two equal parts: a half partridge is a fair portion for [one].

Grouse

[This] may be carved in the same way as partridge. It is well to know that the backbone of the grouse is highly esteemed by many and considered...to possess the finest flavour.

☕COFFEE

Coffee is made from the seeds of the berries of the genus *Coffea*, a family of shrubs and small trees. The flavour of the seeds, or beans, bears little resemblance to the flavour of coffee until they are roasted, which changes the chemical structure of the seeds.

The two main types of coffee beans are *C. arabica* and *C. robusta* (also known as *C. canephora*). Arabica is the more flavourful and less bitter of the two, and consequently the more expensive. Within these two species there are many varietals, such as Colombian, Java, Jamaican blue mountain and Kopi Luwak. The last is made from beans that have been consumed by and passed through the digestive tract of the Asian palm civet, a small mammal, and is the most expensive coffee in the world.

COFFEE BREWING

Coffee is the result of the infusion of ground coffee beans in hot water. Its concentration and taste depend on the temperature of the water, how finely the coffee is ground, the amount of time the water and coffee are in contact, and the pressure at which they are mixed. How best to mix the two has been the subject of much ingenuity and invention.

The simplest way to make coffee is to mix coarse ground beans with boiling water in a jug and, after letting it stand, pour it through a handheld strainer into a cup. In principle, this can be done without a strainer because the coffee will eventually settle at the bottom of the cup; in practice this results in a somewhat grainy drink.

The cafetière, or press pot, is similar, but the strainer is built into the pot in the form of a plunging sieve. Once the grounds are saturated, the plunger is pressed down, leaving the grounds at the bottom and the coffee on top.

Alternatively, medium ground coffee may be held in a paper filter and the coffee poured over it. Because the coffee and water are in contact for a short time, only the most soluble components of the coffee will dissolve, and the taste is noticeably different from the above two methods.

The Moka Express, invented in Italy in the 1930s, is an elegant two-piece coffee maker. It takes advantage of the steam pressure which builds in the lower chamber to force water through finely ground coffee into the upper chamber. The higher pressure yields a cup in between that obtained by the filter method and a professional espresso machine.

An espresso machine is a high precision piece of equipment which forces hot water through compact, finely ground coffee at high pressure. The result is the famous espresso, a strong, distinctive coffee marked by the telltale presence of a crema, or fine golden froth.

CHEMEX COFFEE-MAKER

James Bond is a heavy coffee drinker. In Ian Fleming's *From Russia with Love*, we are given a glimpse of Bond's morning ritual. 'Breakfast was Bond's favourite meal of the day. When he was stationed in London it was always the same. It consisted of very strong coffee, from De Bry in New Oxford Street, brewed in an American *Chemex*, of which he drank two large cups, black and without sugar.' De Bry is no longer in business, but the Chemex coffee-maker can still be obtained. It is the simplest and most elegant way to make coffee.

The Chemex (www.chemexcoffeemaker.com) was invented by German-born American Peter Schlumbohm in 1941. It has no moving parts, but consists only of a heat-resistant glass vessel with an hourglass shape. A filter is placed in the upper half, where the coffee brews before passing to the lower half. It was voted one of the 100 best industrial designs of modern times and is on permanent display at the Museum of Modern Art in New York.

CAFFEINE CONTENTS

Coffee is one of the best sources of caffeine, the natural stimulant found in the seeds and leaves of a number of trees and shrubs. The typical caffeine contents of various substances are shown below. The amount of caffeine in coffee and tea depends significantly on bean and leaf variety, production and preparation. Note that the serving sizes used below are 250 ml (0.44 pints) or 40 g (1.4 ounces); in practice this can vary considerably.

Average daily UK intake (mg caffeine)	280
Caffeine tablets	*mg caff./pill*
Vivarin	200
Stay Alert gum	100
No Doz	100
Pro Plus	50
Soft drinks	*mg caff./250 ml*
Red Bull	82.5
Jolt Cola	50.0
Mountain Dew	39.1
Diet Coke	32.8
Dr Pepper	29.6
Pepsi-Cola	26.4
Diet Pepsi-Cola	25.4
Coca-Cola	24.0

Lethal dose for 50% of people (mg caffeine)	10,000
Coffee and tea	*mg caff./250 ml*
Coffee, brewed (typical)	140
Coffee, instant (typical)	100
Tea, black (typical)	85
Tea, fruit (Pickwick)	80
Tea, green (typical)	60
Coffee, decaffeinated (typical)	5
Chocolate	*mg caff./40 g*
Unsweetened choc. (typical)	35
Hershey's Special Dark	29.2
Semi-sweet choc. (typical)	25
Milk chocolate (typical)	10
Hershey's Bar	9.4
Kit Kat	5.7

❦BREAKFAST

There are few things more rousing in the morning than a cooked breakfast. The cheerless, so-called Continental breakfast – coffee diluted with milk and a croissant – is unlikely to summon you from slumber. Fruit is for women, cereal for children; a working man needs a hearty meal to start the day.

FULL ENGLISH BREAKFAST

'To eat well in England', noted W. Somerset Maugham, 'you should have a breakfast three times a day.' The most splendid cooked breakfast is the full English, which is made up of most of the following:

eggs	black pudding	fried potatoes
toast	grilled tomatoes	pancakes
bacon	fried mushrooms	coffee (p 144)
sausage	baked beans	orange juice

While it may not be practical to prepare a full breakfast every day, with some practice you will be able to rustle up bacon and eggs without thinking. Here are some essential recipes which should help you rise and shine.

SCRAMBLED EGGS JAMES BOND

In the Ian Fleming short story '007 in New York', included in more recent editions of *Octopussy and The Living Daylights* (Books, p 182), we learn the recipe of Bond's favourite meal – breakfast:

> He would have one more dry martini at the table, then smoked salmon and the particular scrambled eggs he had once (Felix Leiter knew the head-waiter) instructed them how to make.
>
> For four individualists:
> 12 fresh eggs   Salt and pepper   5–6 ounces fresh butter
> Break the eggs into a bowl. Beat thoroughly with a fork and season well. In a small copper (or heavy-bottomed saucepan) melt 4 ounces butter. When melted, pour in the eggs and cook over a very low heat, whisking continuously with a small egg whisk. While the eggs are slightly more moist than you would wish for eating, remove the pan from heat, add the rest of the butter and continue whisking for half a minute, adding the while finely chopped chives or fines herbes. Serve on hot buttered toast in individual copper dishes (for appearance only) with pink champagne (Taittinger) and low music.

ESQUIRE OMELETTE

The most elegant way of preparing eggs is to make an omelette. *Esquire's Handbook for Hosts* (Books, p 174) offers these instructions for making a perfect specimen. Just before folding you may add your favourite filling.

Crack into a bowl two eggs (for each person) and season them with a pinch of salt and a half pinch of pepper. Beat it unmercifully for five minutes, until the whites and yolks are completely mixed; the more the eggs are beaten, the lighter the omelet will be; and beat it with a silver fork. Do not use fancy kitchen utensils like an egg beater unless you are callous to the contempt of professional chefs.

Take a frying pan and put into it a teaspoonful of best olive oil; do not use butter as it might burn. Heat the oil in the pan until it becomes terribly hot on the brisk flame. When the oil starts to smoke, fume and crackle, pour the eggs into the pan and agitate them gently for no longer than forty to fifty seconds; never dry them out by leaving them longer on the range, as a dried-out or burned omelet in uneatable. Now remove the pan to a somewhat less hot spot on the range and fold the omelet with your fork – the side nearest the handle first – into a half-moon shape. Smear a bit of butter over it; take the handle of the pan in your right hand, a hot plate with a napkin underneath it in your left and with a rapid movement turn the pan right over the center of the plate. If you have done all this properly you may crow like a cock: 'Ko-ko-ri-ko!' for that is how the French chefs greet a perfect omelet when it is ready. But do not forget that efficiency and quickness count above all, and that an omelet must always be made to order; it is better that the man wait rather than eggs.

MAKING BACON

Bacon is pork that has been cured (immersed in water mixed with salt and other preservatives), originally practised as a means of preservation. There are two main kinds, called back bacon and streaky bacon in British English, or Canadian bacon and bacon in US English. Streaky bacon contains much more fat than back bacon, and is recognizable by its marbled texture.

The best way to cook bacon, particularly the streaky sort, is over low heat for 30 minutes or more, whether it be by frying, baking or grilling. This is the only way to reduce the fat without burning the meat, and it also improves the flavour. It takes longer, of course, but the bacon does not need much attention while it cooks. A thorough investigation into the different ways of cooking bacon, including frying, microwaving, broiling, grilling and slow baking, and the results of each, can be found at www.cookingforengineers.com (Websites, p 177).

❦CHILLI

Chilli is the archetypal male dish. It is easy to make, mostly red meat and served from a single pot, from which it can in principle be eaten. It is not necessary to have fine ingredients to prepare an excellent specimen. It usually divides the sexes, men finding it addictive and women unremarkable.

DEFINITION OF CHILLI

The best definition of chilli con carne (spelled 'chili' in America) is a literal translation of its Spanish name: peppers with meat. These are the chief and essential ingredients. Chilli originated in the American southwest (but not what is now Mexico) as a simple, palatable preparation of staple foods. Early 19th-century recipes called for beef and suet and as much again chilli peppers, onions and garlic – alas, no tomatoes, which could not always be obtained. The inclusion of beans is particularly contentious. The International Chili Society defines chilli as any kind of meat or combination of meats, cooked with chilli peppers, spices and other ingredients, with the exception of beans and pasta, which are forbidden. This definition regulates its annual cook-off – the largest chilli, and indeed food, competition in the world.

CHILLI PEPPERS

Chilli peppers, sometimes called chillies or peppers, are the fruit of the genus *Capsicum,* which contains many species that are used as a spice or food. Characteristic of chillies is their piquancy (hot taste). This is caused by a substance called capsaicin: an irritant in the form of a single molecule which produces a burning sensation when brought in contact with the mucous membranes.

The piquancy of a chilli pepper grows in proportion to the amount of capsaicin present. It can be quantified by the Scoville scale, which measures the factor by which a liquid extract of chilli must be diluted until it can no longer be detected. For example, a pepper with a rating of 1,000 must be diluted 1 part chilli in 1,000 parts water to be undetectable. A bell pepper, which contains no capsaicin, registers zero, whereas pure capsaicin registers 16 million Scoville units. More Scoville ratings are given opposite.

An alternative and less cumbersome system for measuring heat uses a scale of 1 to 24. It is the base-2 logarithm of the Scoville rating (see Beauty, p 34); adding 1 to the scale corresponds to a two-fold increase in piquancy. The units of this scale are called logarithmic Scoville units, or LSU for short. The minimum rating is 1 LSU for a bell pepper and the maximum is 24 LSU for pure capsaicin, with other chillies falling in between.

CHILLI PEPPER SCOVILLE RATINGS

Chilli or compound	Scoville units	LSU
Pure capsaicin	15,000,000–16,000,000	23.8–23.9
Pepper spray (self-defence)	2,000,000–5,000,000	20.9–22.2
Naga Jolokia (hottest known pepper)	860,000–1,000,000	19.7–19.9
Scotch Bonnet	100,000–320,000	16.6–18.3
Cayenne pepper	30,000–50,000	14.8–15.6
Tabasco sauce	2,500–5,000	11.3–12.3
Anaheim pepper	500–2,000	9.0–11.0
Bell pepper	0	0

JOE COOPER'S CHILLI

4 tbsp olive oil
3 lb cubed lean beef
1 quart (0.9 litres) water
2 bay leaves
6 tbsp chilli powder
10 cloves chopped garlic
3 tbsp paprika

1 tbsp salt
1 tbsp sugar
1 tsp ground cumin
1 tsp oregano or marjoram
1 tsp red pepper
½ tsp black pepper
flour or cornmeal

Serves 6–8. Method: Sear meat in oil over a high heat. Add water and bay leaves, and simmer. Remove bay leaves; add all but the last ingredient and simmer again. Add flour or cornmeal to taste. (Joe Cooper is the author of the famous book on chilli, *With or Without Beans*; see Books, p 174.)

MAN'S CHILLI

1 lb cubed lean beef
3 tsp olive oil
¼ tsp salt
½ tsp black pepper
2 chopped chilli peppers
1 small chopped onion
4 cloves chopped garlic
½ tin chopped tomatoes

1½ tbsp chilli powder
2 tsp ground cumin
1 tsp paprika
1 tsp sugar
½ tsp cayenne pepper
½ tsp oregano
1 beef stock cube
1 tin red kidney beans

Serves 2. Method: Fry beef in 1 tsp oil over high heat. Add salt and black pepper. Fry chilli peppers, onion and garlic separately in 2 tsp oil. Combine with remaining ingredients except beans in saucepan and simmer for at least an hour, adding water to taste. Add beans 30 minutes before serving.

❦ S T E A K

The best steak is served rare or medium-rare. For some men this is an acquired taste, due as much to squeamishness as to anything else. It is a taste worth acquiring, however, and the best way to do so is to cook or order your steak one degree rarer than you would normally have it (medium instead of medium-well, for example). You will soon become used to this, and much the happier for it, and you may wish to repeat the process.

HOW TO COOK A STEAK

Although many men assume grilling is the best way to prepare steak, the very best method is frying. The ideal frying pan is a heavy cast iron one, for two reasons. Because the thick iron base stores a lot of heat, it will stay hot during the initial period of contact with the steak. Second, pans with nonstick coatings are liable to be damaged at the high temperature required to cook a steak. Good steak (T-bone, sirloin, rib eye), correctly cooked, should speak for itself. The seasoning should be simple: salt, pepper and olive oil are the only necessary ingredients. Only pepper should be put on the steak before cooking it; salt is best added afterwards because it draws out the juices from uncooked meat via osmosis (this is the basis of salt-curing).

Heat the pan at the highest possible setting; a gas stove is preferable to an electric one because it gets hotter. First let the pan warm up for a few minutes, then add a small amount of olive oil – only a teaspoonful (4 ml). Let the pan continue to heat until the oil begins to smoke, taking care not to let it catch fire. At this point drop the room-temperature steak on to the pan so that it lands flat. It will make an awful noise and splatter so be sure to wear a cook's apron. The steak will immediately stick to the pan, which is what you want; do not agitate it in any way. Leave it there for 1½–4 minutes (more precise times are described below), then pull it off from both sides with an upward motion and turn it over. (Scraping it off with a spatula is likely to break the thin crust which keeps the juices of the steak from escaping.) Leave it to cook on the second side for the same amount of time, adding salt to the cooked side.

When the time is up pull the steak off again and place it on a plate with the cooler side down, salting the second side. Cover it loosely with foil and let it sit for 4 minutes before eating it. It is during this essential period that the inner and outer juices equilibrate. The resulting steak will appear more cooked by one degree than it would have had you cut straight into it.

The amount of time to cook each side depends on how done it should be. For a 1-inch (2.5 cm) thick steak, cook it approximately 1½–2 minutes per side for rare, 3 for medium and 4 for well done. These times will vary with the cut of meat and pan temperature and should be adjusted accordingly.

IDLING

Idleness: want of occupation; habitual indolence (*Oxford English Dictionary*)

Samuel Johnson · Every man is, or hopes to be, an Idler. (*The Idler*, 1758–1760)

Honoré de Balzac · In order to be fashionable, one must enjoy rest without having experienced work... Like steam engines, men regimented by work all look alike... The man instrument is a social zero.

Raymond Chandler · [Poker is] as elaborate a waste of human intelligence as you could find outside an advertising agency.

Ian Fleming · The scent and smoke and sweat of a casino are nauseating at three in the morning. (First sentence, *Casino Royale*, 1953)

Anonymous · You don't have to be a beer drinker to play darts, but it helps.

Izaak Walton · I love such mirth as does not make friends ashamed to look upon one another next morning. (*The Compleat Angler*, 1653)

Tom Hodgkinson · Characteristic of the idler's work is that it looks suspiciously like play. (*The Idler*, 1993–2007)

Samuel Johnson · The Idler, who habituates himself to be satisfied with what he can most easily obtain, not only escapes labours which are often fruitless, but sometimes succeeds better than those who despise all that is within their reach and think every thing more valuable as it is harder to be acquired. (*The Idler*, 1758–1760)

Benjamin Franklin · It is not lesiure that is not used. ❧ The busy man has few idle visitors; to the boiling pot the flies come not. ❧ A life of leisure and a life of laziness are two things. (*Poor Richard's Almanack*, 1732–1757)

❦DRINKING GAMES

While drinking games are an aid to quaffing quickly, the object of most games is to *avoid* getting drunk, at least relative to other players. Here is a collection of popular and elegant games. Penalties are either buying a round or drinking, the latter of which can take three forms:

A drink Reduce the contents of your glass by two fingers' width;
A glass Imbibe a standard serving (see p 122);
Emptying a glass Any leftover drink must drip, not pour, from the glass.

Pennies in a pitcher

This simple game allows considerable psychological and strategic play. Everyone sits in a circle, and a pitcher or large glass (at least 2 pints) of beer is passed round clockwise. Each time a person receives the pitcher, he must drink from it. The person to the right of the one who empties the contents must buy the next round. The strategy is bistable: if the glass if near-full, it is advantageous to drink only a small amount, and pass; whereas if it is near-empty, it is best to finish it. Alternatively, the game can be turned into a betting game. Each time someone drinks from the pitcher, he must add a fixed amount of money to a pot. Whoever finishes the pitcher collects the money.

Six shooter

This simple game (a.k.a. Six pack) is fast paced and cannot be kept up for long. It is played with a die and six shot or beer glasses, numbered one through to six. To start, all six glasses are filled half-way. A player rolls the die, and if the corresponding glass is not empty, he must drink its contents and roll again. If it is empty, he fills it with as much spirit or beer as he wishes, and play continues to his left. The last one standing is the winner.

Drop the dime

Secure a napkin over a wide-mouthed glass with tape or a rubber band, and place a penny or other small coin on the centre top. Each person in turn touches a lit cigarette to the napkin, burning away a small piece of it. Whoever causes the coin to drop through the napkin must drink a glass. With a little practice, an intricate web supporting the coin will emerge.

I've never…

Each person announces in turn something that he has never done: for example, 'I've never used an electric razor' or 'I've never been dumped by a girlfriend.' Everyone who *has* used an electric razor or been dumped stands and drinks from his glass. Clearly, it is advantageous to announce one's rarer omissions, thereby maximizing the number of others who have to drink.

The name game

In this simple game of word association (a.k.a. Drink while you think) everyone sits round a table with a glass of beer. Someone begins with a well-known name. The person to his left must immediately begin drinking until he thinks of a name in which the first name begins with the same letter as the previous last name. If a player finishes his glass, he does not answer but refills it and play continues to his left. The ubiquity of questionable names can be voted on. For example, the game might go as follows: Ian Fleming → Fred Astaire → Arnold Schwarzenegger → Sean Connery.

Boat race

Named after the annual Oxford and Cambridge rowing competition, this classic game is played at universities throughout the world. It is a beer-drinking relay race in which two or more equal-sized teams compete. Sitting along a table, each team member has before him a glass of beer. Players are not allowed to touch their glasses before their turn. The game begins with the first member of each team emptying his glass. On placing it back on the table, the next in line begins to drink his. The first team to finish wins.

Quarters

This game has a large following, especially in the US. The goal is to throw a medium-sized coin (a UK 10 pence piece, 0.50 euros piece or US quarter) so it bounces off a hard table into a specified glass. An old-fashioned drinking glass can be used for beginners; a shot glass for more seasoned players. If the attempt fails, the coin is passed clockwise; if the attempt succeeds, the thrower chooses who must drink the next drink and throws again.

Master of thumbs

This game can be played in the background of others. One person is chosen to be Master of Thumbs. Every time he places his thumb on the edge of the table, everyone else must too. The last to do so must empty his glass, and becomes the new Master. To discourage cheats, anyone who has his thumb on the table when the Master does not must also finish his glass.

Shot-glass chess

The king of games is played with 32 shot glasses as per standard chess rules. Each time a piece is lost, the loser must drink what it contains. Shot glass sets are commercially available with the requisite six types of glasses. Alternatively, if there are two different types of glasses at hand, one for each player, the identity of a piece can be set by the drink it contains:

King:	whisky	Rook:	Benedictine	Knight:	red wine
Queen:	vodka	Bishop:	Chartreuse	Pawn:	beer

❦DASTARD'S TRICKS

These tricks are dirty, but none of them relies on sleight of hand. They should enable any man to win a few honest drinks a week.

Lift three matches

Put three matches on the table and bet your friend that you can lift all three with a fourth. To do so, assemble the matches into a tripod formation, with the flammable tips touching, as shown. Use the fourth match to ignite the tripod, blow both out and lift the three fused matches with the fourth.

Guess a number

Tell your friend to 'pick a random digit', and have him write it down. On a separate piece of paper, write the numbers 3, 5 and 7. Now bet him even money that his number is one of your three. If your friend chose his number randomly, he would win 70% of the time. But people don't choose random numbers; they pick numbers they *think* are random. The distribution of choices is shown below, taken from 1,770 participants (M. Kubovy and J. Psotka, *J. of Exp. Psychology: Human Perception and Performance,* **2**, 291 (1976)). The numbers 3, 5 and 7 are chosen 54% of the time, which is about the probability with which you should win the bet – a 17% return on investment.

0	1	2	3	4	5	6	7	8	9
1%	3%	6%	14%	9%	13%	11%	27%	12%	4%

Snaps is the name of the game

This excellent party trick is used to telepathically transmit a message from one person (the sender) to another (the receiver). Someone in the party tells all but the receiver a well-known person, place or thing. The sender begins by saying: 'Snaps is the name of the game'. The word is 'sent' to the receiver apparently by a mysterious sequence of finger snaps, but really by spelling it out, according to the following code: consonants are the first letter of every phrase said by the sender; and vowels correspond in rank to the number of snaps of the fingers: 'a' = one snap; 'e' = two snaps; 'i' = three snaps; and so on. If the sender wishes instead to spell out the second word of the message, he begins with: 'Snaps is the name of the game, OK?' For example, if the message is William Shakespeare, the game might go as follows: 'Snaps is the name of the game, OK? – Silence, please. – Here we go. – [Snap] – Keep thinking. – [Snap Snap] – Sooner rather than later!' By this point the receiver has likely guessed the message.

Hold a lit cigarette by its ends

Without being noticed, press your thumb against an ice-cold glass for 30 seconds. While doing so, bet your friend that you can hold a lit cigarette length-wise between two fingers. The trick is to hold it be-tween thumb and forefinger with the lit end against the thumb. You won't feel a thing, or burn your thumb, for a few seconds.

Guess anyone's phone number

For this trick you need a phone book of at least 900 pages. Have your friend pick a secret three-digit number, reverse the digits, and take the difference between the two. For example, 123 reversed is 321, and the difference be-tween them is 198. Now ask him to turn to the same page of the phone book as the number he arrived at, go to the fifth entry, and read off the first ini-tial of the surname. Little does your friend know that the above manipula-tion of his number can only result in one of ten numbers: 0 (in this case you must start over), 99, 198, 297, 396, 495, 594, 693, 792 and 891. You simply need to memorize – or write on a small card – the nine initials from the nine pages (they will all be different) and their phone numbers.

Lift a glass from above

Bet your friend that you can lift a shot glass without touching its bottom or sides. To do so, light a glassful of spirits or liqueur (at least 40% ABV) with a lighter and extinguish it by placing your wet palm directly on top of it. If done quickly the flame will extinguish at once and the cooling gas will cre-ate a partial vacuum, affixing the glass to your palm without pain.

Non-transitive dice

Consider the four unusual dice below, sometimes called Efron's dice. With a friend, play the following simple game: your friend picks a die and throws it, then you pick one of the remaining die and throw it, and the high-est number wins. Which die should your friend throw? The answer is it doesn't matter which die he chooses. You should always choose the die shown to the left of his (below); if he chooses the left-most die, then you should choose the right-most die. In every case you will win with prob-ability two-thirds. These dice are called non-transitive because, even though die A beats die B, B beats C and C beats D, die D nevertheless beats die A.

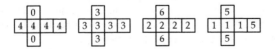

❦SUPERLATIVES

Best advice	Never apologize [1]
Best age of your bride at marriage	½ your age + 7 (p 41)
Best American fashion influence	Blue jeans (p 50); penny loafer [2]
Best beer	Westvleteren 12
Best Bond novel (film)	*From Russia with Love* (*Goldfinger*)
Best book on men's clothes	Hardy Amies, *The Englishman's Suit*
Best bottle to take to a drinks party	Whisky and a candle [3]
Best (and worst) buttonhole flower	Carnation [4]
Best cigar	Trinidad Fundadore [5]
Best cigarettes to be seen smoking	Silk Cut; Marlboro Red
Best cloth	Vicuna, from the coat of the wild South American camelid
Best cocktail	Caipirinha (p 120)
Least-documented common male ailment	Blue balls (p 13)
Hottest curry	Phal, generally available if not always on the menu
Second-best dandy	Count d'Orsay [6]
Worst drink to order in a pub	Half-pint [7]
Best drinking accessory	Curved metal hip flask for the breast pocket
Best drinking game	Shot-glass chess (p 153)
Best endurance sport	Tour de France; Iditarod Sled Dog Race
Best guns	Holland & Holland (shotguns); Purdey (rifles)
Best hat(ter)	Boater; Bowler (James Lock & Co., London)
Best jeans for men	Levi's; Diesel
Best liqueur	Green Chartreuse (p 122)
Best male fashion eras	The late Plantagenet, Regency and 1950s Edwardian revival periods [8]
Best men's film	*Deliverance* (1972)
Most naff fashion item (accessory)	sleeveless T-shirt (white silk scarf)
Best regiment	22nd SAS Regiment [9]
Best second club	The Garrick [10]
Best shirtmakers	Turnbull & Asser (UK); Charvet (France)
Best shoemakers	Lobb; G. J. Cleverley
Best smoking accessory	Parabolic mirror solar cigarette lighter
Strongest spirit (commercially available)	Everclear [11]
Best sports biography	*Arnold: The Education of a Bodybuilder* (p 174)
Best tailors	Anderson & Sheppard; Huntsman & Sons; Henry Poole & Co.; Kilgour, French & Stanbury
Best tie	Seven-fold tie, made from a single piece of silk with no lining
Best tie knot	Nicky (p. 64) [12]
Best way to give up smoking	Take up snuff (p 138)
Best overall whisky distillery	Highland Park (p 115)

SELECTED NOTES

1 'It is a good rule in life never to apologise. The right sort of people do not want apologies, and the wrong sort take a mean advantage of them', writes the British author P. G. Wodehouse.

2 Soon after loafers became fashionable in the 1930s and 40s, copper pennies were inserted into the strap across the vamp. Swells prefer to use 1943 wartime steel pennies, issued when copper was scarce.

3 Between refills, force the lighted candle into the bottle. No one expects a vessel with a candle in it to contain anything drinkable.

4 'Best', argues fashion writer John Taylor, 'because its calyx (the cup beneath the bloom from which the petals grow out) is bulky enough to be held firmly in place by the best buttonhole – which should be between 1 inch and 1⅛ inches long.'

5 Although the Trinidad has been privately produced by the El Laguito factory in Havana, Cuba, for many years as gifts of state, it became commercially available in limited quantities in 1998. It was made in a single size only, the Fundadore at 7½ inches × ring gauge 39, until 2003 when the Reyes, Coloniales and Robusto Extra sizes were introduced.

6 The best, of course, was Beau Brummell, who turned men's dress away from finery and extravagance to understatement, restraint and studied indifference, now so ingrained in masculine costume.

7 Despite being standard issue in France, ordering a half-pint is suspect in Britain and other countries. Order a pint or go home.

8 Not, as many argue, the 1930s, during which men's and women's fashion de-emphasized sex. The eras opposite 'idealized the "natural" but virile shape – emphasizing masculinity with shoulder focus and hose, breeches or trousers which revealed the shape of the leg', writes Taylor.

9 Generally considered the most elite special force in the world. The now-famous SAS mission to find Iraqi Scud missile launchers in 1991 was recounted in Andy McNab's addictive book *Bravo Two Zero*.

10 Not the same as the second-best club. A man's second club, given that he belongs to one of the smart Regency gentlemen's clubs (and the best club is indisputably White's), should be spirited, garrulous and collegiate, and the best of these is the Garrick.

11 Everclear is nearly pure grain alcohol, or ethanol, which comes in two strengths: 151 proof (75.5% ABV) and 190 proof (95% ABV). The latter is very flammable.

12 A symmetric knot, in between the four-in-hand and half-Windsor in size. The earliest-known description of the Nicky is by Italian tie-shop owner Ernesto Curami. It was rediscovered by David Kelsall as an improvement on the Pratt knot and reported in the *Sunday Telegraph* in 1991.

❦ C O N K E R S

The traditional game of conkers is played using the nuts of the common horse-chestnut tree (*Aesculus hippocastanum*). A hole is drilled through the centre of the conker and a thick string or shoelace is threaded through it with a stopping knot tied at the end to retain the nut. Conkers left to dry for a year are harder than freshly fallen ones, though the latter can be hardened by baking them in the oven for several hours.

Players take turns swiping each other's conker, and continue until one of the conkers is sufficiently wrecked to fall off the string. The score associated with a conker is reckoned as follows. Every conker starts off with a score of zero. A conker gains a point for every win, plus the score of every conker it defeats: for example, if a conker with a score of two beats a conker with a score of four, the winning conker's new score is seven, one for winning and four for inheriting the points of the defeated. Thus if 100 new conkers were fought until only one remained, it would have a score of 99, a point for every defeated conker. A conker with a score of n is called an n-er, apart from $n = 0$, in which case the conker is called a none-er.

WORLD CONKER CHAMPIONSHIP RULES

The World Conker Championships are held in Ashton, England, on the second Sunday in October. The official rules (edited for clarity) are as follows:

> The game begins with a coin toss; the winner may elect to strike or receive.
> The length of string between knuckle and nut must be at least 8 inches.
> Each player is allowed three attempted strikes before swapping positions.
> An attempt must be aimed at the nut; deliberate mis-hits are not allowed.
> The game continues until one of the conkers is smashed.
> A small piece of nut or skin shall be judged out. To remain in competition, a conker must be substantial enough to mount an attack.
> If both nuts smash at the same time then the match shall be replayed with new conkers.
> Any nut knocked from the lace but not smashed may be rethreaded and the game continued.
> A player causing a knotting of the laces (a snag) will be noted. Three snags will lead to disqualification.
> If a game lasts five minutes, then play is halted and the 'five-minute rule' comes into effect: Each player is allowed nine further attempted strikes at the opponent's nut, again alternating three attempts each. If neither conker has been smashed by the end, then the player with the most strikes during this period is judged the winner.

PROPERTIES OF AN N-ER

Unlike in most sports, all conkers are undefeated. To lose is to be destroyed. A conker's score tells us something about its strength, although it also leaves room for surprises. Lurking behind a none-er could be a future champion. Alternatively, a 10-er could be a weak nut in disguise, having defeated a series of easy competitors. In general, conkers with higher scores will be stronger and rarer. But just how strong is an *n*-er, and how many of them are about? How many more conkers is an *n*-er likely to defeat?

Below is a table of statistics for *n*-ers.[1] The proportion is the percentage of conkers with a given score at any one time: half of all conkers are none-ers, $\frac{1}{8}$ are 1-ers, $\frac{1}{16}$ are 2-ers, $\frac{5}{128}$ are 3-ers and so on. The median strength measures the hardness of a conker, where 0 is the weakest and 1 the hardest. It is the fraction of random conkers (none-ers) that the median *n*-er could beat. The life expectancy indicates, on average, the score that the median *n*-er will go on to achieve before being beaten, assuming it only plays none-ers. It is about 2.44 × *n*.

N-ER STATISTICS

Score	Proportion	Strength	Life expect.	Score	Proportion	Strength	Life expect.
none-er	50%	0.500	1.0-er	10-er	0.80%	0.939	25.4-er
1-er	12.5%	0.707	3.4-er	20-er	0.30%	0.968	49.8-er
2-er	6.25%	0.794	5.8-er	30-er	0.16%	0.978	74.2-er
3-er	3.91%	0.841	8.3-er	40-er	0.11%	0.983	98.6-er
4-er	2.73%	0.870	10.7-er	50-er	0.08%	0.986	123-er
5-er	2.05%	0.891	13.2-er	60-er	0.06%	0.989	148-er
6-er	1.61%	0.906	15.6-er	70-er	0.05%	0.990	172-er
7-er	1.31%	0.917	18.0-er	80-er	0.04%	0.991	196-er
8-er	1.09%	0.926	20.5-er	90-er	0.03%	0.992	221-er
9-er	0.93%	0.933	22.9-er	100-er	0.03%	0.993	245-er

[1]These *n*-er statistics can be mathematically derived or simulated by considering an imaginary playground of some large number *M* of conkers. All conkers are assigned a random strength between 0 and 1 and start as none-ers. Two randomly chosen conkers are played against each other and the harder conker wins; we do not take into account here differences in skill. The winner's score increases in the usual way and the loser is replaced by a new none-er. Thus the total number of conkers is always *M*. More information on the theory of conkers can be found at the author's homepage (see Colophon, p 213).

❦ D A R T S

While regional variations of the game of darts were played in England during the 19th century, the game as we know it was created in 1896 when Brian Gamlin arranged the 20 numbers around the board as shown below.

RULES

In the standard game of darts, players take turns throwing three darts in an effort to reduce an initial score – usually 301 or 501 or 701 or 1001 – to zero. Scoring is as follows. All wedges are face value, apart from the double and triple regions, which are two and three times face value. The bull is 50 and the outer bull ('the 25') is 25. No points are awarded for darts landing outside the double ring or bouncing off the wire. The last dart thrown must land in the double ring or bull and bring the score to exactly zero; this is called checking out. How long a game lasts greatly depends on the skill of the players. In principle, 501 can be reached with nine darts: seven triple-20s, triple-19 and double-12, among many other nine-dart combinations.

Checking out is one of the most strategic parts of the game. The maximum score with which the game can be won with three darts is 170: two triple-20s and a bull. It can be won with all scores below this except 159, 162, 163, 165, 166, 168 and 169. Sometimes it is more important when checking out to hit an even or odd wedge than a specific value. Even-rich regions are 18-4, 6-10, 16-8; odd rich-are 17-3-19-7.

SET-UP

The centre of the bull should be 5 feet 8 inches off the ground. The oche, a raised ridge beyond which a player cannot step but can lean, is parallel to the face of the board and is 7 feet 9¼ inches from a plumb line dropped from it.

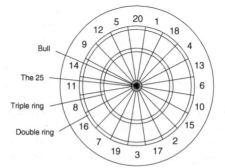

BEST PLACES TO AIM

The distribution of the numbers 1–20 around the board is far from random. They are strategically placed such that the advantage of high numbers is offset by low-number neighbours; this penalizes inaccurate throwing. One way of measuring the difficulty of an ordering is to add up the differences between consecutive numbers around the board. By this reckoning, the most difficult ordering of the numbers yields a total of differences of 200. Gamlin's ordering is near perfect: the differences add up to 198.

While the very best players can always hit a given wedge, the aim for beginners and amateurs is less predictable. Therefore they should seek the most points-rich regions on the board. The location of these regions depends on just how bad a player's aim is. The table below shows the average face value for darts thrown with increasingly large spreads. The bold numbers are the face values of the wedges. A spread of zero means that you can hit a given wedge; a spread of one means that, if you aim for the wire between two numbers, you will hit one of them; a spread of two means that you can hit a wedge or one of its two nearest neighbours; and so on.

What are the best parts of the board to aim at? Overall, the left side is more generous than the right, with 19-7-16 and 11-14-9 especially valuable. Consult the table below for more detailed hot and cool spots*.

AVERAGE SCORE FOR A SINGLE DART

Spread					Right half of board					
0	**20**	**1**	**18**	**4**	**13**	**6**	**10**	**15**	**2**	**17**
1		10.5	9.5	11.0	8.5	9.5	8.0	12.5	8.5	9.5	10.0
2	11.5	10.0	10.2	9.8	9.0	8.8	10.2	10.5	9.0	9.8
3		10.8	10.1	10.0	9.4	8.9	9.5	10.4	9.8	9.4	10.1
4	10.9	10.4	10.1	9.7	9.1	9.2	9.9	10.1	9.6	9.8

Spread					Left half of board					
0	**3**	**19**	**7**	**16**	**8**	**11**	**14**	**9**	**12**	**5**
1		11.0	13.0	11.5	12.0	9.5	12.5	11.5	10.5	8.5	12.5
2	10.5	12.0	12.2	11.8	10.8	11.0	12.0	11.0	9.5	10.5
3		11.2	12.1	12.0	11.2	10.9	11.5	11.5	10.2	10.0	11.0
4	10.7	11.7	12.1	11.6	11.1	11.2	11.5	10.9	10.1	10.5

*The expected point scores here are not uniform but weighted averages, biased towards the number or wire aimed for. For spread 1, the weights are ½ and ½; for spread 2, ¼, ¾ and ¼; for spread 3, ⅛, ⅜, ⅜ and ⅛. In general, if the spread is *s*, the denominator is 2^s and the numerators are the binomial coefficients.

♣ P O K E R

The rules for poker are not complicated, but the game allows for considerable strategic and psychological play. Texas Hold'em poker is by far the most popular version. It is the most common form of poker in American casinos and is the main event at the World Series of Poker.

TEXAS HOLD'EM RULES

The game is played with a standard 52-card pack, and aces counting high, by two or more players. Eventually two private (called hole) cards and five public (called community) cards will have been dealt, and the object of the game is to form the highest hand using any combination of one's two hole cards and the five community cards.

The dealer (whether he actually deals or not) is marked by a disc. Before any cards are dealt, the person to the left of the dealer contributes to the pot the small blind (usually half the minimum bet) and the person to the left of him contributes to the pot the big blind (usually the minimum bet). Each person is dealt two hole cards, face down. The first round of betting begins with the player to the left of the two blinds, and rotates clockwise until it returns to the dealer. At his turn a player may do one of the following:

Call make a bet equal to the most recent bet in the round;
Raise bet more than the most recent bet in the round; or
Fold quit the game, forfeiting any chips he may have bet.

After the first round of betting, players have four options: in addition to call, raise and fold, a player can now 'check', which means to remain in the game but bet no money, so long as no one before him in the rbound has made a bet. Three more betting rounds follow (henceforth beginning with the player to the dealer's left), each after more community cards are dealt. These three dealings are known as the:

Flop first three community cards, dealt before the second round of betting;
Turn fourth community card, dealt before the third round of betting;
River fifth community card, dealt before the fourth round of betting.

If during any round of betting all but one player have folded, the remaining player wins the pot but needs not show his hole cards. If after the fourth and final round of betting two or more players remain, they enter a showdown. Here the players turn their two hole cards face up, and the player with the highest hand formed by any combination of his two hole and the five community cards wins the pot. If two players have the same hand, then the player with the highest hole card not forming part of his hand (the kicker) wins. If there are no kickers (both players' hole cards are part of their winning hands) or the kickers are the same, the pot is divided equally between them. The next round begins with the dealer disc passed clockwise by one player.

ORDER OF HANDS

Given a 52-card deck, there are 2,598,960 distinct five-card hands possible. The order of hands (which are never broken by suit) is as follows:

Hand	Definition	Example	No.	Prob.(%)
Royal flush	10–A, same suit	10◇ J◇ Q◇ K◇ A◇	4	0.00015
Straight flush	seq. of five, same suit	4♠ 5♠ 6♠ 7♠ 8♠	40	0.0015
Four of a kind	four of same rank	8♠ 8♡ 8♣ 8◇	624	0.024
Full house	pair + three of a kind	5♣ 5◇ 9♡ 9♠ 9◇	3,744	0.14
Flush	five of same suit	3♠ 6♠ 7♠ J♠ A♠	5,108	0.20
Straight	sequence of five	7♡ 8◇ 9♠ 10◇ J♡	10,200	0.39
Three of a kind	three of same rank	9♠ 9♡ 9♣	54,912	2.1
Two pair	pair + pair	2♣ 2◇ 8♡ 8◇	123,552	4.7
One pair	two of same rank	10♠ 10◇	1,098,240	42
No pair	none of the above		1,302,540	50

ORDER OF PRE-FLOP HANDS

Before the flop, each player has the option of folding on the basis of his first two (pre-flop) cards, thereby avoiding any losses if his cards are poor. There are 1,326 distinct possible pre-flop hands, but these can be reduced to 169 by bearing in mind that in poker suits have no relative value. In *Hold'em Poker for Advanced Players*, David Sklansky and Mason Malmuth arranged the better hands into eight groups, where group 1 contains the most valuable hands, group 2 the next most valuable hands, and so on; hands are not ordered within a group. The 'т' denotes 10, and 's' means same suit.

Group 1	AA	KK	QQ	JJ	AKS						
Group 2	TT	AQS	AJS	KQS	AK						
Group 3	99	JTS	QJS	KJS	ATS	AQ					
Group 4	T9S	KQ	88	QTS	98S	J9S	AJ	KTS			
Group 5	77	87S	Q9S	T8S	KJ	QJ	JT	76S	97S	AXS	65S
Group 6	66	AT	55	86S	KT	QT	54S	K9S	J8S	75S	
Group 7	44	J9	64S	T9	53S	33	98	43S	22	KXS	T7S	Q8S
Group 8	87	A9	Q9	76	42S	32S	96S	85S	J8	J7S	65	54
	74S	K9	T8	43							

☙BLACKJACK

Blackjack is the most popular betting card game. It is played with one or more packs, and each player and a dealer are dealt two cards, with only one of the dealer's cards showing. Each player bets against only the dealer. The object is to get closer to 21 than the dealer without going over, called going bust, where cards 2 through 10 are worth face value; the jack, queen and king are worth 10 (denoted t below); and the ace is worth 11 or, would that cause a bust, 1. After the cards are dealt, each player has four options, which he can repeat until he stands, doubles down or busts.

> *Hit* receive an additional card;
> *Stand* receive no additional cards;
> *Double down* double the bet, receive one additional card, then stand;
> *Split* if the player's two cards are a pair, he can double his wager, split them into two hands and play them independently.

The dealer's play is strictly formulaic: he must hit on 16 or less and stand otherwise. If both the player and the dealer bust, the dealer wins; if they tie, no money is exchanged. If the player's first two cards total 21 (blackjack), the dealer pays 3:2, unless he has the same, and no money is exchanged.

BASIC STRATEGY

Below are the best options for a player's hand given the dealer's showing card. It assumes: dealer stands on 17; infinite number of packs; double on any two cards; double after split allowed; dealer peaks.

Player's hand	2	3	4	5	6	7	8	9	10	A		Player's hand	2	3	4	5	6	7	8	9	10	A
5–8	·	·	·	·	·	·	·	·	·	·		A,8 A,9	s	s	s	s	s	s	s	s	s	s
9	·	D	D	D	D	·	·	·	·	·		2,2 3,3	P	P	P	P	P	P	·	·	·	·
10	D	D	D	D	D	D	D	D	·	·		4,4	·	·	·	P	P	·	·	·	·	·
11	D	D	D	D	D	D	D	D	D	·		5,5	D	D	D	D	D	D	D	D	·	·
12	·	·	s	s	s	·	·	·	·	·		6,6	P	P	P	P	P	·	·	·	·	·
13–16	s	s	s	s	s	·	·	·	·	·		7,7	P	P	P	P	P	P	·	·	·	·
17	s	s	s	s	s	s	s	s	s	s		8,8	P	P	P	P	P	P	P	P	P	P
A,2 A,3	·	·	·	D	D	·	·	·	·	·		9,9	P	P	P	P	P	s	P	P	s	s
A,4 A,5	·	·	D	D	D	·	·	·	·	·		T,T	s	s	s	s	s	s	s	s	s	s
A,6	·	D	D	D	D	·	·	·	·	·		A,A	P	P	P	P	P	P	P	P	P	P
A,7	s	D	D	D	D	s	s	·	·	·												

Header: Player's hand | Dealer's showing card

KEY · = hit s = stand D = double down P = split

ARTS & SCIENCE

A riddle · Travelling down a road, you come to a fork. One path leads to paradise, the other to death, but you do not know which path to take. At the start of each path stands a guard. One guard always tells the truth, the other always lies, and again you do not know which is which. You can ask one guard a single question about which path to choose. What would it be?

Ernest Hemingway · There is nothing to writing. All you do is sit down at a typewriter and bleed.

Albert Einstein · Reading, after a certain age, diverts the mind too much from its creative pursuits. Any man who reads too much and uses his own brain too little falls into lazy habits of thinking.

Samuel Johnson · Knowledge is of two kinds. We know a subject ourselves, or we know where we can find information upon it. (Boswell, *Life of Johnson*, 1791)

Richard Feynman · People who wish to analyse nature without using mathematics must settle for a reduced understanding.

Lord Chesterfield · Wear your learning, like your watch, in a private pocket; and do not pull it out and strike it merely to show that you have one (*Lord Chesterfield's Letters*, 1776)

Anonymous · What is mind? No matter. What is matter? Never mind.

Joseph Long · When I was your age we didn't have integration. We had to add up differential units by hand. (Caltech, 1993)

Benjamin Franklin · Read much, but not too many books. ❧ Would you persuade, speak of interest, not of reason. ❧ There are lazy minds as well as lazy bodies. ❧ He's a fool that cannot conceal his wisdom. (*Poor Richard's Almanack*, 1732–1757)

❦ USEFUL FACTS

Sometimes the best way to remember something is to reduce it to a list before committing it to memory. Below is a list of lists, ordered by length, from the ancient world and the modern.

THREE

Parts of man	*Graces*	*Fates*	*Magi*
Mind	Aglaia	Clotho	Melchior
Body	Thalia	Lachesis	Gaspar
Spirit	Euphrosyne	Atropos	Balthazar

Enemies of man	*Christian graces*	*Eminent good works*	*Primary colours*
The world	Faith	Prayer	Red
The flesh	Hope	Fasting	Yellow
The devil	Charity	Almsgiving	Blue

FOUR

Cardinal virtues	*Elements*	*Loves*	*Last things*
Prudence	Earth	Affection	Death
Justice	Air	Friendship	Judgement
Fortitude	Fire	Eros	Heaven
Temperance	Water	Charity	Hell

Fundamental forces	*Estates*	*Freedoms*	*Gospels*
Gravity	Nobility	Of speech	Matthew
Electromagnetic	Clergy	Of worship	Mark
Strong	Commoners	From fear	Luke
Weak	Press	From want	John

FIVE

Pillars of Islam	*Orders of architecture*	*Platonic solids*	*Tastes*
Profession of faith	Doric	Tetrahedron	Salty
Prayer	Ionic	Cube	Sour
Charity	Corinthian	Octahedron	Sweet
Fasting	Tuscan	Dodecahedron	Bitter
Pilgrimage	Composite	Icosahedron	Savoury

SIX

Ages of the world	Orders of Mishnah	Rugby nations	Quarks
Adam to	Zeraim	England	Up
Noah to	Moed	France	Down
Abraham to	Nashim	Ireland	Strange
King David to	Nezikin	Italy	Charm
Babylonian exile to	Kodashim	Scotland	Bottom
Advent of Christ to now	Tohorot	Wales	Top

SEVEN

Wonders of the world	Sacraments	Liberal arts	Ages of man
Colossus of Rhodes	Baptism	Grammar	Infancy
Gardens at Babylon	Confirmation	Logic	Childhood
Pharos of Alexandria	Eucharist	Rhetoric	Lover
Pyramids of Egypt	Penance	Arithmetic	Soldier
Statue of Zeus	Holy orders	Music	Justice
Temple of Diana	Matrimony	Geometry	Old age
Tomb of Mausolus	Extreme unction	Astronomy	Dementia

Blunders of the world	Champions of christendom	Deadly sins	Opposing virtues
Wealth w/o work	St George	Lust	Chastity
Pleasure w/o conscience	St Andrew	Gluttony	Temperance
Knowledge w/o character	St Patrick	Greed	Liberality
Commerce w/o morality	St David	Sloth	Diligence
Science w/o humanity	St Denis	Wrath	Meekness
Worship w/o sacrifice	St James	Envy	Kindness
Politics w/o principle	St Anthony	Pride	Humility

EIGHT

Beatitudes

Blessed are the...	for...	Planets
poor	theirs is the kingdom of heaven	Mercury
mourners	they shall be comforted	Venus
meek	they shall inherit the earth	Earth
hungry	they shall be filled	Mars
merciful	they shall obtain mercy	Jupiter
pure	they shall see God	Saturn
peacemakers	they shall be called children of God	Uranus
persecuted	theirs is the kingdom of heaven	Neptune

NINE

Muses and their attributes		*Worthies*	*Choirs of angels*
Calliope	Epic poetry	Hector	Seraphim
Clio	History	Alexander the Great	Cherubim
Euterpe	Lyric song	Julius Caesar	Thrones
Thalia	Comedy	Joshua	Dominions
Melpomene	Tragedy	David	Virtues
Terpsichore	Dance	Judas Maccabaeus	Powers
Erato	Love song	King Arthur	Principalities
Polyhymnia	Sacred song	Charlemagne	Archangels
Urania	Astronomy	Godfrey of Bouillon	Angels

TEN

Scout essentials (p 95)	*Essential exercises*	*SMS input*	
Canteen or water bottle	Curls	0	_
Extra clothing	Tricep extensions	1	.,-?!'@:;/1
First-aid kit	Wrist curls	2	abc2
Map and compass	Bench press	3	def3
Matches and fire starter	Military press	4	ghi4
Pocket knife	Calf-raises	5	jkl5
Rain gear	Squats	6	mno6
Sun protection	Leg curls	7	pqrs7
Torch	Sit-ups	8	tuv8
Trail food	Chin-ups	9	wxyz9

TWELVE

	Birthstones		*Apostles*	*Olympians*
Jan	garnet	dark red	Peter	Zeus
Feb	amethyst	purple	Andrew	Hera
Mar	aquamarine	pale blue	James	Poseidon
Apr	diamond	clear	John	Hermes
May	emerald	green	Philip	Hestia
Jun	pearl	white	Bartholomew	Demeter
Jul	ruby	red	Thomas	Aphrodite
Aug	peridot	pale green	Matthew	Athena
Sep	sapphire	blue	James son of Alphaeus	Apollo
Oct	opal	variegated	Jude	Artemis
Nov	topaz	yellow	Simon	Ares
Dec	turquoise	sky blue	Judas Iscariot	Hephaestus

♥ USEFUL FIGURES

There are seven symbols used to construct roman numerals: I, V, X, L, C, D and M. Putting a line over a symbol is equivalent to multiplying it by 1,000.

I	1	VII	7	XL	40	C	100	DCC	700
II	2	VIII	8	L	50	CC	200	DCCC	800
III	3	IX	9	LX	60	CCC	300	CM	900
IV	4	X	10	LXX	70	CD	400	M	1,000
V	5	XX	20	LXXX	80	D	500	MM	2,000
VI	6	XXX	30	XC	90	DC	600	MMVIII	2,008

BIG AND SMALL NUMBERS

The prefixes to the left can be combined with SI units. Some conventional larger numbers are googol (10^{100}), centillion (10^{303}) and googolplex ($10^{10^{100}}$).

deca	da	$\times 10$	ten	deci	d	$\times 10^{-1}$	tenth
hecto	h	$\times 10^2$	hundred	centi	c	$\times 10^{-2}$	hundredth
kilo	k	$\times 10^3$	thousand	milli	m	$\times 10^{-3}$	thousandth
mega	M	$\times 10^6$	million	micro	μ	$\times 10^{-6}$	millionth
giga	G	$\times 10^9$	billion	nano	n	$\times 10^{-9}$	billionth
tera	T	$\times 10^{12}$	trillion	pico	p	$\times 10^{-12}$	trillionth
peta	P	$\times 10^{15}$	quadrillion	femto	f	$\times 10^{-15}$	quadrillionth
exa	E	$\times 10^{18}$	pentillion	atto	a	$\times 10^{-18}$	pentillionth
zetta	Z	$\times 10^{21}$	sextillion	zepto	z	$\times 10^{-21}$	sextillionth
yotta	Y	$\times 10^{24}$	septillion	yocto	y	$\times 10^{-24}$	septillionth

SI UNITS

The Système International d'Unités, or SI units, is a coherent system of base 10 (metric) units. With the exception of imperial units (see p 170), it is the customary system of units throughout the world.

Base units			
metre (m)	length	mole (mol)	amount of substance
kilogram (kg)	mass	candela (cd)	luminous intensity
second (s)	time	*Associated units*	
ampere (A)	electric current	are (a) = 100 m^2	unit of area
kelvin (K)	temperature	litre (l) = <u>0.001</u> m^3	unit of volume
		Note: 1 l of water weighs 1 kg	

IMPERIAL UNITS

Imperial units are the traditional British units of measurement. They are used in the United Kingdom, much of the the British Commonwealth and, with some differences, the United States.

Apothecaries' capacity

pint	20 fluid ounces
fluid ounce	8 drachms
drachm	3 scruples
scruple	20 minims

Apothecaries' weight

pound	12 ounces
ounce	8 drams
dram	3 scruples
scruple	20 grains

Area

square mile	640 acres
acre	4 roods
rood	1,210 square yards
square yard	9 square feet
square foot	144 square inches

Avoirdupois (common) weight

ton	20 hundredweight
hundredweight	4 quarters
quarter	2 stones
stone	14 pounds
pound (lb)	16 ounces
ounce (oz)	16 drams

Capacity (UK)

bushel	4 pecks
peck	2 gallons
gallon	4 quarts
quart	2 pints
pint	4 gills
gill	5 fluid ounces

Length

league	3 miles
mile	1,760 yards
yard (yd)	3 feet
foot (ft)	12 inches
inch (in)	3 barleycorns

Surveyors' length

mile	8 furlongs
furlong	10 chains
chain	4 rods
rod	25 links
link	0.66 feet

Troy weight (precious metal)

pound	12 ounces
ounce	20 pennyweights
pennyweight	24 grains

CONVERSION BETWEEN UNITS

inch	2.54 centimetres
foot	0.3048 metres
mile	1.609344 kilometres
acre	0.4047 hectares
ounce (avoirdupois)	28.35 grams
ounce (apoth. & troy)	31.10 grams

pound	0.4536 kilograms
fluid ounce (UK, apoth.)	28.41 ml
quart	1.136 litres
temp (°C)	temp (K) − 273.15
temp (°F)	$(9/5 \times$ temp (°C)$) + 32$

KEY   All integers and underlined decimal numbers are exact.

OTHER UNITS

Alcoholic strength   see p 123

Angular measure
circle   360 degrees
degree   60 minutes
minute   60 seconds
circle 2π radians

Astronomical distance
parsec 3.08×10^{13} km
light year 9.46×10^{12} km
astronomical unit 1.50×10^{8} km

Beauty
Helen   25.6 Helenas
10 Helenas   beauty to die for

Cooking & drinks capacity   see p 123

Gem weight
gram   5 carats
carat   100 points

Gym (typical)
workout   8 exercises
exercise   3 sets
set   10 repetitions

Memory
terabyte (TB) 2^{40} bytes
gigabyte (GB) 2^{30} bytes
megabyte (MB) 2^{20} bytes
kilobyte (kB) $1,024 = 2^{10}$ bytes
byte (B)   8 bits

Microscopic length
micron (μ) 10^{-6} m
angstrom (Å) 10^{-10} m

Nautical measures
cable   100 fathoms
fathom   6 feet
league (at sea)   3 nautical miles
nautical mile (intl)   1,852 m
knot   1 nautical mile/hour

Paper sheets
bale   10 reams
ream   20 quires
quire   25 sheets

Paper size
letter 8.5×11 in
legal 8.5×14 in
A4 210×297 mm
A0 $841 \times 1,189$ mm
B0 $1,000 \times 1,414$ mm
C0 $917 \times 1,297$ mm
A0 = 2 A1 = 4 A2 = 8 A3, etc.
Same for B0 and C0.

Shoe size   see p 46

Typography
0.9961 inches   6 picas
pica   12 points

Wine bottle sizes   see p 106

MATHEMATICAL CONSTANTS

γ	Euler constant	0.57722	$\sqrt{3}$	Square root of three	1.73205
$\sqrt{2}$	Square root of two	1.41421	e	Base of natural log	2.71828
ϕ	Golden ratio	1.61803	π	Pi	3.14159

❦ B O O K S

Below is a collection of classic books for men, many of which are the definitive work in their field. In general the earliest date of publication is listed. Some of the books have remained continuously in print, others have been reissued after a dormant period. Those that are out of print and those that are out of copyright can often be found second-hand or free on the following websites, among others:

Out of print
www.abebooks.co.uk
www.bibliofind.com

Out of copyright
www.gutenberg.org
www.digital.library.upenn.edu/books

This list attempts to strike a balance between old classics and more recent publications where the dust has not settled between trendy and trusted.

50 MOST ESSENTIAL BOOKS FOR MEN

The Book of the Courtier	Baldassare Castiglione	1528
The Compleat Angler	Izaak Walton	1653
Lord Chesterfield's Letters	Philip Stanhope	1776
Pelham; or,	Edward Bulwer-Lytton	1828
the Adventures of a Gentleman		
A Hero of Our Time	Mikhail Lermontov	1840
Manners for Men	Mrs Humphry	1897
★ *Scouting for Boys*	Robert Baden-Powell	1908
The Stag Cook Book	C. Mac Sheridan	1922
The Pipe Book	Alfred Dunhill	1924
The Gentleman's Companion, vols 1 & 2	Charles Baker, Jr	1939
★ *The Ashley Book of Knots*	Clifford Ashley	1944
Brideshead Revisited	Evelyn Waugh	1945
★ *The Fine Art of Mixing Drinks*	David A. Embury	1948
★ *Esquire's Handbook for Hosts*	Esquire	1949
★ *Scarne on Cards*	John Scarne	1949
With or Without Beans	Joe Cooper	1952
A Family Album	The Duke of Windsor	1960
Dandies	James Laver	1968
★ *Esquire's Encyclopedia of*	O. Schoeffler & W. Gale	1973
20th Century Men's Fashions		
★ *Arnold: The Education of a Bodybuilder*	Arnold Schwarzenegger	1977
Spirits and Liqueurs	Peter Hallgarten	1979
★ *The Gentlemen's Clubs of London*	Anthony Lejeune	1979

★ *The James Bond Bedside Companion*	Raymond Benson	1984
★ *The Ultimate Pipe Book*	Richard Carlton Hacker	1984
★ *The SAS Survival Handbook*	John Wiseman	1986
The Theory of Poker	David Sklansky	1987
The Tie	Sarah Gibbings	1990
★ *The Elements of Typographic Style*	Robert Bringhurst	1992
A History of Men's Fashion	Farid Chenoune	1993
★ *Beer Companion*	Michael Jackson	1993
The Englishman's Suit	Hardy Amies	1994
Sex and Suits	Anne Hollander	1995
A James Bond Omnibus	Ian Fleming	1997
Tree Houses You Can Actually Build	D. Stiles & J. Trusty Stiles	1998
Gentleman	Bernhard Roetzel	1999
★ *Malt Whisky Companion*	Michael Jackson	1999
The 85 Ways to Tie a Tie	Thomas Fink & Yong Mao	1999
London Man	Francis Chichester	2000
The Boutonnière	Umberto Angeloni	2000
The Faber Book of Smoking	James Walton	2000
The Chap Manifesto	G. Temple & V. Darkwood	2001
★ *Dressing the Man*	Alan Flusser	2002
The Modern Gentleman	P. Mollod & J. Tesauro	2002
US Army Survival Manual 3-05.70	Department of Defence	2002
Who's a Dandy?	George Walden	2002
Mr Boston Official Bartender's and Party Guide	Chris Morris (ed.)	2005
★ *Diffords Guide to Cocktails: v. 6*	Simon Difford	2006
★ *Hugh Johnson's Pocket Wine Book*	Hugh Johnson	2006
Manliness	Harvey Mansfield	2006
★ *The Dangerous Book for Boys*	Conn & Hal Iggulden	2006

KEY   ★ means that the book is the definitive work in its field

SELECTED NOTES

The Compleat Angler Walton's guide to catching and eating different species of fish is the most printed book in the English language after the Holy Bible and *Pilgrim's Progress*. It describes the spirit of fishing as well as the mechanics, much of which has little changed.

A Hero of Our Time The short story 'Princess Mary' offers a telling insight into the mind of a woman falling in love.

The Gentleman's Companion These two volumes were reissued in 2001 as *Jigger, Beake, and Glass: Drinking Around the World*; and *Knife, Fork and*

Spoon: Eating Around the World.

Scouting for Boys This is the original Scouting handbook by the founder of the Scouts, Robert Baden-Powell. It was edited by Elleke Boehmer and reissued by Oxford University Press in 2005. Readers will notice that modern-day Scouting has drifted far from what Baden-Powell originally set up, which focused on boys, God, adventure, common sense and manly pursuits.

The Ashley Book of Knots Universally regarded as the most comprehensive and entertaining book on knots, it contains nearly 4,000 knots and over 7,000 drawings. It is still in print. 'It is a prodigy', writes *The Observer*. 'Knots, in the world of books, have thus been tied forever.'

The Fine Art of Mixing Drinks This is, simply put, the most influential treatise on cocktails ever written. It is 'the Escoffier of cocktail books. More than a compilation of recipes, it is delightful, urbane reading for all who aspire to prepare drinks which are refreshingly palatable, not just potable', according to the publisher. No longer in print, it remains timely and it is worth tracking down a second-hand copy.

Esquire's Handbook for Hosts This splendid book, which is surprisingly insightful 60 years later, was republished in its original form in 1999 by Black Dog & Leventhal. The comprehensive manual is divided into three parts: Eat: the world's best chefs wear pants; Drink: liquor is quicker; And Be Merry: how to be happy though host.

With or Without Beans The subtitle is 'Being a compendium to perpetuate the internationally famous bowl of chili (Texas style) which occupies such an important place in modern civilization'.

Esquire's Encyclopedia of 20th Century Men's Fashions A detailed, comprehensive overview of the trends in men's dress, though it does not of course examine the last three decades. Copies are now considered prize possessions, and second-hand copies are expensive.

Arnold: The Education of a Bodybuilder Written with Douglas Kent-Hall early on in Schwarzenegger's career, it remains the best book on weights, even more for its tale of extraordinary mental discipline than its back-to-basics exercise prescriptions. The first half is autobiographical and the second details exercises and lifting routines.

The SAS Survival Handbook For 26 years the author served with the SAS (Special Air Forces), generally regarded as the most elite special force in the world. His book is the definitive all-terrain survival manual, a grown-up version of *Scouting for Boys*.

The Elements of Typographic Style Not an obvious choice but a welcome lesson in, and example of, beautiful design, proportion and layout. 'I wish to see this book become the Typographers' Bible', writes Hermann Zapf.

Beer Companion Many men, especially those outside continental Europe, have only experienced the tip of the beer iceberg, usually in the form of pale lager. Michael Jackson is arguably the world's most knowledgeable beer expert, and this award-winning book examines beer history, classification and notes on beers from around the world.

The Englishman's Suit This slim volume is, word for word, the best book on men's dress. It is short, witty, authoritative and outspoken. Hardy Amies was longtime dressmaker to the queen and founder of the eponymous Savile Row tailoring company.

A James Bond Omnibus Many men are not aware that Ian Fleming's original Bond novels are more entertaining and consistent than their film adaptations. This is a single-volume collection of the Fleming novels *From Russia With Love*, *Dr No* and *Goldfinger*, often considered the three best Bond novels. There are 14 Bond books by Fleming in all, a list of which can be found on p 182.

The 85 Ways to Tie a Tie The story of the knotted neckcloth and the modern necktie and how to tie both, with forays into history, mathematics and men's dress along the way. The book was inspired by two mathematics papers by the authors in which they prove that there are exactly 85 necktie knots and explain how to tie them. The papers are for experts; the book is for laymen.

The Chap Manifesto 'A rallying point for the classic bloke beleaguered in postmodern confusion, *a cri de coeur* from the manly bosom, a hail-well-met to gentlemen of all pinstripes.' Written along the lines of *The Chap* magazine, it precedes *The Chap Almanac* (2002) and *The Best of The Chap* (2005).

Dressing the Man One of the best and most comprehensive books on men's dress. Also worth noting are Flusser's *Clothes and the Man* (1985), a less glossy but equally authoritative volume, and *Style and the Man* (1996), a guide to good men's clothes shops around the world.

Who's a Dandy? This slim volume is in two parts. The first is an exploration of modern dandyism; the second, a new translation of the French dandy Jules Barbey d'Aurevilly's 19th-century essay on George Brummel (a.k.a. Beau Brummel).

Diffords Guide to Cocktails: v. 6 The best guide to cocktails currently in print. Also noteworthy is Difford's *Sauceguide: Drink & Drinking* (2002). Difford's *Guide* series are extensively researched, beautifully typeset and illustrated and are written in clear, entertaining prose.

Manliness Harvard government professor Mansfield makes a spirited defence of the importance of manliness and the cultural differences between the sexes. What to many is common sense is scandalous to others, and this book has sharply divided readers and critics.

❦WEBSITES

Unlike books (p 172), websites are free and never go out of print – just down. Here are some necessary and eccentric sites for men, with a bias towards depth over breadth. All start 'www' unless otherwise shown.

50 MOST ESSENTIAL WEBSITES

General

www.askmen.com	Essays and forum on all men's questions
www.mensjournal.com/feature/0408/bestwebsites.html	
	Top 100 sites for men

Health

www.malehealth.co.uk	Information from the Men's Health Forum
www.menstuff.org	The national men's resource
www.webmd.com	Better information. Better health
www.medlineplus.gov	Trusted health information

Sports

195.102.4.163/cgf1/calendar_front.asp	Online sports calendar
www.wikipedia.org/wiki/2008_in_sports	2008 sports calendar
www.football-linx.com	World-wide football links
www.explorersweb.com	The most extreme parts of the world

Women

www.stagweb.co.uk	Stag night suggestions and best man advice
www.members.garbersoft.net/spartacus/home.htm	Men's rights
www.fathers.com	Centre for fathering
marriage.rutgers.edu	The sociology of marriage

Dress

www.dandyism.net	Insufferably bored since 1828
www.askandyaboutclothes.com/forum/index.php	Men's dress forum
www.englishcut.com	Savile Row tailor's blog
asuitablewardrobe.dynend.com	Thoughts on classic men's clothing

Town

www.repairclinic.com	Don't throw it out, now you can fix it
www.wackyuses.com	Little-known uses for well-known products
www.ehow.com	How to do just about everything
www.last.fm	Listen to music similar to what you already like

Country

www.wildwoodsurvival.com	Wilderness survival , wilderness mind
equipped.com/fm21-76.htm	Pdf of US Army Survival Manual FM 21-76
www.scouts.org.uk	Official website of the Scout Association in the UK
www.selfbuild.com	Self build and DIY forum

Drinking

www.ratebeer.com	Beer reviews, forums and information
www.dcs.ed.ac.uk/home/jhb/whisky	Full single malt whisky tour
www.wineanorak.com	Online wine magazine
www.webtender.com	6,000 drinks recipes and bartender's handbook

Smoking

www.forestonline.org	A haven for smokers and freedom of choice
www.fakefags.co.uk	Don't let health warnings take the fun out of fags
www.cigars-review.org	History, directory and reviews of cigars
www.snuffhouse.org	Dedicated to nasal snuff

Cooking

www.coffeegeek.com	Coffee, espresso, cafés and coffee culture
www.cookingforengineers.com	Have an analytical mind? Like to cook?
www.barbecuen.com	Tutorials, tips, techniques and recipes
www.chilicookoff.com	Official website of the International Chili Society

Idling

www.worldconkerchampionships.com	World Conker Championships
www.bjmath.com/bjmath/	Mathematics of gambling
www.patrickchaplin.com	Darts culture and history
www.peter-upton.co.uk/sub1.htm	Table-top football game Subbuteo

Arts & Science

www.howstuffworks.com	For the engineering geek inside every man
www.gutenberg.org	Over 20,000 free books available for download
www.mathworld.wolfram.com	The most extensive mathematics resource
www.tjbd.co.uk	Sketch of the literary James Bond character

Time

www.tondering.dk/claus/calendar.html	FAQ about calendars
aa.usno.navy.mil	Sun, moon times and astronomical ephemera
www.almanac.com	*The Old Farmer's Almanac* online
www.timeanddate.com/calendar	Calendar for any year and country

❦ERNEST HEMINGWAY

Hemingway was born in Chicago on July 21, 1899. After finishing school he worked as a cub reporter for the Kansas City *Star*. He was determined to see action in the First World War, however, and after six months of journalism he served as an ambulance driver for the Italian Red Cross. He was wounded and decorated for his rescue of an Italian soldier.

Hemingway moved to Paris in the early 1920s, where he befriended other expatriate American writers, including Gertrude Stein and Ezra Pound. He wrote his first novels there, although it was not until *The Sun Also Rises* that he was established as a first rate writer. War and outdoor pursuits – hunting, deep-sea fishing and bullfighting – would become themes in Hemingway's life and writing. He covered the Spanish Civil War in the 1930s, which would be the basis of *For Whom the Bell Tolls*. He spent much of the Second World War on a boat off the Cuban coast, as much looking to sink German submarines as drinking and big-game fishing.

The Old Man and the Sea was the last of his books to appear during his lifetime, and soon after its publication he won the Nobel Prize in literature. In 1961 Hemingway committed suicide, like his father, brother and sister before him, with a self-inflicted shotgun wound to the head. He had married four times and produced three sons. 'The world is a fine place and worth the fighting for', he had once written in *For Whom the Bell Tolls,* 'and I hate very much to leave it'.

WRITING

Hemingway's terse style, which has had such a significant and widespread influence on American literature, was marked by spartan work choice, limited use of qualifiers and simple sentence structure – a conspicuous inconspicuousness, to borrow a description from men's dress. This simplicity was deceptive, however, and did not come easily (cf. Hemingway, p 165): he was an inveterate revisionist, sometimes reworking a manuscript a hundred times. He remains one of the few writers whose identity is apparent from the style of a single sentence.

Despite Hemingway's reckless lifestyle and his frequent bouts with depression, he kept up a disciplined program of writing. For him the writer's life was a lonely one, and it depleted him. 'I learned never to empty the well of my writing', he wrote in *A Moveable Feast*, 'but always to stop when there was still something there in the deep part of the well, and let it refill at night from the springs that fed it'.

BOOKS

A number of Hemingway's works below were published after his death in 1961. Some of these were unfinished and required significant pruning.

Novels and stories		*True at First Light*	1999
Three Stories and Ten Poems	1923	*Under Kilimanjaro*	2005
in our time (limited printing)	1924		
In Our Time	1925	*Nonfiction*	
The Torrents of Spring	1926	*Death in the Afternoon*	1932
The Sun Also Rises	1926	*Green Hills of Africa*	1935
(originally *Fiesta* in the UK)		*A Moveable Feast*	1964
Men Without Women	1927	*The Dangerous Summer*	1985
A Farewell to Arms	1929		
Winner Take Nothing	1933	*Other*	
The Snows of Kilimanjaro	1936	*By-Line* (journalism)	1967
To Have and Have Not	1937	*88 Poems* (poetry)	1979
The Fifth Column and the		*Dateline: Toronto* (journalism)	1985
First Forty-Nine Stories	1938		
For Whom the Bell Tolls	1940	*Re-collected works*	
Across the River		*The Essential Hemingway*	1964
and Into the Trees	1950	*The Nick Adams Stories*	1972
The Old Man and the Sea	1952	*The Complete Short Stories*	
Islands in the Stream	1970	*of Ernest Hemingway*	1987
The Garden of Eden	1986	*The Collected Stories*	1995

BIOGRAPHIES

Of the many biographies of Hemingway, the five below are notable. The premier Hemingway website, www.timelesshemingway.com, says: 'The bios by Lynn, Baker and Meyers [are] "the big three" and any serious EH scholar or enthusiast should have these works in his or her possession.' *The New York Times* says Mellow's biography 'stands with the best work done on the writer to date'. Most ambitious of all is Reynolds' five-volume set.

Ernest Hemingway: A Life Story	Carlos Baker	1969
Hemingway: A Biography	Jeffrey Meyers	1985
Hemingway: Life and Work	Kenneth Lynn	1987
Hemingway: A Life Without Consequences	James Mellow	1992
The Young Hemingway (1986);	Michael Reynolds	1986–1999

Hemingway: The Paris Years (1989); *The American Homecoming* (1992); *The 1930's* (1997); *The Final Years* (1999)

❦JAMES BOND

Of all 20th-century literary characters, the British spy code-named 007 has had the biggest influence on the modern perception of masculinity. James Bond is the central character of Fleming's 14 books and the inspiration for 21 official films and countless other publications. The 3,000 pages penned by Fleming, however, remain the authoritative record of Bond, and in them can be found a coherent picture of the man.

BIOGRAPHY

James Bond was (likely) born in 1924, the son of Andrew Bond of Glencoe, Scotland, and Monique Delacroix of Switzerland. His family motto is *Orbis non sufficit* (The world is not enough). Bond's father was an arms dealer for Vickers, what is now part of BAE Systems Land & Armaments, and as a consequence much of Bond's childhood was spent abroad. When Bond was 11 his parents died climbing in the Aiguilles Rouges and he was taken in by his aunt Charmian Bond in Pett Bottom, Kent, a stone's throw from what is now the Duck Inn restaurant. A year later Bond entered Eton College, follow-ing his father's instructions, but had to be re-moved after two halves due to 'alleged trouble with one of the boys' maids'. He transferred to

Fleming's vision of Bond, from the *Daily Express*.

his father's old school, Fettes, where by comparison he prospered: he was an avid judo wrestler and lightweight boxer and spoke French and Ger-man, of which he had had early exposure abroad, with ease.

At 17 Bond finished school and began study at the University of Geneva; this was interrupted when he joined the Royal Navy Volunteer Reserve in 1941. By the end of the war he had achieved the rank of commander and his service record soon drew the attention of M (Miles), the director of the UK's Secret Intelligence Service (MI6). It was at this stage that Bond became 'as-sociated with certain aspects of the ministry's work'. After his second assas-sination, Bond was awarded a double-o number, indicating a licence to kill, and it is from this point that a number of his missions have been docu-mented. In 1954 Bond was made a Companion of the Order of St Michael and St George (CMG). He was later offered a knighthood for his services to MI6 but refused for the sake of professional anonymity. At the end of *On Her Majesty's Secret Service*, Bond married Contessa Teresa di Vicenzo

(Tracy), daughter of Marc-Ange Draco; she was killed shortly after the wedding by Ernst Stavro Blofeld, Bond's longstanding nemesis. Nonetheless, Bond is known to have had at least one illegitimate child, through the Japanese agent Kissy Suzuki whom he met in *You Only Live Twice*.

APPEARANCE

At 6 feet and 165 pounds, Bond is slim, almost wiry (body mass index = 22.4). He has blue-grey eyes, a rather cruel mouth, a long vertical scar on his left cheek and short, dark hair which falls to his forehead in a wandering comma. On the back of his hand is a scar in the shape of the Russian character Ш, carved by a smersh agent in *Casino Royale*. His dress is simple but elegant: single-breasted blue serge or houndstooth check suits (probably from a tailor just off the Row; certainly not Italian) with a white shirt and slip-on shoes. His tie is black knit silk, evidently tied in a four-in-hand or half-Windsor (Bond thought the Windsor knot was 'the mark of a cad'; see p 65). Alas, his bow tie is black satin rather than barathea.

Bond has few possessions but they are fine: a wide, flat gun-metal cigarette case; a black oxidized Ronson lighter; and a Rolex Oyster Perpetual watch. Contrary to the films, Bond prefers Bentleys; in order, he drives a 1930 (or 1933) Mark IV convertible, a 1953 Mark VI and a Mark II Continental, all of them grey with navy or black interior. He occasionally dines at the London club Blades, modelled after Boodle's (see p 76).

HABITS

Bond is an able amateur sportsman, particularly at skiing, golf and hand-to-hand combat, the last being the subject of his book-in-progress, *Stand Firm*. He rode the Cresta Run from Top.

The British spy dislikes tea but frequently drinks coffee, brewed in an American Chemex. His taste in food is refined if unadventurous, with a preference for traditional English fare. His favourite meal is breakfast, for which we are given his recipe in the short story '007 in New York' (see p 146). Bond smokes approximately 60 cigarettes a day, usually a mix of Turkish and Balkan tobaccos, with three gold bands on the filter, indicative of his naval rank. He is a heavy drinker. Despite his cinematic preference for vodka martinis, Fleming's Bond prefers whisky. Throughout the books his most common drinks are 25% whisky or bourbon, 11% sake, 10% champagne and 6% vodka martini.

Bond's secretary, Mary Goodnight, suggested for Bond this simple if simplistic epitaph: 'I shall not waste my days in trying to prolong them. I shall use my time.'

BOOKS AND FILMS

Ian Fleming wrote 12 novels and two collections of short stories about Bond, published once a year between 1953 and 1966:

Casino Royale	1953	*For Your Eyes Only*	1960
Live and Let Die	1954	*Thunderball*	1961
Moonraker	1955	*The Spy Who Loved Me*	1962
Diamonds are Forever	1956	*On Her Majesty's Secret Service*	1963
From Russia with Love	1957	*You Only Live Twice*	1964
Dr No	1958	*The Man with the Golden Gun*	1965
Goldfinger	1959	*Octopussy and The Living Daylights*	1966

The Bond series was extended by Kingsley Amis, who wrote *Colonel Sun* in 1968 under the pseudonym Robert Markham. Between 1981 and 1996 John Gardner wrote 14 novels and two film novelizations, and between 1997 and 2002 Raymond Benson wrote six novels and three novelizations. Of the many nonfiction books on Bond, three can be considered classics:

The James Bond Dossier	Kingsley Amis	1965
James Bond: The Authorized Biography of 007	John Pearson	1973
The James Bond Bedside Companion	Raymond Benson	1984

There are 21 official Bond films, with the 22nd scheduled for release in late 2008. Bond has been played by six actors, though Fleming saw only Sean Connery (SC). According to Vesper Lynd in *Casino Royale*, we know that Bond resembled singer Hoagy Carmichael, and on this basis Timothy Dalton (TD) looks most like the spy. The other actors are George Lazenby (GL), Roger Moore (RM), Pierce Brosnan (PB) and Daniel Craig (DC).

Dr No	SC	1962	*Moonraker*	RM	1979
From Russia with Love	SC	1963	*For Your Eyes Only*	RM	1981
Goldfinger	SC	1964	*Octopussy*	RM	1983
Thunderball	SC	1965	*A View to a Kill*	RM	1985
You Only Live Twice	SC	1967	*The Living Daylights*	TD	1987
On Her Majesty's	GL	1969	*Licence to Kill*	TD	1989
Secret Service			*GoldenEye*	PB	1995
Diamonds are Forever	SC	1971	*Tomorrow Never Dies*	PB	1997
Live and Let Die	RM	1973	*The World Is Not Enough*	PB	1999
The Man with the	RM	1974	*Die Another Day*	PB	2002
Golden Gun			*Casino Royale*	DC	2006
The Spy Who Loved Me	RM	1977	*Bond 22*	DC	2008

TIME

The fyrste moneth is Januarye, the childe is without might tyll hee bee 6 yeere olde, he can not helpe him selfe.

The 6 yeere that is the first time of the springinge of all flowres, and so the childe till 12 yeere groweth in knowledge and learning, and to doo as he is taught.

Marche is the buddinge time, and in that 6 yeere of Marche the Childe wax-eth bygge and apte to doo seruice, and learne scyence from 12 to 18, such as is shewed hym.

Aprill is the springing tyme of flowres, and in that 6 yeere he groweth to mans state in heyght and bredthe, and wax-eth wise and bolde, but then beware of sensualitie, for he is 24.

Maye is the season that flowers byn spreade, and bee then in theyr vertue with sweet odours. In these 6 yeeres he is in his most strength, but then let him geather good maners betyme, for if his tary past that age it is an hap if euer he take them, for then he is 30 yeare.

In June he beginneth to close his mynde, and then hee waxeth rype, for then he is 36 yeere.

In July he is 42, and he begynneth a lyt-tle to declyne, and feeleth hym not so prosperous as he was.

In August he is by that 6 yeere 48 yeere and then he goeth not so lustely as he dyd, but studieth howe to geather to fynde him in his olde age to liue more easely.

In September he is 54 yeere he then pu-rueyethe against the winter to cherish himselfe withall and keepe neere to-gether the goods y^t he gat in his youth.

Then is a man in October 60 yeere full, if he haue ought he gladdeth, and if haue nought he weepeth.

Then is man 66 in Nouember, he stoupeth and goeth softly, and leeseth all his beauty and fayrnesse.

In December he is 72 yeeres, then had he leuer haue a warme fire then a fayre lady, and after this age he goeth into de-crepitie to waxe a childe again, and can not welde him selfe, and then young folkes be wery of his company but if they haue much good they beene full lytell taken heede of.

Kalendar of Sheepehards, 16th c., in *Oxford Companion to the Year*.

❦PROPERTIES OF 2008

NAMES, CYCLES AND ERAS

Roman numerals	MMVIII	Julian period	6721
Athenian numerals	XXΠIII	Age of Earth (creationist)	7207
Binary (base 2)	11111011000	Liturgical cycles (e. 29 Nov)	A/2
Octal (base 8)	3730	Chinese year (b. 7 Feb)	Rat
Hexadecimal (base 16)	7D8	Grecian (Seleucidae) year	2320
Prime factorization	$2 \times 2 \times 2 \times 251$	French Rep. yr (b. Sep 22)	CCXVII
Phinary	1010001010001011	Saka (Indian) year	1930
	.0001000000100001	Japanese era year	Heisei 20
Dominical letter	F/E	Muslim year (b. 10 Jan)	1429
Epact	22	Jewish year (AM, b. 30 Sep)	5769
Golden number	XIV	Masonic year (AL)	6008
Solar cycle	1	Regnal year (b. 6 Feb)	57
Roman indiction	1	Roman year (AUC)	2761

SELECTED NOTES

Roman numerals Described on p 169.

Athenian numerals The Athenian number system uses I for 1, Π for 5, Δ for 10, H for 100, X for 1,000 and M for 10,000. Writing a symbol inside Π indicates five times its value.

Binary In other words, 2008 = 1024 + 512 + 256 + 128 + 64 + 16 + 8.

Hexadecimal The letters A–F represent the numbers 10–15.

Prime factorization The smallest positive numbers which when multiplied give 2008.

Phinary Expressed in base ϕ (the Golden ratio, see p 212), where, for example, $.1 = \phi^{-1}$ and $.11 = \phi^{-1} + \phi^{-2}$. Remarkably, all integers can be so expressed with a finite number of digits.

Dominical letter The letter corresponding to the date in January on which the first Sunday of the year falls: A=1, B=2 and so on.

Epact The age of the ecclesiastical moon in days on 1 January, minus one.

Golden number The place in the 19-year Metonic cycle after which the phases of the moon return to the same days of the month (19 solar years equals 235 lunar cycles).

Solar cycle The place in the 28-year cycle after which the calendar (days and dates) repeats itself.

Roman indiction The place in the 15-year cycle initiated in the late Roman Empire for the organization of tax, used until medieval times in written records alongside the year.

Julian period The number of years since 4713 BC, now used only by astronomers.

Age of Earth Among strict creationists, the most accepted year for the creation of the world is 5199 BC.

Liturgical cycles Readings at Masses cycle over three years for Sundays (A, B, C) and two years for weekdays (1, 2).

Regnal year The number of whole years the current British monarch has reigned plus one, starting from the day of accession.

CURIOUS MATHEMATICAL PROPERTIES

Most numbers have interesting properties, if you look hard enough. In *Ramanujan*, the English mathematician G. H. Hardy recounts: 'I remember once going to see [Ramanujan] when he was lying ill at Putney. I had ridden in taxi cab number 1729 and remarked that the number seemed to me rather a dull one, and that I hoped it was not an unfavourable omen. "No", he replied, "it is a very interesting number; it is the smallest number expressible as the sum of two cubes in two different ways."' ($1729 = 1^3 + 12^3 = 9^3 + 10^3$.) In *The Penguin Dictionary of Curious and Interesting Numbers*, D. G. Wells suggests that 48 is the first uninteresting number, but concludes that for this reason it is interesting after all.

The number 2008 has the following interesting properties:

2008 is *even* because it is divisible by two.

2008 is *composite* (not prime), having prime divisors 2 and 251. The proper divisors of 2008 are 2, 4, 8, 251, 502 and 1,004.

2008 is the first number to need 19 lines when shown on a digital clock.

$2^{2008} + 3$ is prime, and so is $(10^{2008} + 2)/6$.

2008 is *happy* because, if you take the sum of the squares of its digits, and iterate this process on the answer until it converges, the result is 1.

2008 is *untouchable* because it cannot be expressed as the sum of the divisors of any other number excluding the number itself.

2008 is the sum of 3 positive cubes in two different ways.

2008 is *odious* because it has an odd number of 1s in its binary expansion.

The number of numbers less than 2008 that are relatively prime to it is 1,000.

2008 is the sum of all 3-digit Lucas numbers (Lucas numbers begin 1, 3, 4, 7, 11, 18, 29,..., where $1 + 3 = 4$, $3 + 4 = 7$, and so on).

2008 is *deficient* because the sum of its divisors apart from itself is less than itself.

2008 is a *pentary palindrome* because it reads the same in both directions in base 5: 31013.

2008 is an *apocalyptic power* because 2^{2008} contains three consecutive 6s.

❦ CALENDAR

2007

January						
S	M	T	W	T	F	S
	■	2	3	4	5	6
7	8	9	10	11	12	13
14	15	16	17	18	19	20
21	22	23	24	25	26	27
28	29	30	31			

February						
S	M	T	W	T	F	S
				1	2	3
4	5	6	7	8	9	10
11	12	13	14	15	16	17
18	19	20	21	22	23	24
25	26	27	28			

March						
S	M	T	W	T	F	S
			W	2	3	
4	5	6	7	8	9	10
11	12	13	14	15	16	I
18	19	20	☛	22	23	24
25	26	27	28	29	30	31

April						
S	M	T	W	T	F	S
1	2	3	4	5	■	7
★	■	10	11	12	13	14
15	16	17	18	19	20	21
22	E	24	25	26	27	28
29	30					

May						
S	M	T	W	T	F	S
		1	2	3	4	5
6	■	8	9	10	11	12
13	14	15	16	17	18	19
20	21	22	23	24	25	26
27	■	29	30	31		

June						
S	M	T	W	T	F	S
					1	2
3	4	5	6	7	8	9
10	11	12	13	14	15	16
17	18	19	20	☛	22	23
24	25	26	27	28	29	30

July						
S	M	T	W	T	F	S
1	2	3	4	5	6	7
8	9	10	11	12	13	14
15	16	17	18	19	20	21
22	23	24	25	26	27	28
29	30	31				

August						
S	M	T	W	T	F	S
			1	2	3	4
5	6	7	8	9	10	11
12	13	14	15	16	17	18
19	20	21	22	23	24	25
26	■	28	29	30	31	

September						
S	M	T	W	T	F	S
						1
2	3	4	5	6	7	8
9	10	11	12	13	14	15
16	17	18	19	20	21	22
☛	24	25	26	27	28	29
30						

October						
S	M	T	W	T	F	S
1	2	3	4	5	6	
7	8	9	10	11	12	13
14	15	16	17	18	19	20
21	22	23	24	25	26	27
28	29	30	31			

November						
S	M	T	W	T	F	S
				1	2	3
4	5	6	7	8	9	10
11	12	13	14	15	16	17
18	19	20	21	22	23	24
25	26	27	28	29	S	

December						
S	M	T	W	T	F	S
						1
2	3	4	5	6	7	8
9	10	11	12	13	14	15
16	17	18	19	20	21	☛
23	24	■	■	27	28	29
30	31					

2008

January						
S	M	T	W	T	F	S
		■	2	3	4	5
6	7	8	9	10	11	12
13	14	15	16	17	18	19
20	21	22	23	24	25	26
27	28	29	30	31		

February						
S	M	T	W	T	F	S
					1	2
3	4	5	6	7	8	9
10	11	12	13	14	15	16
17	18	19	20	21	22	23
24	25	26	27	28	29	

March						
S	M	T	W	T	F	S
						W
2	3	4	5	6	7	8
9	10	11	12	13	14	15
16	I	18	19	☛	■	22
★	■	25	26	27	28	29
30	31					

April						
S	M	T	W	T	F	S
		1	2	3	4	5
6	7	8	9	10	11	12
13	14	15	16	17	18	19
20	21	22	E	24	25	26
27	28	29	30			

May						
S	M	T	W	T	F	S
				1	2	3
4	■	6	7	8	9	10
11	12	13	14	15	16	17
18	19	20	21	22	23	24
25	■	27	28	29	30	31

June						
S	M	T	W	T	F	S
1	2	3	4	5	6	7
8	9	10	11	12	13	14
15	16	17	18	19	☛	21
22	23	24	25	26	27	28
29	30					

July						
S	M	T	W	T	F	S
		1	2	3	4	5
6	7	8	9	10	11	12
13	14	15	16	17	18	19
20	21	22	23	24	25	26
27	28	29	30	31		

August						
S	M	T	W	T	F	S
					1	2
3	4	5	6	7	8	9
10	11	12	13	14	15	16
17	18	19	20	21	22	23
24	■	26	27	28	29	30
31						

September						
S	M	T	W	T	F	S
	1	2	3	4	5	6
7	8	9	10	11	12	13
14	15	16	17	18	19	20
21	☛	23	24	25	26	27
28	29	30				

October						
S	M	T	W	T	F	S
			1	2	3	4
5	6	7	8	9	10	11
12	13	14	15	16	17	18
19	20	21	22	23	24	25
26	27	28	29	30	31	

November						
S	M	T	W	T	F	S
						1
2	3	4	5	6	7	8
9	10	11	12	13	14	15
16	17	18	19	20	21	22
23	24	25	26	27	28	29
S						

December						
S	M	T	W	T	F	S
	1	2	3	4	5	6
7	8	9	10	11	12	13
14	15	16	17	18	19	20
☛	22	23	24	■	■	27
28	29	30	31			

★ Easter   ☛ New season begins   ■ Bank holiday (England & Wales)

E St George's Day   **W** St David's Day   **S** St Andrew's Day   **I** St Patrick's Day

❦ ASTRONOMICAL EVENTS

All times are Greenwich Mean Time (GMT), also called Universal Time (UT).

MOON IN 2008

The moon phase dates and times are accurate worldwide, although the hour must be adjusted outside GMT.

● *New Moon*		〗 *First Quarter*		○ *Full Moon*		☾ *Last Quarter*	
8 Jan	11:37	15 Jan	19:46	22 Jan	13:35	30 Jan	05:03
7 Feb	03:44	14 Feb	03:33	21 Feb	03:30	29 Feb	02:18
7 Mar	17:14	14 Mar	10:46	21 Mar	18:40	29 Mar	21:47
6 Apr	03:55	12 Apr	18:32	20 Apr	10:25	28 Apr	14:12
5 May	12:18	12 May	03:47	20 May	02:11	28 May	02:57
3 Jun	19:23	10 Jun	15:04	18 Jun	17:30	26 Jun	12:10
3 Jul	02:19	10 Jul	04:35	18 Jul	07:59	25 Jul	18:42
1 Aug	10:13	8 Aug	20:20	16 Aug	21:16	23 Aug	23:50
30 Aug	19:58	7 Sep	14:04	15 Sep	09:13	22 Sep	05:04
29 Sep	08:12	7 Oct	09:04	14 Oct	20:02	21 Oct	11:55
28 Oct	23:14	6 Nov	04:03	13 Nov	06:17	19 Nov	21:31
27 Nov	16:55	5 Dec	21:26	12 Dec	16 37	19 Dec	10:29
27 Dec	12:22						

EARTH IN 2008

The solstices mark the points in the Earth's orbit where its axis is maximally tilted towards the sun; the equinoxes, where its axis is perpendicular to the sun. Because the Earth's orbit is slightly elliptical, its distance from the sun varies throughout the year, although this has only a nominal effect on the seasons. The point of shortest distance is called perihelion; the point of longest, aphelion.

Vernal equinox	05:48	20 Mar	Perihelion	00	3 Jan
Summer solstice	23:59	20 Jun	Aphelion	08	4 Jul
Autumnal equinox	15:44	22 Sep			
Winter solstice	12:04	21 Dec			

An eclipse occurs when one object moves into the shadow of another. When the Earth casts its shadow on the moon, it is called a lunar eclipse; and when the moon casts its shadow on the Earth, it is called a solar eclipse (technically an occultation – a true eclipse only for an observer on the moon). Both occur in 2008 as follows:

	First contact	Enters totality	Leaves totality	Last contact	
Annular solar eclipse	03:20	03:29	04:22	04:31	7 Feb
Total lunar eclipse	01:43	03:01	03:52	05:09	21 Feb
Total solar eclipse	09:21	09:24	11:18	11:21	1 Aug

	First contact	Max. coverage	Last contact	
Partial lunar eclipse	19:36	21:10	22:45	16 Aug

SEASONS

Although ancient, the division of the year into four parts, or seasons, is not universal. At the equator, the association of seasons with hot and cold breaks down: the length of the day is 12 hours all year round. Here two seasons, rainy and dry, provide a more useful division. Subtropical regions sometimes assume three: hot, rainy and cool. Even today there is no broad agreement about when one season ends and another begins. The most commonly used starting points are the equinoxes and solstices (p 187): thus winter, for example, begins on the shortest day of the year and continues until the days and nights are of equal length. More sensible is the Elder Pliny's division, with winter approximately centred on the winter solstice, and so on. The Irish calendar and British meteorological convention associate seasons with months, winter beginning with 1 November and 1 December respectively.

	Irish calendar	Elder Pliny	UK Met. office	Astronomical	in 2008
Spring begins	1 Feb	8 Feb	1 Mar	Vernal equinox	20 Mar
Summer begins	1 May	10 May	1 Jun	Summer solstice	20 Jun
Autumn begins	1 Aug	11 Aug	1 Sep	Autumnal equinox	22 Sep
Winter begins	1 Nov	11 Nov	1 Dec	Winter solstice	21 Dec

Part of the confusion rests with the fact that the shortest and longest days do not correspond with the coldest and hottest. Because it takes weeks for the Earth's surface to warm and cool in response to more or less sunshine, the temperature lags behind the period of greatest sunshine by about 40 days, depending on location.

	in 2008		approximately
Shortest day (7h 50m)	21 Dec	Coldest day	1 Feb
Longest day (16h 38m)	20 Jun	Hottest day	1 Aug

ZODIAC

The zodiac is the imaginary band in the heavens marked out by the path of the sun and 8 degrees to either side. It is broken into 12 segments, each of which is associated with a star sign (*zodia*, little beasts). These have by convention taken on fixed periods within the year.

Sign	Association	Symbol	Man of signs	Duration
Aries	ram	♈	head	21 Mar–20 Apr
Taurus	bull	♉	neck, throat	21 Apr–20 May
Gemini	twins	♊	arms, shoulders	21 May–20 Jun
Cancer	crab	♋	chest	21 Jun–22 Jul
Leo	lion	♌	heart, upper back	23 Jul–22 Aug
Virgo	virgin	♍	belly	23 Aug–22 Sep
Libra	scales	♎	lumbar region	23 Sep–22 Oct
Scorpio	scorpion	♏	genitals	23 Oct–22 Nov
Sagittarius	archer	♐	thighs	23 Nov–21 Dec
Capricorn	sea-goat	♑	knees	22 Dec–19 Jan
Aquarius	water bearer	♒	legs, ankles	20 Jan–19 Feb
Pisces	fish	♓	feet	20 Feb–20 Mar

METEOR SHOWERS

Because meteor showers result from the Earth's passage through trails of dust left by comets, they tend to be annual events. The major annual showers can vary in intensity from year to year, depending on how recently the parent comet passed. The showers last several days, sometimes weeks; the dates below are the peak days of major showers, although these can vary by a day or two. Viewing is optimal with a dim moon; see p 187 for moon phases.

Name	Meteors/hr	Parent comet	
Quadrantids	30–50	minor planet 2003 EH$_1$	3–4 Jan
Lyrids	10–20	Thatcher	21–22 Apr
Eta Aquarids	10–20	Halley	4–6 May
Delta Aquarids	20–30		28–29 Jul
Alpha Capricornids	0–10		29–30 Jul
Perseids	50–100	Swift-Tuttle	12–13 Aug
Draconids	0–10	Giacobini-Zinner	8–9 Oct
Orionids	10–20	Halley	21–22 Oct
Taurids	0–10	Encke	1–10 Nov
Leonids	20–30	Temple-Tuttle	17–18 Nov
Geminids	50–100	3200 Phaethon	13–14 Dec
Ursids	10–20	Tuttle	19–22 Dec

❦SAINTS' DAYS

The association of certain days with saints and martyrs has been customary since the early Church. Alongside days marking the events of Christ's life, these have been formalized as follows. (Movable dates are shown for 2008.)

CHURCH OF ENGLAND

The Church of England observes the feast days in *The Book of Common Prayer*:

All Sundays in the year		St Barnabas	11 Jun
Circumcision of Our Lord	1 Jan	St John the Baptist	24 Jun
Epiphany	6 Jan	St Peter	29 Jun
Conversion of St Paul	25 Jan	St James	25 Jul
Purification of the		St Bartholomew	24 Aug
Blessed Virgin	2 Feb	St Matthew	21 Sep
St Matthias	24 Feb	St Michael & All Angels	29 Sep
Annunciation	25 Mar	St Luke	18 Oct
Monday after Easter	9 Apr	SS Simon & Jude	28 Oct
Tuesday after Easter	10 Apr	All Saints	1 Nov
St Mark	25 Apr	St Andrew	30 Nov
SS Philip & James	1 May	St Thomas	21 Dec
Ascension		Nativity of Our Lord	25 Dec
(6th Thu after Easter)	1 May	St Stephen	26 Dec
Monday after Whit Sunday	12 May	St John the Evangelist	27 Dec
Tuesday after Whit Sunday	13 May	Holy Innocents	28 Dec

ROMAN CATHOLIC CHURCH

In the Catholic Church, saints' days are divided into Solemnities, Feasts and Memorials. Memorials, which are the least significant, are not listed here.

Solemnities

All Sundays in the year		Corpus Christi	
Solemnity of Mary	1 Jan	(9th Thu after Easter)	22 May
Epiphany	6 Jan	Sacred Heart	
St Joseph	19 Mar	(10th Sat after Easter)	31 May
Annunciation	25 Mar	Birth of St John the Baptist	24 Jun
Ascension		SS Peter & Paul	29 Jun
(6th Thu after Easter)	1 May	Assumption	15 Aug
Holy Trinity		All Saints	1 Nov
(8th Sun after Easter)	18 May		

Christ the King		Immaculate Conception	8 Dec
(Sun nearest to 23 Nov)	23 Nov	Nativity of Our Lord	25 Dec

Feasts

Baptism of the Lord		Triumph of the Cross	14 Sep
(Sun after 6 Jan)	13 Jan	St Matthew	21 Sep
Conversion of St Paul	25 Jan	SS Michael, Gabriel	
Presentation of the Lord	2 Feb	& Raphael	29 Sep
Chair of St Peter	22 Feb	St Luke	18 Oct
St Mark	25 Apr	SS Simon & Jude	28 Oct
SS Philip & James	3 May	Dedication of Lateran	
St Matthias	14 May	Basilica	9 Nov
Visitation of the BVM	31 May	St Andrew	30 Nov
St Thomas	3 Jul	St Stephen	26 Dec
St James	25 Jul	St John	27 Dec
Transfiguration of the Lord	6 Aug	Holy Innocents	28 Dec
St Lawrence	10 Aug	Holy Family (Sun after 25	
St Bartholomew	24 Aug	Dec and before 1 Jan;	
Birthday of the BVM	8 Sep	if none, 30 Dec)	28 Dec

Country-specific Solemnities and Feasts

Some countries have extra Solemnities and Feasts to honour local saints and martyrs. In the UK these are as follows:

Solemnities			St Columba	I	9 Jun
St David	W	1 Mar	SS John Fisher		
St Patrick	I	17 Mar	& Thomas More	E	22 Jun
St Andrew	S	30 Nov	St Oliver Plunkett	I	1 Jul
			St Gregory the Great	E	3 Sep
Feasts			40 Martyrs of England		
St Brigid	I	1 Feb	& Wales	E	25 Oct
St David	E	1 Mar	6 Welsh Martyrs		
St John Ogilvie	S	10 Mar	& Companions	W	25 Oct
St Patrick	S E W	17 Mar	All Saints of Ireland	I	6 Nov
St George	E W	23 Apr	All Saints of Wales	W	8 Nov
Beatified Martyrs of			St Margaret of Scotland	S	16 Nov
England & Wales	E	4 May	St Columban	I	23 Nov
St Augustine			Thomas Becket	E	29 Dec
of Canterbury	E	27 May			

KEY   E = England   W = Wales   S = Scotland   I = Ireland

In the US, there is one additional Feast: Our Lady of Guadalupe on 12 Dec.

❦ HOLY DAYS AND FASTS

The two principal days of Christian significance are Christmas, set by the solar cycle, and Easter, set by the lunar cycle. From the date of Easter all movable holy days and fasts are fixed by their separation in number of days, apart from Advent Sunday and Christ the King.

HOLY DAYS

		in 2008
Epiphany	6 Jan	6 Jan
Presentation of the Lord	2 Feb	2 Feb
Ash Wednesday	7th Wed before Easter	6 Feb
Annunciation (Lady Day)	25 Mar	25 Mar
Palm Sunday	Sun before Easter	16 Mar
Maundy Thursday	Thu before Easter	20 Mar
Good Friday	Fri before Easter	21 Mar
Easter	see below	23 Mar
Rogation Sunday	5th Sun after Easter	27 Apr
Ascension Day	6th Thu after Easter	1 May
Whit Sunday (Pentecost)	7th Sun after Easter	11 May
Trinity Sunday	8th Sun after Easter	18 May
Corpus Christi	9th Thu after Easter	22 May
All Saints' Day	1 Nov	1 Nov
All Souls' Day	2 Nov	2 Nov
Christ the King	Sun before Advent Sunday	23 Nov
Advent Sunday	Sun nearest to 30 Nov	30 Nov
Christmas Day	25 Dec	25 Dec

EASTER DAY

Easter is the first Sunday after the first full ecclesiastical moon falling on or after the vernal equinox; if the full moon falls on a Sunday, Easter is the following Sunday. The ecclesiastical moon is not the astronomical moon but a tabulated theoretical moon which closely approximates it, deemed full on its 14th day. The equinox is defined to be 21 March. The earliest and latest dates of Easter are 22 March and 25 April; the most likely date, 19 April.

The Book of Common Prayer gives a prescription for determining the date of Easter. The problem is somewhat complicated, and the 1662 instructions fill three pages. Devising an elegant and concise prescription has attracted the attention of amateur and professional mathematicians alike. The following algorithm (P. Kenneth Seidelmann, ed., *Explanatory Supplement to the Astronomical Almanac*) is a refined version of Oudin's 1940 algorithm. It gives the month and day of Easter for any Gregorian calendar year.

AN ALGORITHM FOR EASTER DAY

Let 'year' be the Christian year AD, 'month' the number 3 (March) or 4 (April) and 'day' a number between 1 and 31. In all divisions the integer is kept and the remainder discarded. The operation 'mod' is the opposite: the remainder is kept and the integer discarded. For example, $23/5 = 4$ and $23 \bmod 5 = 3$. In the case of year = 2008, we find from below that $A = 20$, $B = 13$, $C = 1$, $D = 1$ and $E = 6$. This gives month = 3 (March) and day = 23. The algorithm is guaranteed to repeat only after 5,700,000 years.

$$A = \tfrac{\text{year}}{100} \qquad B = \text{year} \bmod 19 \qquad C = \left(A - \tfrac{A}{4} - \tfrac{8A+13}{25} + 19B + 15\right) \bmod 30$$

$$D = C - \tfrac{C}{28}\left(1 - \tfrac{29}{C+1}\,\tfrac{21-B}{11}\right) \qquad E = \left(\text{year} + \tfrac{\text{year}}{4} + D + 2 - A + \tfrac{A}{4}\right) \bmod 7$$

$$\text{month} = 3 + \tfrac{D-E+40}{44} \qquad \text{day} = D - E + 28 - 31 \times \tfrac{\text{month}}{4}$$

FASTS

In order to correspond in length to the 40 days which it commemorates, it is customary to omit from the Lenten fast the six Sundays preceding Easter – Sundays always being feast days. Fasting, which originally meant avoiding all food, now indicates that only one meal should be had; it should not be confused with abstinence, avoiding only meat.

		in 2008
Lent	Ash Wednesday to Sat before Easter, inclusive	6 Feb–22 Mar
Advent	Advent Sunday to 24 Dec, inclusive	30 Nov–24 Dec

	Wednesday, Friday and Saturday on or after	
Spring Embertide (Ember days)	1st Sunday of Lent	13, 15, 16 Feb
Summer Embertide	Whit Sunday (Pentecost)	14, 16, 17 May
Autumn Embertide	Triumph of the Cross (14 Sep)	17, 19, 20 Sep
Winter Embertide	St Lucy's Day (13 Dec)	17, 19, 20 Dec

	Monday, Tuesday and Wednesday after	
Rogation Days	Rogation Sunday	28, 29, 30 Apr

The two principal periods of abstinence or fasting, Advent and Lent, are customarily preceded by celebrations and feasts. The days before Lent are called Shrovetide, which culminates on Shrove Tuesday, also known as *Mardi Gras* (Fat Tuesday). On the Sunday before Advent Sunday, popularly known as Stir-up Sunday, wives are encouraged to begin preparations for Christmas. The day's collect from *The Book of Common Prayer*, which reads 'Stir up, we beseech thee, O Lord, the wills of thy faithful people', is commonly taken to be an indication to begin making the Christmas puddings.

❦HOLIDAYS

Holiday, while derived from, and once synonymous with, 'holy day', now refers to any day of national festivity, which may or may not have religious significance. The Reformation diminished their number in England, particularly the popular saints' days and their religious and secular customs. Today the UK has conspicuously fewer days of festivity than its Catholic neighbours.

There is a movement afoot in the home countries – England, Scotland, Wales and Northern Ireland – to celebrate their national days, which have long been neglected. In 2006 Scotland made St Andrew's Day a bank holiday, and England is considering the same for St George's Day.

	Moveable holidays	*in 2008*
Handsel Monday	1st Mon in the New Year	7 Jan
Plough Monday	1st Mon after 6 Jan (Epiphany)	7 Jan
Shrove Tuesday	7th Tue before Easter	5 Feb
Mothering Sunday	3rd Sun before Easter	2 Mar
Commonwealth Day	2nd Mon in Mar	10 Mar
Easter	see p 192	23 Mar
Father's Day	3rd Sun in Jun	15 Jun
Harvest Festival	Sun closest to the autumnal equinox	21 Sep
Remembrance Sunday	Sun closest to 11 Nov	9 Nov
Stir-up Sunday	Sun before Advent Sun	23 Nov

	Fixed holidays		
New Year's Day	1 Jan	Orangemen's Day (I)	12 Jul
Twelfth Day	6 Jan	Trafalgar Day	21 Oct
Burns Night	25 Jan	All Saints' Day	1 Nov
Candlemas Day	2 Feb	All Souls' Day	2 Nov
St Valentine's Day	14 Feb	Guy Fawkes Day	5 Nov
St David's Day (W)	1 Mar	Armistice Day	11 Nov
St Patrick's Day	17 Mar	St Andrew's Day (S)	30 Nov
All Fools' Day	1 Apr	Christmas Day	25 Dec
St George's Day (E)	23 Apr	Boxing Day	26 Dec
May Day	1 May	Hogmanay (S)	31 Dec
Oak Apple Day	29 May		

For bank holidays, see p 196; for Red-letter and flag days, see p 197.

KEY   E = England   W = Wales   S = Scotland   I = Ireland

US HOLIDAYS

Only America has fewer holidays than the UK, as one New Yorker notes:

> Our Protestant Faith affords no religious holiday & processions like the Catholics. From the period of the Jews & Heathens down thro the Greeks & Romans, the Celts, Druids, even our Indians all had & have their religious Festivals. England retains numerous red letter days as they are called which afford intervals of rest, together with the Christmas, Easter & Whitsun holidays, for all the public offices Banks &c., but with us, we have only Independence, Christmas & New Year, 3 solitary days, not enough & which causes so much breach of the Sabbath in this city... John Pintard, 1823

While the United States does not technically have any national holidays, it observes nationwide ten annual days and one day every four years. These are called federal holidays, during which government employees do not normally work. They are marked ★ below.

	Moveable holidays	*in 2008*
★ Inauguration Day*	20 Jan, but if Sun, 21 Jan	n/a
★ Martin Luther King's Birthday	3rd Mon in Jan	21 Jan
Mardi Gras	7th Tue before Easter	5 Feb
★ Washington's Birthday	3rd Mon in Feb	18 Feb
Easter	see p 192	23 Mar
Arbor Day	last Fri in Apr	25 Apr
Mother's Day	2nd Sun in May	11 May
★ Memorial Day	last Mon in May	26 May
Father's Day	3rd Sun in Jun	15 Jun
★ Labor Day	1st Mon in Sep	1 Sep
★ Columbus Day	2nd Mon in Oct	13 Oct
Election Day	Tue after 1st Mon in Nov	4 Nov
Sadie Hawkins Day	Sat closest to 9 Nov	8 Nov
★ Thanksgiving	4th Thu in Nov	27 Nov

*Only in years following a presidential election.

	Fixed holidays		
★ New Year's Day	1 Jan	★ Independence Day	4 Jul
Groundhog Day	2 Feb	Halloween	31 Oct
St Valentine's Day	14 Feb	All Saints' Day	1 Nov
St Patrick's Day	17 Mar	All Souls' Day	2 Nov
All Fools' Day	1 Apr	★ Veterans Day	11 Nov
Cinco de Mayo	5 May	★ Christmas	25 Dec
Flag Day	14 Jun	Boxing Day (Canada)	26 Dec

❦UK CIVIL DAYS

PUBLIC (BANK) HOLIDAYS

Holy days and holidays not falling on a Sunday are sometimes marked with the cessation of work. In the UK these are called public holidays, of which there are two kinds: common law (by custom and habit) and statutory. In England, Wales and Northern Ireland, Christmas and Good Friday are common-law holidays. Statutory holidays, also known as bank holidays, took the place of holy days and feast days during the 19th century. The Bank of England closed on more than 40 saints' days and festivals before 1830; by 1834 the number had been reduced to four. Today, with eight public holidays per year, the UK has the second-fewest of all European countries; only The Netherlands has fewer with seven. Most public holidays are observed on days of no religious or cultural significance whatsoever.

	England and Wales	*in 2008*
New Year's Day	1 Jan*	1 Jan
Good Friday	Fri before Easter	21 Mar
Easter Monday	Mon after Easter	24 Mar
Early May bank holiday	1st Mon in May	5 May
Spring bank holiday	last Mon in May	26 May
Summer bank holiday	last Mon in Aug	25 Aug
Christmas Day	25 Dec*	25 Dec
Boxing Day	26 Dec*	26 Dec

	Scotland	
Same as England and Wales apart from:		*in 2008*
2 January	2 Jan*	2 Jan
Not Easter Monday		
Summer bank holiday	1st Mon in Aug	4 Aug
St Andrew's Day	30 Nov*	1 Dec

Thus the 2008 days are: 1, 2 Jan; 21 Mar; 5, 26 May; 4 Aug; 1, 25, 26 Dec.

	Ireland (Northern)	*in 2008*
Same as England and Wales apart from:		
St Patrick's Day	17 Mar*	17 Mar
Battle of the Boyne (Orangemen's Day)	12 Jul*	14 Jul

Thus the 2008 days are: 1 Jan; 17, 21, 24 Mar; 5, 26 May; 14 Jul; 25 Aug; 25, 26 Dec.

*If Sunday, the Monday after is a bank holiday; if Saturday, the Monday may be a bank holiday. If 25 and 26 December are Saturday and Sunday, the Monday and Tuesday after are bank holidays.

RED-LETTER DAYS

The more important saints' days, holy days and days associated with the royal family are called Red-letter days, originally printed in red ink in early church calendars. On these days the High Court Queen's Division judges wear, when sitting, scarlet robes. (Moveable dates are shown for 2008.)

Conversion of St Paul	25 Jan	St Barnabas	11 Jun
Purification	2 Feb	Official BD of HM the Queen	
Accession of HM the Queen	6 Feb	a Sat in Jun, appointed annually	
Ash Wednesday (see p 192)	6 Feb	St John the Baptist	24 Jun
St David's Day	1 Mar	St Peter	29 Jun
Annunciation	25 Mar	St Thomas	3 Jul
BD of HM the Queen	21 Apr	St James	25 Jul
St Mark	25 Apr	St Luke	18 Oct
Ascension Day (see p 192)	1 May	SS Simon & Jude	28 Oct
SS Philip & James	1 May	All Saints	1 Nov
St Matthias	14 May	Lord Mayor's Day	
Coronation Day	2 Jun	(2nd Sat in Nov)	8 Nov
BD of HM Duke of		BD of HRH Prince of Wales	14 Nov
Edinburgh	10 Jun	St Andrew's Day	30 Nov

FLAG DAYS

Government buildings fly the Union flag (see UK National Days, p 198) on the days below throughout the UK, apart from the three saints' days, when the flag is flown in the respective nation only. (Moveable dates are for 2008.)

BD of Countess of Wessex	20 Jan	Official BD of HM the Queen	
Accession of HM the Queen	6 Feb	a Sat in Jun, appointed annually	
BD of Duke of York	19 Feb	BD of Duchess of Cornwall	17 Jul
St David's Day (w)	1 Mar	BD of the Princess Royal	15 Aug
BD of Earl of Wessex	10 Mar	Remembrance Sunday	
Commonwealth Day		(Sun closest to 11 Nov)	9 Nov
(2nd Mon in Mar)	10 Mar	BD of HRH Prince of Wales	14 Nov
BD of HM the Queen	21 Apr	Wedding day of the Queen	20 Nov
St George's Day (E)	23 Apr	St Andrew's Day (s)	30 Nov
Europe Day	9 May	Opening of a session of Parliament	
Coronation Day	2 Jun	Prorogation	
BD of HM Duke of		of a session of Parliament	
Edinburgh	10 Jun	(both Greater London area only)	

KEY   BD = birthday   E = England   W = Wales   S = Scotland

☙UK NATIONAL DAYS

The UK does not have a national day of celebration; rather, the four constituent countries celebrate their national days independently. It does, however, have its own flag (the Union flag), which derives from the superposition of three heraldic crosses: the cross of St George, and the saltires (X-shaped crosses) of St Andrew and St Patrick. These are the respective flags of England, Scotland and, until 1922, Ireland. The first two were combined in 1606, with the third added in 1801. (Wales was legally part of the kingdom of England when the first Union flag was created.)

The national days of the four home countries are as follows:

WALES, 1 MARCH

Motto Cymru am byth (Wales for ever).

Flag Red dragon on a green and white field.

National day 1 March, St David's Day, Flag day in Wales, Red-letter day, RC Solemnity in Wales and RC Feast day in England.

Customs An old custom, mentioned in Shakespeare's Henry V, is the wearing of leeks in hats on St David's feast day: 'but why wear you your leek today? Saint Davy's day is past'. Alternatively, a daffodil can be worn, which is the national flower of Wales.

Patron St David (Dewi in Welsh), bishop in Mynyw, is 'perhaps the most celebrated of British saints', according to *Butler's Lives*. He died *c.* 600, but his principal biographer, not writing until 1090, combined much fiction with fact. David founded, among others, an abbey in Menevia, Wales, known for its severe asceticism.

NORTHERN IRELAND, 17 MARCH

Motto No consensus, but arguably *Quis separabit?* (Who shall separate?).

Flag Until 1972, Cross of St George with crown, red hand and white star.

National day 17 March, St Patrick's Day, RC Solemnity in Ireland and RC Feast day in England, Wales and Scotland.

Customs St Patrick's Day is the most widely celebrated of all UK national days. It always occurs in Lent, but it is customary to break one's fast on this day, especially in Ireland, where it is an RC Solemnity. In Britain much Guinness beer is drunk. In America, people are meant to wear something green; if they do not they may be pinched with impunity. A number of US cities dye their rivers green.

Patron St Patrick, archbishop of Armagh, apostle of Ireland, was born *c.* 389 of Romano-British origin. In his adolescence he was captured and sent to Ireland as a slave, but escaped after six years to return to his family. It was at this time that he determined to return to the island to evangelize, which he later did, setting up a see at Armagh in 444. He died *c*. 461, having converted, in 30 years, the whole of Ireland to Christianity.

ENGLAND, 23 APRIL

Motto Dieu et mon droit (God and my right).

Flag Cross of St George (red cross on a white field).

National day 23 April, St George's Day, Flag day in England and RC Feast day in England and Wales.

Customs There has been a revival of St George's Day celebrations during the last few years. On this day men wear red roses in their buttonholes (see Accessories, p 68). St George's flag is flown.

Patron St George, martyr, protector of the kingdom of England. All that can be said with confidence about this saint is that he died a martyr's death in Palestine *c*. 300. Although it is unlikely that St George set foot in England, his cult in that country precedes the Norman Conquest. He gradually came to replace St Edward the Confessor as the patron saint of England after being promoted by Edward III.

SCOTLAND, 30 NOVEMBER

Motto Nemo me impune lacessit (No one provokes me with impunity).

Flag Cross of St Andrew (white X-shaped cross on a blue field).

National day 30 November, St Andrew's Day, Flag day in Scotland, Red-letter day, CofE Feast day, RC Solemnity in Scotland and RC Feast day.

Customs Scotland's other day of national celebration is Burns' Night, 25 January, and is the more popular of the two. However, St Andrew's Day has been much promoted in recent years, and in 2006 the Scottish parliament designated St Andrew's Day a bank holiday, which will first be celebrated in 2007.

Patron St Andrew, apostle, was from Bethsaida in Galilee, the brother of Simon Peter. The first of Christ's disciples, he is sometimes called the Protoclete, or First-called. Little is known about his later life, though he is said to have been crucified on an X-shaped cross, hence St Andrew's Cross.

KEY   CofE = Church of England   RC = Roman Catholic

❦INAUSPICIOUS DAYS

DISMAL DAYS

From medieval times certain days, collectively called *dies mali*, or 'evil days', were held to be unwise for starting any enterprise. Thus the word dismal was originally a noun referring to these unlucky days, only later taking on its descriptive sense of causing gloom. The most common accounts list two days per month:

January	1 25	May	3 25	September	3 21
February	4 26	June	10 16	October	3 22
March	1 28	July	13 22	November	5 28
April	10 20	August	1 30	December	7 22

MONDAYS

While all Mondays are associated with questionable fortune, the first Mondays in April and August and the last in December (in 2008, 7 Apr, 4 Aug and 29 Dec) are particularly inauspicious:

> Anyone who lets blood of man or beast on them will not last the week, anyone who accepts a drink, or eats goose, will die within the fortnight, and any child, male or female, born on them will come to a bad end.
>
> B. Blackburn and L. Holford-Strevens, *Oxford Companion to the Year*

DOG DAYS

Dog days, generally accepted to be from 3 July to 11 August, correspond to the hottest days of the year (though not the longest, see p 187). In ancient times they were thought to result from the coincidence of the rising and setting of the sun and the star Sirius, the major star of the constellation Canis Major (Big Dog). Sirius is the brightest of the stars seen from Earth, and the combined heat of it and the sun was thought to be the cause of this sweltering period. It is traditional to avoid blood-letting and medical treatment and to abstain from women. As Poor Robin (1675) indicates, not everyone agrees with the latter:

> Husband give me my due, the woman saies;
> The man replies, 'Tis naught Wife these Dog daies;
> But she rejoins, Let women have their rights,
> Though there be Dog daies, there are no Dog nights.

LEAP DAY

In 2008, February 29 is a leap day, and on this day women may by tradition propose to men. There are two other prescribed days of feminine initiative: In France, on the feast day of St Catherine of Alexandra (25 November), women may ask men in marriage. In the US, on Sadie Hawkins Day (8 November in 2008), women are meant to invite men on a date, a refreshing variation but in direct conflict with *The Rules'* first prescription (First Date, p 38): don't talk to a man first (and don't ask him to dance).

Leap days are necessary because of an astronomical discrepancy. Because the length of the year is 365.2422 days, to keep the seasons and the months aligned it is necessary from time to time to insert an extra day in the year. Years which have 365 days are called common years, and those with 366 days are called leap years. The extra day is always added to the end of February, and this day – February 29th – is called a leap day. The rule for determining leap years is as follows: years divisible by 4 are leap years, but those divisible by 100 are not, but those divisible by 400 are after all. This approximates the year by $365\frac{97}{400} = 365.2425$ days, exceeding the tropical year by only 27 seconds. No plan has been put forward to address this discrepancy, which will have accumulated to one day by the year 4800.

FRIDAY THE 13TH

Friday the 13th is the coincidence of two events in themselves associated with ill fortune. Friday, the day on which Adam fell and Christ was crucified, is thought to be the least lucky of the weekdays: 'Sneeze on a Friday, sneeze for sorrow'; 'Cut your nails on a Friday, cut them for woe.' The number 13 is prime, and is the number of men who sat at the Last Supper. In Dan Brown's novel *The Da Vinci Code*, the decimation of the Knights Templar under King Philip IV of France occurred on Friday, 13 October 1307.

Friday the 13ths occur on average once every 213 days, but they are not evenly distributed; some years have one, some two and some three. The table below repeats every 28 years from 1901 to 2099. The 13th is (marginally) more likely to be a Friday than any other day of the week.

Years				*Fri 13th in*			*Years*			*Fri 13th in*		
2001	2007	2018		Apr	Jul		2009	2015	2026	Feb	Mar	Nov
2002	2013	2019	2024	Sep	Dec		2010	2021	2027	Aug		
2003	2008	2014	2025	Jun			2012			Jan	Apr	Jul
2004				Feb	Aug		2020			Mar	Nov	
2005	2011	2016	2022	May			2028			Oct		
2006	2017	2023		Jan	Oct							

❦INTERNATIONAL DAYS

The United Nations officially recognizes a number of days to be observed internationally throughout its member countries. Notably, there are days for women, youth and children, but not for men. (Moveable dates are for 2008.)

Victims of the Holocaust	27 Jan	Slave trade & its abolition	23 Aug
Mother language	21 Feb	Literacy	8 Sep
Women's rights		Preservation of the ozone layer	16 Sep
& international peace	8 Mar	Peace	21 Sep
Elimination of		Maritime during last week in Sep	
racial discrimination	21 Mar	Older persons	1 Oct
Peoples struggling against		Habitat (1st Mon in Oct)	6 Oct
racism (week)	21–27 Mar	Space (week)	4–10 Oct
Water	22 Mar	Teachers	5 Oct
Meteorological	23 Mar	Post	9 Oct
Road safety (week)	during Apr	Mental health	10 Oct
Mine awareness & assistance		Natural disaster reduction	
in mine action	4 Apr	(2nd Wed in Oct)	8 Oct
Health	7 Apr	Food	16 Oct
Book & copyright	23 Apr	Eradication of poverty	17 Oct
Press freedom	3 May	United Nations	24 Oct
Those who lost their lives		Development information	24 Oct
during WWII	8–9 May	Disarmament (week)	24–30 Oct
Families	15 May	Preventing the exploitation of the en-	
Telecommunication	17 May	vironment in armed conflict	6 Nov
Cultural diversity for		Tolerance	16 Nov
dialogue & development	21 May	Road traffic victims	
Biological diversity	22 May	(3rd Sun in Nov)	16 Nov
Peoples of non-self-governing		Africa industrialization	20 Nov
territories (week)	25–31 May	Children	20 Nov
United Nations peacekeepers	29 May	Television	21 Nov
No-tobacco	31 May	Elimination of violence	
Innocent children victims		against women	25 Nov
of aggression	4 Jun	Palestinian people	29 Nov
Environment	5 Jun	AIDS	1 Dec
Combat desertification & drought	17 Jun	Abolition of slavery	2 Dec
Refugee	20 Jun	Disabled persons	3 Dec
Public service	23 Jun	Volunteer day for economic	
Against drug abuse &		& social development	5 Dec
illicit trafficking	26 Jun	Civil aviation	7 Dec
Support of victims of torture	26 Jun	Human rights	10 Dec
Cooperatives (1st Sat in Jul)	5 Jul	Mountain	11 Dec
Population	11 Jul	Migrants	18 Dec
Indigenous people	9 Aug	South–South cooperation	19 Dec
Youth	12 Aug	Human solidarity	20 Dec

INDEX

COLOPHON

DESIGN

This book was designed and typeset by Thomas Fink in QuarkXPress on a Macintosh computer, departing from the typesetting program Latex used in the 2007 edition. Most figures were drawn with xfig and Omnigraffle.

FONT

The text was set in Palatino, a font designed by Hermann Zapf in 1948. Based on the fonts of the Italian Renaissance, it is one of the most popular and admired of the serifed typefaces and is thought to be highly legible. Chapter titles are set in 14 pt, quoted passages in 7.83 pt and the remainder in 8.7 pt. Subsections are set in small caps and all numbers in text figures.

PAGE

The proportion of the text block is ϕ:1, where the Golden ratio $\phi = (\sqrt{5} + 1)/2 = 1.618$. ϕ can be derived from the regular pentagon (below) and it can be approximated by the ratio of two consecutive Fibonacci numbers (1, 2, 3, 5, 8, 13, 21, 34, 55, 89,…); the ratio approaches ϕ as the series continues.

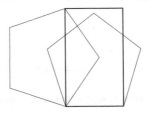

TYPOGRAPHICAL SUMMARY

Text block proportion	1.618:1	Number of chapters	12
Text block height	161.8 mm	Number of sections	87
Text block width	100 mm	Number of pages	224
Ratio of margins (inside:		Number of words	71,000
top:outside:bottom)	2:3:4:6	Number of figures	29
Typeface	Palatino	Number of index entries	781
Text size, principal	8.7 pt	Chapter head block height	14 lines
Text size, displayed	7.83 pt	Chapter head size (caps)	14 pt
Lines per page	42	Section head size (caps)	8.7 pt
Characters per line	73	Subsection head size	
Leading	10.93 pt	(small caps)	8.7 pt
Vertical spacer	1 line	Chapter head tracking	70
Indent	4.5 mm	Section head tracking	50
Gutter width	5 mm	Subsection head tracking	30

❦ (SECTION SYMBOL)

Section names are preceded by a hedera (❦), a typographical ornament or dingbat in the shape of an ivy leaf. Decorative hederae can be found in ancient inscriptions and medieval manuscripts. Here it is also used as a flag.

DIFFERENCES FROM THE 2007 EDITION

This edition of *The Man's Book* is 32 pages longer than the 2007 edition. The central Almanack has been removed and four new chapters and 31 new sections have been added. The font size is slightly smaller but the spacing between lines and subsections has been increased. Sections have been broken up into subsections.

LOCATION

This book was written and researched at the British Library, the Cambridge University Library, the London Library and the author's house in London.

HOMEPAGE

www.tcm.phy.cam.ac.uk/~tmf20